The American People are The Fourth Branch

CHIEF MAC DA'IBHIDH

Fulton Books
Meadville, PA

Published by Fulton Books 2022

ISBN 978-1-63710-623-5 (paperback)
ISBN 978-1-63710-624-2 (digital)

Printed in the United States of America

ABOUT THE BOOK

In the beginning there were to be Four Branches of the American Government; Executive, Legislative, Judicial, and The People. Just as the words; *"check and balance"* do not appear anywhere in the Constitution, the structure for both; checks and balances and *"The People being the Fourth Branch, "*are in the United States Constitution. The foundation was laid in the Constitution of the United States that the people were to be the most *critical form of balance* that would keep their governing body in *check*. There were many reasons that the people would be the most critical component for success. But mainly as men and women gain power they become prone to corruption or become highly susceptible to inauspicious influences thoroughly convinced it is the right reason for the decision they make. Those governed and most impacted by the laws were to be the most critical and weighted check, balancing the weight of decisions by those who are immune from the laws they enact. So it was from the beginning.

When comparing man's beginning on earth to man's new beginnings, three hundred years would seem as *a short time.* But in that short time a nation would rise to become a great power. As the nation grew in world stature it somehow forgot its strength is derived from a free people. What would begin as The American People being The Fourth Branch; in *a short time* would change into The People being The Fourth Branch as the end neared. All in preparation for the new beginning. Within this book are three stories.

One of the stories is of a little boy that sees God when he is between four to five years old. He is a witness but, the boy is not believed. So, he then gives false testimony. Can't do that no matter the age. It caused a change. Once so innocent as to see God in all his Glory then suddenly the child knew bad. He falls away but still strives as all must to survive.

The second story is a continuation of the first. Much later in life, the boy becomes an elder who realizes that all along he has cared deeply about people. The man prays for answers to the terrible unraveling he witnesses all about him and sees a pathway for a *reprieve* or *respite* for *the people*. A message of *restoration of balance for* an unbalanced government. A way towards Unification for a Union which is dissolving. Once again, he sees truth. Some would listen and scoff. Then there were those who understood the amendment would restore balance to an unbalanced government. But those who understood also knew the proposal was so sound that the influential, wealthy or powerful would never allow the amendment to come to fruition. If the man had the opportunity to present the amendment to the people; would he be believed?

The third story is a creative tale of a Biblical Patriarch's life as a boy as he grows into becoming a man around 1029 years before the Great Flood of AM 1656. His name is Enoch and the year of the story is around AM 627. The setting is earth around 627 years after man's creation. Life on earth for Enoch is not like what the majority for this generation thinks. His life is not going to be like his peers as he grows either.

The life stories of the two boys are for a comparison and contrast of seeking love and truth for people some 5000 years apart on earth.

In the Qur'ān, Enoch is known as a man named Idris; a Prophet of truth and sincerity (Mary 19:56). Enoch was known by Hebrews, to be the Patriarch of the seventh generation from Adam found in Genesis Ch 5, Luke 3:37&38 and Jude 1:14 (KJV). Enoch was known by the Hebrews to be *taken by God or translated by God into heaven that he should not see death.* Genesis 5:24 and Hebrews 11:5 (KJV), and Ecclesiasticus 44:16 (DRV). The strength of Enoch's faith in God to provide better things for past generations and current generations through their faith in God was conveyed by Paul to Hebrews in Palestine (*From the Epistle of Paul to Hebrew Christians in Palestine 11:5 & 40, (about 63 AD) & Ecclesiasticus 44:16*).

Paul went on to explain in his letter to Timothy, the Bishop of Ephesus (2 Timothy 3:16 KJV): "All Scripture is given by inspiration of God, and is profitable for doctrine, for reproof, for correction, for instruction in righteousness. 17, That the man of God may be perfect, thoroughly furnished unto all good works."

So that all is made clear, being *perfected* should not cause anyone in this generation concern at all. God clearly understands that nobody's perfect. God just wants what any good father wants from all of his children. He wants us to call him. He wants us to talk to him. Its just that the best way to talk with him is to pray. And the best way to talk (pray) to him is by reading the Bible (Scripture). If only we seek Him, he will do the rest and your path to Him will be revealed unto you. He will even bless you with hidden treasures and valuable gifts along the way. But remember the world can ensnare and entraps us, at times causing us to face challenges, obstacles, or tests. Are we all great test takers? No! Even the best at tests can meet their match and be brought to their knees. So, what does your good father in heaven do when we fail our tests? He sends the greatest *teacher* in the world and beyond to teach you. He can even send a *helper*.

Can this book's writings prove God's existence? Of course not! No book proves the existence of God except the Bible. The Bible. which contains the Divine Word of God, helps others find God. Then through faith and belief, proof of God will only exist between God and whom the Creator has chosen or elected to receive proof of His existence. Proof or not doesn't matter because its through faith and belief we come to **_know_** God. It is hoped that the three stories combined can help *generate an interest for this generation in the Bible, Jesus Christ, and our Father in heaven and not necessarily in that order either!*

Please enjoy the book with attention to detail as intended but, please allow yourself some benevolence in excusing the writings when they seem to fall short in some spelling, grammar or composition. The processes of writing and self-editing in an affordable way within the design set parameters for this generation were proven to be very difficult for someone of a passing generation.

GROUNDWORK

It is written that God spoke through Prophets. Sometimes in previous writings a divine entity arrives in person to speak with someone and is revealed as a messenger, an angel, or our Lord. In the earliest of written reference there are a few that actually spoke with God—Adam and Eve, Cain, Noah, Abraham, Isaac and Jacob, Moses, Job, Jonah—and there are but a few more still that are written of. For us, the lamp that removes the darkness and enlightens our path is to believe His Word walked in the flesh in our midst. Then a believer can speak to God through prayer as we journey along. Still, fewer actually walked with God as did Enoch and Noah (Genesis 5:24 &6:9 KJV).

Our ability to comprehend what *walked with God* truly means is very limited. Our mind tends to drift with current worldly limitations and expectations. Try to imagine it is exactly as written. To be part of the initial phases of a path's construction during a time of unimaginable wickedness and lawlessness would require consistent Divine Intervention.

On a side note: Although Enoch "walked" with God, the Book of Enoch was not canonized as biblical. The Book of Enoch was written by who could considered to be God's First Scribe. Some 366 writings, some considered to be prophetic (Scripture) were delivered unto surviving generations by Noah on the Ark. Noah was Enoch's great-grandson. Since Jesus was God's Word in the flesh, basically he was the "Teachings" walking amongst us and would've been as One with the originator of all writings, teachings, or Scripture. Paul, whose testimony contributed to approximately 50 percent of the New Testament, referenced the Book of Enoch. So too did Jude in the Book of Jude in the Bible. It was James and Jude who were stepbrothers of Jesus (Mark 6:3 DRV & Jude 1:1 KJV) and were martyred, and both have canonized testimony of their brother Jesus in the New Testament. All who were familiar with the teachings of their day knew of the Book of Enoch, the reason for the Great Flood, and would've understood details about the Nephilim /ˈnɛfɨˌlɪm/ נְפִיל, Naphíl or Naphil, the history of Angels mating with humans, and the two hundred Fallen Angels who departed from heaven with the Rebellious One. Humans had many inherent gifts Angels simply could not possess. In Deuteronomy (meaning "these are the words") 1:28, the Israelites rebuked God for they were afraid to fight the Amorites after being told by men of their own the greatness of the Amorite cities, and moreover, those sent to reconnoiter saw "sons of Anakim" (giants). These giants or Anakim could've been descendants of Fallen Angels who possibly somehow survived the great flood. There is no doubt evil still roams the earth freely and is not at all completely destroyed.

Although remnants of Anakim, Fallen Angels, and Nephilim remain in the Old and New Testaments, this knowledge is just as Enoch once was. Enoch was a man who walked with God then was no more. With each "age" came a change in the way God constructed the path home. Where one route seemed to end in actuality another route had already been cleared and was revealed for the next age (generations). So too knowledge of Enoch is no more. But Fallen Angels also known as principalities still exist and are called aliens by this generation. Nephilim are here in vast numbers but mainly remain unseen lest they be manifest by authority. This generation should know some were to have eternal life. Their children were not. Names and appearances may have changed for each generation, but the intentions of the fallen angels remain unchanged. Their priority is of their own designs and for the lives of their own children, not at all for human desires, intentions, or goals toward the good of humanity. Although names and appearances change, the striking at the heels of man remains, for they strive to overthrow that which was never intended to be theirs or their heirs'. They were not created to have heirs, reproduce, or have intercourse.

Some have had discussions with God. Some have pleaded with God because they are in dire need or were told to do something or shown what they must do or what they must tell others. Some have argued with God, usually unconvinced that they are capable of what is to be. But there is an extreme difficulty which arises that comes with others understanding these conversations. Actually, anyone can ask God for wisdom, and surprisingly enough, God will freely give. There are plenty who live and die totally unnoticed except for those they touch. Those are the children who volunteer. Some say they are selected first and only think they Volunteer. Read on from one who once felt certain at the beginning of his journey that he volunteered.

Pauquette, *a tiny package*

He was baptized in the Wisconsin River near a little park in Portage, Wisconsin, on Tuesday, August 18, 2015. Visiting in Wisconsin, he called on an old friend, a pastor who happened to be finishing up some pastor training in northern Wisconsin and was heading home the following day. "Hey, Bubba, will you baptize me?"

Bubba replied, "Sure. Where and when?" He replied, "Looking at the map, there is a place two hours north of him and two hours south of you, kinda on your way back home in Portage, Wisconsin. A place called Pauquette. Tomorrow about 4:00 p.m.?"

"Good."

Neither had ever been to Pauquette. The name seemed to have no meaning. Bubba asked, "Would you rather be baptized in the Jordan River in Wisconsin?" Understanding the name Jordan River would have more of a biblical connection. No. For some reason, it would be Pauquette. Bubba, somewhat puzzled at his passing up a rare baptism opportunity in a river which would have a very deep connection, agreed. They would meet at a small park in Portage, Wisconsin, the next day.

He understood and knew he would have to cry out to the Lord prior to being born again. So he had found in a pamphlet that was given some time before, at a minor league Charleston SC River Dog baseball game, what to say. And since for some reason his death was to be there, he looked up the meaning of *Pauquette*. It was originally a French word, meaning "small or tiny package."

So well into the Wisconsin River, ready to be handed over to God by his good friend Bubba, he nervously and humbly said out loud, "Dear God, I am a sinner and need forgiveness. I believe that Jesus Christ shed His precious blood and died for my sin. I am willing to turn from sin. I now invite Christ to come into my heart and life as my personal savior."

But then he continued, "God, accept me as a *pauquette* to you. A small gift or a tiny package to do your will. Be it the smallest of kind gestures, such as opening a door for or helping little old ladies or the grandest of actions."

Bubba couldn't help it. He giggled or chuckled a little. He slowly turned and gave a slight grin as it if to acknowledge He himself, although he meant what he just said. He also recognized how silly it must've sounded to another. And he followed with a nod, "Ready." Bubba then immediately followed, saying the most wonderful and kindest of words to God he and his wife had ever heard.

Bubba told him he could hold his nose if he wanted. He nodded. He knew he would be all right he could slowly blow air through his nose if a problem arose. Bubba laid one hand on his chest and one on his back. He grabbed the hand on his chest with both hands, laying trust and faith in Jesus and God. Bubba gently lowered him back into the river.

He kept his eyes open a second or two then closed them. After a few more short seconds, Bubba raised him from the river. As he was helped upright, he tried to remain focused for any change. Anything? Well, the sky was partly cloudy as before. A slight breeze. Overriding any ability of situational awareness became stability. The river bottom made up boulders of infinitesimal shape and size, making their exit from the river extremely difficult. He noticed a little embarrassment at the amount of help he was receiving from Bubba. Bubba seemed to notice this slight exhibit of emotion and quickly attributed his own stability from previous experiences and offered assistance. The man gladly accepted the help. Bubba had slipped on a pair of older tennis shoes prior to water entry. He had only prepared himself with sandals.

He'd have to admit he looked to the sky, looking for the Holy Spirit. Grayish and cloudy. Clouds moving quite noticeably. But no dove. Only a hawk, seemingly hunting, circled above. Extracting themselves from the river, they returned up a steep embankment, grabbing shrubbery for stability. All three began the walk while chatting quite excitingly across a small bridge and Pauquette Park to a bathroom. There they could change into dry clothes for the long drive in separate directions they were to take. He and his wife two hours south. Bubba about four hours west. As they walked across a small bridge with a babbling brook passing underneath, he looked up again. Nothing. No change. Gray sky. Clouds moving low and fast. The hawk still flying directly above the three. One of three pointed. A hawk. Yup, a hawk.

Exiting the bathroom, fresh from a dip in the river, they noticed a young couple just outside the bathroom at a picnic table. With absolutely no one else around, someone was quick to ask the young couple, Wasn't it a school day? Bubba was even faster to ask, "Do you know Jesus?"

Both answering simultaneously, a slightly different response but adamant in exact confirmations. "Oh yes! Very well indeed. Extremely well." And they both went on to explain, yet the girl, becoming aware she was overtalking her boyfriend, relented to quietness. Introducing themselves, they asked the young couple. They both responded with the young man saying his name was, "Noah."

Overwhelmed, he exclaimed, "That's awesome. Noah was at my baptism!"

As they said their goodbyes, shaking hands, he turned and said to the group that the young couple had made his day, because Noah was at his baptism. Walking away, making small talk, he looked up. The hawk was still there.

This book is a *pauquette* for you.

Forgiveness

Why read anything that one who lives in the midst of man Unforgiven by man's law has written? Who is it that cannot forgive?

Or is it a what? Why is it that a man cannot be forgiven? Is it an act which is unforgivable, something one has done which cannot be forgiven, or is it the human being, something which lives and breathes, physically changes each day, grows older and ages, which itself makes it impossible? Is it who or is it what that cannot forgive?

Humans are not really capable of the requirements placed upon one from another. Usually because humans tend to place greater expectations upon others than they would place upon themselves. When to stand steady in resolve, when to say what is desired to be heard. Let's be clear there is far greater ease in saying what is desired than what is necessary or required. Which is why what is necessary usually goes unheard. One of the greatest impacts on his life resulted from man's lack of sincere interest and attentive compassion required for an event of rare and unique magnificence. Well, he was grateful it all didn't happen two hundred years earlier. He surely would've been put to death. There was no other day as important as the day he saw God. He knew it! How could others ever possibly grasp or fathom the event? At the time, he certainly couldn't. It was only half a century later would he begin to comprehend the magnitude of a past moment long, long ago.

How does the child know whom its father is? Always there since birth, but where is the proof? Even when not physically present, the father is always in accompaniment. As the child grows older, its belief and faith grows beyond acceptance to the point of fact. The child will come to know (eido/bay'-do) whom its father is.

Eido/bay'-do: Know was translated from the Greek word *'eido'* and is pronounced as *'bay'-do'* meaning; *Inward, in the consciousness. And in John 8:55 KJV additionally meant able to hear in the mind as One.*

Without substantiation, belief becomes a near impossibility. For this reason, it is they, the few, who are the chosen for proof or revelation. But since they are the few, truth remains elusive to pass on or share. Harder yet to believe without proof, transubstantiation (pleroo) occurs to the average man.

Pleroo: Greek; *filling within, inward, or inwardly.*

When an opportunity for higher learning or enlightenment smashes all that is concrete, especially when the source is a little boy, it requires valuable traits and wisdom not normally found in man. To him, he saw the problem others had was the ability to believe. Not for him, because he knew what he saw, but that treasured commodity can be nearly impossible to attain. Belief from others which he desired to support his own. Belief requires trust that the information is from a reputable source. Establishment of rapport. What if the source has no rapport? Will it ever be possible that the message is more important than messenger? Is it possible the need becomes great enough, that the people take it upon themselves to magnify the message to fulfill its purpose?

A Child's Beginning

When he was younger than two years old, he tried to scale an electrical cord. The cord extended from a hot clothing iron resting upright on an ironing board downward, plugged into an electrical outlet a few inches from the floor. This would be the little boy's first attempt in training and the learning experiences of rope-climbing skills. The iron was on and hot, very hot. The iron once filled with water could release steam into the clothing to assist in removing wrinkles. Pushing a button located on the handle, usually with one's thumb, would produce the odd yet loud sound achieved from the spontaneous reaction of water, immediately changing to a steam cloud. The resultant sounds from water contacting an extremely hot object make can culminate throughout the air. Using these techniques, a homemaker could easily morph an unkempt and unseemly family member into a sharp dressed man. Might even assist the wearer's transition into the state of being handsome and debonair. Hand-ironing clothes takes sacrifice of one's time, some skill and knowledge of technique, but most of all, it requires "caring." A skill and trait not completely lost in today's modern society but certainly trending on the way out in exchange for the untucked and belt buckle modeled front and center and wearing of pants down to the knees exposing the underwear looks. Not to mention the form-fitting stretch pants or leotard with nothing covering them, leaving the impression of a color of choice naked embedded in the mind. Exposing yesterday's losses for this day's gains can be very enlightening at times, but let us get back to his training.

His mom had just left to answer the phone in the kitchen. Thinking back, he remembered noticing the cord might steady his rise to his feet. His mom told him the rest. The horror she felt when she heard the sounds of calamity in the next room, realizing what the sounds could mean. Hearing the screams, dropping the phone, bolting toward, and when she rounded the corner into the room, her baby lay with the hot iron on his face. For some reason, the child lay with the hot iron covering one side of his face. She rushed him to PGH Peninsula General Hospital Salisbury, Maryland. From there, doctors called a burn specialist at Johns Hopkins University in Baltimore, Maryland. The burn specialist in Baltimore asked, "What has been done for treatment of the burn so far?"

The reply from PGH doctors in Salisbury attending the two-year-old was, "A cold, wet rag has been applied."

The burn specialist asked, "Who applied the cool, wet rag?"

PGH replied, "The patient's mother."

John Hopkins said that the cool, wet rag applied immediately was the best treatment and to let the burn specialist know if they could be of any other assistance for treatment of the burn on the little boy's face. After leaving a child alone near a hot iron to answer a phone, the doctor doing nothing probably extended no relief from guilt. The little boy's mom would bear the burden of extreme guilt and sorrow. At least until forgiveness was accepted inwardly.

Having no recollection of any of the events except "trying to climb a cord," one evening, he asked his mom to tell his new wife the story of the hot iron on his face and the wet rag. His mom tenderly explained. Sometimes with emotion apparent. They moved in close. Within reach, the two gently touched his face pointing out the scar. Over twenty years after the accident. What could they see that he couldn't? Up close and personal, they both gazed onto his face. Occasionally glancing in his eyes, making contact. With a light touch, his mom slid her finger from his forehead over and down by his cheek. Finally, his wife exclaimed, "I see it!" What? He never saw it. He wanted to see the scar also.

Seizing the moment, all three hurriedly rushed into the bathroom. Him first. With all three faces now in a small mirror, he thought he might see the small inverted *V* from what must have been a horrible burn. What could've been a horrible and terrifying scar from childhood curiosity today was invisible even to the most astute observer. Recollecting praises of his mom's actions from burn specialist a hundred miles away would always cause a beaming pride. What must've been a truly horrific and guilt-ridden tragedy. The little boy's mother did the best and only thing anyone can do for such a horrible burn to the face.

He never truly realized what had actually happened until he was born again. Only after being baptized would he eventually be receptive of the wisdom to comprehend the day he saw God. That was the day God turned his face toward him. After more than fifty-five years later, he would come to know that God never turned away. He would come to know without the love and faith in people that Jesus knew, he would not be writing these words today. It is not that God cannot save some one, for surely He can do all things. It is the law that God wrote that we follow for a pathway back to Him. It is natural that God should not intervene, for if God does intervene, His majestic intervention disturbs the natural state of things. Could God intervene without disturbing the natural state of things? Yes. But when God intervenes, he usually does so in a way that some or someone would come to know him. But the decision was made long ago that changed man and women forever more. There would be no undoing the change. This is why God works through man. God very much prefers His children to come into their own, to know Him as any father would. God much prefers agreements and covenants. Just as your father does, so too your Creator. God's direct intervention normally is only required when the natural state of things is in jeopardy of being altered toward irreversible catastrophic consequences for all. Which is why all are truly free to do whatever we please or free to pursue our happiness. But with this choice comes responsibility for good and bad outcomes, and accountability which can lead to death. It is only through the laws that Jesus lived and filled that we might enjoy heaven on earth. God cannot walk with the corrupted as they sin, but they do not have to be alone for Jesus will walk with the sinner or attend to the sinner in the blink of an eye that the person might die and be born again with a new heart that is able to stand in the presence of God's face without permanent stoppage.

Such a little boy, around four years old, maybe five, experiencing life-altering events of such great magnitude. If he ever wanted to be normal, never again should he give much thought to the few minutes of that day. Knowing what he saw but never able to share. He tried to fit in but sometimes just couldn't. How does anyone forget, especially when events happened continuously throughout his life with meanings, giving reasons which always pointed back to that day? Events such as this become known as the unseen. What is seen and known as truth has to be unseen. The brain has to erase the event. The mind has to wipe the event clean. The brain and mind have to make what was seen; unseen. As in Post Traumatic Stress Disorders (PTSD), man has learned that making a life altering event go away in its entirety is not really possible. And, making that which has been seen and known; an unseen and unknown is not really possible either. Born near Dagsboro, Delaware, he was about two years old when his family moved to Chesapeake Heights, a rural area just outside Salisbury, Maryland. This neighborhood title, Chesapeake Heights, might seem to give more affluence than deserving. The homes were built in the 1950s on three streets about half a mile long, each with connecting streets every tenth of a mile, basically forming the blocks of a neighborhood in Wicomico County. Located on the Delmarva Peninsula, an area one foot below sea level, surrounded by farm land and wooded areas, his neighborhood was about thirty miles from Ocean City, Maryland, "the beach." Many people would drive the several-hour trip from major cities of the northeast, Philadelphia, Baltimore, and Washington, DC, to enjoy summers at the beach.

Known as the Lower Eastern Shore on the Delmarva Peninsula, Delaware, Maryland, and Virginia all share its wealth and beauty. Ocean City, Maryland, was once part of a long barrier peninsula.

As far back as the early 1800s, hurricanes began cutting inlets. The overfilled Indian River Bay, Delaware, waters receded back to the ocean. Amplified during tide change from high to low tide created the Indian River Inlet. Hurricanes, bringing lots of rain, wind, sand erosion, and tidal change would cause water to wash back at low points over the long barrier peninsula. The Great Hurricane of 1933 separated Ocean City, Maryland, from Assateague Island, Maryland, as the waters receded just south of the Isle of Wright Bay, Maryland. Bethany, DE, South Bethany, DE, Fenwick Island, DE, and Ocean City, Maryland, are bordered on this twenty-mile-long barrier island.

Growing up, he and his family were able to enjoy some weekends at the beach. His dad would rent a beach house for a one-week vacation in Ocean City, Maryland. He enjoyed the beach, swimming and body surfing small to large waves, building sand castles, looking for fiddler crabs with a flashlight at night, and just relaxing on towels or blankets, just as long as he was at the beach. Spending time near the ocean was entertaining and yet relaxing. For excitement the family could go to the boardwalk. There were bumper cars, roller coasters, Ferris wheels, games to win prizes, funnel cakes, cotton candy, candy apples, and caramel popcorn. All made in front of you. The smells were incredible along the boardwalk. Fresh air off the ocean and all the different foods. The "boardwalk" fries were awesome. There were always extremely long lines. French fries deep fried in peanut oil, but the only condiments available were salt and vinegar. Most would get a bucket to share with friends. Soak the fries with vinegar and load the salt. A little bit of the British or English "fish and chips" left four hundred years later on the east coast. And the hand-tossed pizza. Pizza so good he would burn the roof of his mouth every time he ate it. He'd try but seemingly just couldn't wait long enough for the pizza to cool.

Back then, renting a beach house in advance, families took great risk with what the weather could bring. Stuck with the time frame of prior renting and when Dad could get off work, we kids had to adapt to what to do with rough surf, tropical storms, hurricanes, and power loss in summer during these vacations. Great fun and terrific memories! Adaptability was key to having fun. Knowing when to test swimming skills, understanding what to do in rip current, and when to stay out of the water were all part of summer vacation's terrific memories. Oh yeah, when he was young, he actually made some water rescues and saves. Sure, what good swimmer didn't hit the water running and get deep enough to do a shallow dive? Get up, run, and dive again till swimming and ducking waves was a must. It was a good feeling when parents said "Thank you." Well, sometimes. Sometimes the kids would get disciplined for not recognizing the rip and getting pulled out way over their head. "Stay on the raft!" we would holler. "Someone will get you." And we would. Swim with the rip. Eventually, the water gets deep enough, and the rip dies off. Return alongside the rip. It was on many occasions people panicked because they felt they were being pulled too far out and fight the rip, trying to come straight back or they'd slide off the raft. That's not really a good idea at all. Honestly, on a few occasions, the water was just way too rough. There were some heavy wooden boats spaced every block or so that would require teamwork and time. In most cases, hollering encouragement from shore most were saved. Undertow was a whole other story. Very dangerous for a novice swimmer to be pulled under in rough surf. Learning how to back-float is extremely beneficial and catching surface waves beside the undertow is the way to go. Even the best of swimmers can get caught off guard. Just having a good time in the water, playing around, and suddenly realize you're in trouble. Everyone can have good time, but communication and situational awareness among your group and sharing with others helps a lot.

Of course, during the 1960s, stays at the beach were before central air. If his family got lucky, the vacation home came with a window unit. Surely his dad did not pay extra during the early years. Power loss in the summer ensured those closest to the windows in the bedroom got the best sleep, especially after being in the sun all day. No air-conditioning meant arguments at night between brothers over who had the fans blowing directly on them. Arguments had to be settled by Dad. If Dad did not intervene, of course the oldest brother, being the strongest, would end up in the morning totally covered with blankets and the fan blowing directly on his head. His brothers, except he and his youngest brother, had fair skin and burned easier.

Actually, with multiple windows open came an ocean breeze and the sounds of crashing surf. Waves rolling in sometimes peaceful, smooth and with ease. Sometimes crashing with loud thunderous pounding. Softness was very relaxing. The loud surf always attracted the swimmer. He darkened more than burned. For an elementary school play, each pair of kids, a boy and a girl in his grade, was chosen to represent a state of the United States. Even though he and Reba were not Puerto Rican, they were chosen to represent the Commonwealth of Puerto Rico. When he proudly told his mom, she seemed upset. He paid this no mind. No one else was as dark in third grade, and he got to hold Reba's hand; she was cute!

He loved crabbing for the Maryland Blue Crab with his dad. The blue crab's meat is considered a delicacy in restaurants around the country. The crab could easily be trapped or netted using bait in the salt water wetlands of the Lower Eastern Shore. Using cheap chicken parts like chicken neck usually purchased for gravy or soups as bait, tied to strings then attached to a post on shore at one end with the bait disappearing into the dark turbid waters at the other. A crabber can use anything dead for bait. Fish heads or cut-up eel worked fine too. To prevent the bait from floating or be taken by current, a sinker had to be attached near the bait. A crabber could purchase sinkers and bait string at the hardware store. Kite string and bolts, large nuts, or washers for weight would work fine. To catch the crab, one retrieves the bait by pulling the string hand over hand until the crab becomes visible. A savvy crabber learns the blue crab prefers to scavenge and eat prior to certain tidal changes. Prior to the changing of tides, the crab becomes reluctant to let go of its find, making crabbing easier to net and more plentiful the catch. As the line is pulled near, and once the crab becomes visible, the crabber uses a net on a pole to scoop it and dump it in a bushel basket. Usually within two to three hours, they could fill a bushel basket. If they hit the tide change right, twenty to thirty minutes and were done. Sometimes they came home with a bushel full of eighteen-inch claw-to-claw, nine-inch point-to-point, all males, with the lovely blue claw, throwing the females back. The blue crab was commonly sold for fifteen to twenty-five dollars by the bushel depending on size, and affordability. The catch of the Maryland Blue Crab is quite sparse, and great catches of the "jumbo" or "jimmy" are scarce today. The crab was overfished. The commercial fishing industry and water temperature changes of the Chesapeake Bay have reduced their numbers. The temperature may be due to a changing environment today but years ago corporations using salt water for cooling needs returned the used water to the bay warmer in large quantities. Originally, catches were limited by how much one could carry. Today, catches are limited by laws; prices have climbed making bushel purchase almost impossible for the common man. More common to be sold by the dozen.

There were a few extra tricks to learn if one went crabbing. Like how to get the crab out of the net. Switching from a scooping technique coming from under the bait. Flipping the net over while in a slight downward motion dumps the crab into a bushel basket. The crab likes to hold on to the netting, but with a little force and persistence, the crab lets go. Sometimes much easier said than done. Sometimes the crab is feisty and tangles in the net. When many crabs are biting, a crabber is best to have a clean net quickly. The best story is of the man who was nearby. It was crabbing day for him and his dad. All had been going well most of the day until the man netted a big, stubborn female. It's easy to tell the male from the female. The female has a triangular shape or semicircle when mature on the underside of her shell that opens to release her eggs. This underbelly portion of her shell opens and closes and is called an apron. The male's apron has a monument shape on a mound, which opens during mating. When the nearby gentleman tried to free the female crab, well, she became tangled a little. His dad and him really paid little attention for everyone struggles with a tangled crab once in a while. They both heard a cry out in pain. Oh boy, she had the man's finger good. The gentleman hollered, "Get her off!" Blinded by pain and seeing a little blood oozing had forced the gargled scream for attention.

His dad said, "Just put your hand in the water." The gentleman was momentarily confused. Trying to undo her claw which was embedded in the finger while holding the other claw is near impossible. Finally, his dad, encouraging with a little assistance, steering the man's hand downward, while saying "Put your hand in the water and she'll let go." The man did. She let go and swam away. Very relieved and catching his breath, the man said, "You know, I was doing real good. I'd been watching the crab's mouth all day, and wouldn't you know, the damn thing bit me with its hand!"

Crabbing on weekends with his dad was great. Mostly while crabbing, his focus tended more to be about playing around, curiosity about all the creatures of the Lower Eastern Shore wetlands, and he loved swimming. He asked his father, "Why do we use chicken?"

His dad said, "Because it's cheap, but you can use anything dead. Some use fish head." *Anything—wow, that's a little disturbing,* he thought. How about him while he swims, what's in the dark turbid waters? Many unknowns. Jellyfish, sharks, all kinds of creatures that cause pain maybe even death. The sense of adventure and fun seemed to outweigh risk. We seem to have more confidence when our feet are on a sandy bottom, not letting feet or toes touch the muck on the bottom. The surf was one thing, but back in the channels like this, you never know what's on the bottom. He once stepped in a nest of eels barefooted. How did he know it was eels not snakes? The skin of the slimy creatures against the bare skin of his feet and toes, much slimier than that of the reptilian skin. Always being concerned and worried of what could be hidden in the dark turbid waters, so he swam. If those crabs could bite with their hands, certainly the sharks he knew about could bite a leg off or a sting ray could sting him with the barbed poisonous bone protruding near its tail. Just couldn't see what was in the dark, turbid waters but they were all there. Always told by others, "You'll be fine, don't be scared." Is it the same on land? Is there a type of life among us that exists without any possible scientific explanation? Because man is just not capable of completely understanding of all forms of existences?

One time, a crowd gathered at the beach. Of course he ran to investigate. His older brother went too. They gathered around a very colorful jellyfish. Someone said it was Portuguese Man o' War. What's that? They kicked sand over it and walked away. He watched with a little curiosity and said, "What are you doing?" Then getting surprised, he said, "Don't, better not," as he watched his older brother pick it up. His brother screamed bloody murder as it rolled down his arms and chest. He looked at that thing and thought, *Wow, that thing did that?* He thought the pretty colors must be a warning. His brother immediately went into shock, was taken away by ambulance, and that was it. They had to go. His brother came home later from the hospital bandaged all over from acid like burns and had almost died from the shock. He and his brothers made fun of him laid up on the sofa, telling him he looked like "the Mummy" from the old mummy movies.

One Saturday, his dad took him and his two older brothers fishing at Isabella St. Bridge, Salisbury, Maryland. Known for an area of ship building along the Wicomico River in Salisbury. The Wicomico River was tidal filling and emptying into the Chesapeake Bay. Damned at Johnson Pond. About a four- to five-foot spillway, gently, almost lazily but really beautifully spilled a tea-like color of the Lower Eastern Shore's fresh water into the river from the pond. The sound of a small waterfall can be graciously relaxing. A good place to fish. His oldest brother was casting with a rod-and-reel fishing rod and had a knack for fishing just as his grandfather did. His older brother was having some success catching bass, crappie, and other game fish. Full of energy but regulated to a long bamboo pole with hook and earthworm, his dad baited for him. Of course he wanted a fishing rod to cast with. Of course he asked and lamented out loud. He was simply left to figure it out on his own; he just wasn't trusted with a rod-and-reel fishing rod yet. Still wanting to catch fish, he would run to wherever his oldest brother would catch a fish. His brother would move to a different spot once his little brother would slap the water with bobber and hook. The little boy must've been very annoying to a fisherman. Noticing his older brother had slipped away and hooked a nice-sized bass, he immediately lifted his long bamboo pole enough to free the bait from water and began running along the bank toward the much hotter fishing spot. While running, believing he had snagged in a bush, slowing very little. Glancing to check surely a hard tug would free it. Then full speed ahead immediately. Then another snag. *Must be a bush*, he thought. Without looking, he gave an extra hard tug on the pole only to hear a bloodcurdling yell. A loud command but in obvious pain: "Whoa, boy, *whoa*!" Uh-oh.

Stopping to look back, he noticed an older gentleman with a hat on and a bamboo pole. But now, with a hand to the neck. He walked slowly to look as Dad ran forward to help. Not only did the little boy accidentally hook the man in the neck, he had given an extra hard tug, accidentally setting the hook deeper. His dad ran over quickly to assess then proceeded to toss the worm and remove the deeply embedded hook. Couldn't fish. The little boy's pole would be unavailable for a while. Watching for a little bit, he got bored and wandered over by his brother. With shaggy, curly dark-brown hair just covering his ears, his brother glared at him through thick, black-rimmed glasses. Even looked at him over the glasses. With a very noticeable shaking of the head, he went back to casting near the falls.

After the hook was out, his dad made him go to the older man, and apologize. He did but really didn't understand the seriousness and didn't have the remorse he should've. Suddenly, his dad commanded, "Go sit in the car." "But," came the reply. Then, "No! Get in the car." His dad made him sit in the car while they both fished. A seeming forever length of time longer. He didn't really understand back then why his other older brother would rather sit in the car almost the whole time, not fishing as he did. He asked his older brother; he just remembered his older brother said he didn't like fishing and didn't want to stay.

His brother said, "What'd you do this time?"

"Uh, nothing. Guess I hooked some man." This was not the first time he caused his dad to be in a tough position and embarrassed of his son's behavior and certainly not the last.

Not only Truthful Testimony but also, do not Test thy Lord thy God

While in Sunday school, he was taught that God couldn't be seen but was real. He had swam in waters of which creatures could not be seen, but they were there. He asked the Sunday schoolteacher,

"If he's real, why can't you see Him?" She assured him God was real, you just can't see Him. Now that just didn't make sense. Even if you couldn't see all the animals of the dark ocean waters or even the fresh, dark waters of Lower Eastern Shore, they're there. Can prove it! Sharks will kill people and can be caught, killed, and eaten. Crabs and fish are there. Can't see them, but they're there. People catch 'em and eat 'em. Everyone had told him not to worry sharks and other things wouldn't bother him. Sure was a lot of creatures in the dark waters that could hurt him. Oh well, without fear, he swam anyway. Was this Sunday school teachings real? Was this Sunday school teaching similar to the strange creatures in the dark waters? Were there such things as the Unseen that are real, exist, a form of life that can't be seen, but are all about us? He loved all he was being taught about the long-haired guy with sheep and kids. Who seemed to love everyone and cared for everyone, was real but couldn't be seen. He wondered why, if God was real, why couldn't He be seen. Which at first was an extreme puzzlement brought forth an extremely firm belief. Finally, the little boy thought, *That ain't right!* If God was real, one could see Him. No! They're wrong! He believed. No. The little boy knew! If God was real, one could see Him. What could've been awe-inspiring on a beautiful blue and puffy white-clouded day turned into the little boy being cast from church at about five years old. Although he could see, hearing a call can sound quite different and seemingly hard to match with what you have seen or what you see.

"Many are called, but few are chosen."

Being quite young at this church meant not attending while the service was delivered by "the Preacher" to attending adults. Oh, how the little boy longed and yearned to learn more of this long-haired, loving man. But the little boy was prevented. Relegated to filling in pictures with crayons of the man that cared and loved everyone one so much, He would willingly hand Himself over to be so brutally and horrible tortured until death. A type of pain which can only be endured because one is chained to be flogged, then lifted high purposely that the earth would provide for man's evil intentions of its natural constant downward pull. Left to struggle in the midday sun for every last breath taken. Each breath to be taken by pulling one's body weight up with muscle and bone which are firmly nailed into position, timed with the upward thrust from legs either nailed or steadied upon a small perch. For the specific reason of struggle for each and every last breath. The little boy understood very young that people of power and authority could be cold, callous, even viciously cruel. Of the many thousands left to die on a tree in this manner, some with a strong will to live would have their legs broken toward evening to prevent from pushing up with the strongest part of their body. Left with the pain and impossibility of pulling full body weight up basically in the position of the iron cross. The amount of time the iron cross is held is measured in seconds, maybe minutes, by the greatest of gymnasts on a set of rings. The act of delivering death as mercy was only done near major cities or during religious festivals where large gatherings of influential people from all over the world might attend. Nothing was worse than preventing a proper burial and leaving a dead body in a tree overnight. Although throughout the countrysides of the known world, leaving the corpse in a tree was also a teaching lesson by those seeking to extend authority and control over others by fear. Undoubtedly, there would be loyal and devoted family and friends that would risk their lives to sneak in the thousands of corpse trees. Searching stealthily before nightfall to attend to loved ones lovingly and properly. What man would volunteer for this type of brutal death? Merely that others would come to know that they are loved? The little boy lacked so much. He just could not understand the need for this type of love. But truly, the little boy did want to know such love. He wanted to find out. He wanted to learn it.

He gathered and sat with the other children and listened intently while the Sunday school teacher read from a children's bible to them all. He was thoroughly engrossed while listening, becoming absolutely amazed, even utterly astounded at someone so loving and caring and a Divine Being of such great and extraordinary magnificence. After the reading, he and the other children assembled around a table with crayons. They all quietly began coloring biblical pictures of men and women dressed in older-style robing and sheep. To him, the plainness seemed easy to color in. He loved it! Something so magnificent meant we lived in a very wonderful world. There would be so much to look forward to. He wanted to share such wonderment with the other children. But when he began to share his excitement with others, he began to feel odd. What could only be described today as "The odd man out?" Others did not seem receptive. To him, things began to seem so odd, as if they didn't believe. But it all was real. The teacher had just said so. The little boy believed. Others seemed that they could care less. What was it? Didn't anyone really care? Didn't they all believe? Well, to him, that was it. Either it was real, or it wasn't. If it was real, and he believed it was all very real, then he could see them. When he said this to the other kids, they became troubled and upset. So he became a little upset too, but in a way that was firm and resolute in truth. If God was real, well then, he could see Him! The little boy argued this point with the teacher until she became firm and gruff. Then the little boy was the odd boy left out. The other kids kept their distance and wouldn't talk with him anymore.

At first, intentionally displaying humility and intentionally asking in a mere curious voice but loud enough for the teacher to hear a few tables away. "We can see God, right?" The Sunday school teacher, very calmly and assuredly, said, "Oh no. It's not like that."

He cut her off, "But if they're real, we can see them!" Herself becoming firmer, even more animated in expression, began to repeat herself. It was then he could hear no more. He was upset and embarrassed. Something just wasn't right! He slowly unfurled, resting down upon bent knees, head in one hand. Returning to coloring but now halfheartedly. Deflated, he began to wonder, *If they're real, why can't we see them?* Now what the adults said didn't sit well with him. It just didn't make sense. Because he believed. Now he really wanted to see God, wanted to badly. They all were wrong. He knew it!

Shortly thereafter, he stood alone in the front yard and looked to the sky. No one else around. He strained, focusing deep down to his inner core, knowing, *God, if you are real then I can see you.* It came out. Wow, he actually said that out loud. Then slowly, the little boy began to feel something. Inside his inner being and from outside. Everywhere. Then something caused him look to the sky. A pull? Of course, he slowly began to lift his head. It was at this time, he felt nothing, there was nothing else but the sky as it began to change. He stood. He now stood erect hands at side with head angled up in the air. It was a gorgeous blue sky with soft white puffy, pillowy clouds abounding everywhere. The skies in the direction he was looking began to change. Swirling, circular, almost tunnel like, but not into a tunnel at all. Although there seemed to be a swirl, it formed as part of everything that was of the sky. What was being revealed seemed to be there all along. Like what was behind something, no more like a part of what was already there, merely changing, now becoming clear. Maybe, like slowly erasing or dissolving what was between he and they. Now they were perfectly clear. Almost too clear? They were very large. They were ginormous and so clear they were real. Not ghostlike. The details were perfection. They were merely a different form of energy. Not flesh. Their hair and clothing, even the toes of the one closest to him, with his back turned, moved a little. Yes, he wore sandals with robing way down to upper shin. The boy's attention first turned to examine the two with their backs facing him yet with their right sides angled a little toward him, with a larger man opposite them. Wait, they were so big. As his eyes traveled upward for close examination, he thought, *were the two turning to look at him?* What they were sitting at seemed to be a slight angle to the little boy's point of view. Or maybe just a matter of perspective. Although the three appeared to be as mostly the color of the sky, blue and white. Additionally, there were various other different shades of blue, turquoise, purple, and greens that defined their appearance. Some would describe this sighting as a vision, or seeing these appearances as apparitions, or daydreaming, or even hallucinating. *Ha!* That would be a resounding *no!* What he saw was so real he could've touched them. Or they could reach out and touch him or could've hit him? They seemed reserved or very contrite, though. Complete sense of security, harmless, peaceful. Weren't they seemingly too far away? Well, maybe. Distances suddenly seemed to vary when everything that exist manifest into the three Most Holy Divine Beings.

The three of them were sitting at a table. But it was quite a different table than any he had ever seen before. The table seemed to be a little higher than a normal table one might sit at. Even though they sat at the table, they were leaning over, looking intently down into the table. As if the table had depth. Yes, they were looking down into the depths of the table. As they looked intently into the depths of the table, the three were communicating. Not by speaking. There was no lip movement at all. But clearly they were communicating very rapidly. Mentally. Today, we call it or refer to as telepathically. To him, it seemed deeper than that. Working on something back and forth extremely rapidly, almost simultaneously, seemingly in harmony. It was then he noticed the closest two did not know he was there. Now he realized it seemed as though the two were turning toward the little boy. Then slowly, the one closest began to smile and slowly look right down unto him. He saw him! But His smile was so genuinely caring and seemingly in loving amusement; the little boy was not frightened at all. Actually a reassuring and very warm, welcoming smile. After all, the little boy had asked to see. Well, almost, because the little boy believed so deeply he merely stated toward the sky and heavens matter-of-factly, "God, if you're real, I can see you." It was actually deeper than that. What the little boy had said extended from his heart and soul as innocent and humble. Not demanding. It was a sheepish way to say what one knows. The closest One the little boy noticed, now smiling at the boy, had long hair extending outward from under a hood. The exposed soft hair was gently being blown by wind or lightly flowing in the wind. His hair did seem soft and so too his beard and mustache. He was absolutely charming. Aware all three were still there, the little boy's eyes went to the left, examining the One seated at the left of the One closest to him. She smiled down at him. She was really pretty, not really dainty but feminine. She was beautiful; her movements as she shifted to turn and look down upon him were graceful and effeminate. Her smile was genuine sincere and, although amused, seemed to care of or about but then the little boy's gaze shifted to the One across from the two.

Although His clothing was very similar, His clothing seemed to be well-worn, or His robe was "worn extremely casually." Much heavier. Much bigger. Much larger framed. His forearms were exposed. Like a man ready to get down to some hard work. Very large bulbous forearms. His upper chest was exposed. His hood was down. His full head of shoulder length hair was fully exposed and began to be blown about fiercely, wildly as if blown by a strong wind. His beard and His mustache moved in the wind. Even His eyebrows bristled in the wind. The little boy now becoming astonished was slowly able to focus on the eyes and face of the larger One. Because the larger One now gained eye to eye contact with the little boy. His look was quite different. His look was as if the little boy interrupted a general, while the general was coordinating battle stratum in an ongoing war. A very serious look. It was then, the large One made the point, intentionally moving His face closer to him. Surely it wasn't a frown or scorn but very intent, serious, and yes, fearsome indeed. To most, it would've been terrifying or horrifying. But to him, the little boy, after all, he had asked to see. But that face was getting closer, as if he, the little boy, had interrupted, like he could be in trouble. That did it. It was too much. He shook it all off and ran into the house. Yes, he was scared, shaken; after all, the little boy had just experienced a light dose of the true fear of God.

An episode like that might be what has become known as "scaring the bejeezus out of him" (commonly pronounced be-'jē-zus). Well, although the occurrence did not scare the "be-like-Jesus out of him," what would happen next would result in a block or would directly contribute in his great difficulty in coming to know Jesus, being able to "come into his own" and great difficulty in becoming like Jesus or to "be like Jesus."

Although like being in trouble and very traumatic, the experience was very awe-inspiring. It was too much to keep to himself. He wanted to jump with joy. He wanted to tell someone. Wanted to tell everyone. By telling someone would relieve some pressure. He felt if someone else believed, the great internal pressure the little boy was experiencing would be released. But there would never be that type of release. The little boy would never be believed. This would cause a huge letdown, an unbelievable inner turmoil. As the little boy grew, he would search for ways to gain confidence. Always pushing the very limits of all boundaries. Even life and death. It was on many occasions he just plain knew truth, but without any reinforcement, he thought all his struggles were his own. His saving grace, being young and innocent mixed with naivete and immaturity. He deep down believed he never did anything wrong, yet for the one thing that would come next. Even being so young, such an experience could've been and should've been awe inspiring, with the potential to change everything. Change everything indeed. Just not the way anyone would've hoped.

The little boy did not know man cannot stand alone in the real presence of God and live. Too young to know the difference between clean and unclean, only just beginning to know the difference between right and wrong. His first knowing of wrong was when he was told, God and Jesus are real, and exist but can't be seen. What was right for him merely led to another wrong. Not understanding completely why, only knowing what is real can be seen. Too young yet to understand that there can be many ways to "see," to learn and know truth. Being of youth and pureness, his skin was not yet corrupted, the little boy caught a glimpse of what he was not yet supposed to see.

He skipped a process. Critical steps. Procedures that must be learned and must be taken. That look was so intensely fearsome, especially from such an imposing appearance. The one who seemed in charge gave the little boy a look as if he had done something wrong and was about to get in some serious trouble. As the boy grew to adulthood, get in trouble he surely did. Forgetting the smiles which seemed reassuring. The boy felt as though he had interrupted. Is there a penalty against a pure heart that contends with assertion for substantiation? No. Were it not for other two present, would there have been repercussions by the One for such insistence by a little boy or a child with a pure heart? Or is it that the little boy skipped all that is required to come to know faith and learn the power of belief? Surely, without a doubt, the little boy believed with his entire being, that if God was real, the little boy could see Him. So he did. The little boy had all the substantiation he needed to believe. But too young and weak for the required battles, as the boy grew, he fell away. Off a cliff. No one to blame but himself. The little boy should've remained firm and strong. It was as if he would have to forget what happened to fit in everywhere: school, work, recreational activities, everything, everywhere.

Were it not for presence of the other two, was witnessing God's existence possible? Are incomprehensible repercussions unintentional but unavoidable because of a type of spontaneous combustion when corrupt flesh nears God? A type of existence or energy required to produce a cosmos, universe, and an earth which all are alive. A form of life man is incapable to understand or unable to comprehend, yet it is that universe and planetary system which sustains life and is itself alive.

Think of a body sweating. Think of flesh as emitting an aroma (a smell). Think of the body carrying static electricity or even having a small electromagnetic field. This human body also carries many forms of microorganisms inside and out. Good and bad bacteria in the colon. Spontaneous combustion occurs when a material increases in temperature without drawing heat from its surroundings, such as oily rags or hay. Or picture a gasoline fire. It is not that gasoline that ignites quickly; it is the fumes that burn.

Now reason that it is not necessarily the flesh that cannot be in the presence with the makeup of God; it is what the body carry's internally and sometimes unknowingly externally, which emits or radiates, which causes "combustion" when in the presence of the material, makeup, or pure energy of the Creator.

Is there a way? Sometimes if one tosses a lit cigarette into a puddle of liquid gasoline, the lit cigarette is extinguished. Sometimes the ember finds its way through the fumes or vapor without igniting, only to be extinguished by the gas liquid. Removing the vapors turns the highly volatile gas into a harmless, controllable liquid.

Removing the sin which cannot be seen or removing the invisible corruption can only be achieved through forgiveness. Containing the fumes will not prevent possible combustion.

It was what happened next that would prevent anyone else for more than half a century coming to know Him from this child.

His Sunday school lessons were located in an old castle like building located at the center of town in Salisbury, Maryland. At the time, he went to the stone and mortar castle-like structure, the church was a Christ Methodist Church. The first day of Sunday school since his vision or, to him, his first chance to tell someone he saw God. Not just saw God, no, *really* saw God! He was so ecstatic with joy. It was all, very real! He couldn't wait to tell someone. So excited. What may have been a proud and miraculous moment for all turned awful. See, he was just a little boy and knew what he saw had to be. He didn't understand that so few had seen God, and none of those were to be believed. Not without proof anyway. But for him, there was no doubt. To understand the reasons that none have seen God and lived to tell about it, some misunderstandings would have to be cleared up. Maybe as the true story of a little boy who saw God continues, truth might provide a greater understanding for many or provide for clarity that others might see. One thing for sure: the power of belief is so strong; if people believe they can't see God, well then, they can't. Unless of course, God knocks some sense into them, sets a bush on fire with beautiful flames which do not harm the bush, fills a mountain with smoke, flames, during hurricane-type conditions with lightning traveling in every direction. The ground splitting open and quaking in conjunction with the sounds of His voice would be so frightening everyone would fall on their face, screaming that the end of the world is at hand. And by the way, the ones who still stand in defiance would have their eyes burned out while their skull turns to a molten puddle of goo.

The little boy couldn't help himself. At first, while coloring at the table with other children, he began sharing what he had seen. God's real. And that he'd seen Him. First, the boys closest to him. A guy thing? They either actually turned a shoulder or quietly became more intent on their project. Then the cutest girl directly across from him whom he had on frequent occasion compared the quality of their coloring together. Guess it was a kind of reciprocal flirtation but both too young to understand. He certainly did have a clear extra interest in her though. She moved over a seat and moved her crayons too. Becoming a little perturbed at the ignorance around him, he now understood he would have to challenge the teacher in front of everyone. Then if the teacher was convinced, then certainly the other kids would have an opportunity to learn. Upset now but controlled, the little boy declared, "God is real. I saw Him."

The Sunday school teacher's shock and disbelief of a little boy so adamant and firm in his beliefs turned into rigorous and demanding questioning. First, the teacher made completely clear to everyone in the room that it was not possible. It's not like that. Others were shocked at the little boy speaking so boldly and confidently.

Then came the questions from the teacher across the room demanding, "When?"

He tried to confidently answer.

"Where?"

Again, he tried.

"What did he look like?"

A sudden realization came over the little boy. It was clear now the little boy was being verbally disciplined in front of everyone. So the little boy who was making a stand at first on his knees in his chair sank to a seated position. The little boy understood what was beginning to take place. Realization was slowly sinking in.

She got up from her desk, pet student stepping back, giving a slight grin and a look like "You're going to get what you deserve now." As she came over toward him the little boy started to withdraw into the sinking feeling, which started to consume him. The teacher approached in short order and firmly pulled him up out of his chair. She bent over to be inches from his face. That was when he straightened his back, intently turning his little face slowly but purposely toward her face. As far as he recalled, this was the first time he experienced an inward defiance. He now was standing firm in the face of an adult whose intentions were being covered by fake mannerisms of gentleness and kindness. The little boy sensed it and acquired a great disdain for it. Then came seemingly kinder demands to answers and to describe what he saw: what did they look like, what color, what were they sitting at, since he said they were sitting at something. While trying to answer the questions, he slowly began to notice he was not being believed. The questioning only became more intense. Then again came a sarcastic demand, "Well, what were they sitting at?"

He could not answer because he did not know what exactly the three were sitting at. The little boy had no clue what an altar was or a Book of Life, let alone how to explain to someone how they could've possibly be communicating without talking. He could see the outcome of saying something like that, if she could not believe something so simple as the little boy had seen God. Caving into what was seeming like relentless pressure and interrogation, he lied, saying something he thought they would believe. She would not believe the truth, but he knew she would believe a lie and stop with the embarrassing chastisement in front of everyone. And the cute girl. She would never come near him again. Only strange looks from her and her mom. Mostly her mom. Her dad paid him no mind. Nothing. Actually intentional ignorance of the little boy's presence. He decided to tell her something she would believe. So he lied. He said they were sitting at a black pot. That seemed to work. She stopped. Just to make sure, he defiantly added, "And there was a fire under it." Really defiant. With a mad, mean-faced look. Now the little boy knew she would stop. She sure did!

Shouldn't have said that! Besides it not being a true representation of what he actually saw. He lied. That he can never change. There was no color of a fire. He said there was a black pot. No pot. And there was no black color to what he had seen. He also knew then what he knows today, no description of what he saw will ever adequately suit anyone. No one. What would make him so special as to see God? He learned quickly he could never tell anyone again. He would just have to get through this episode he caused. At the time, he had no idea the depth of his actions. Fifty years later, the man would come to understand and know that he did bear false witness. But not necessarily against his neighbor. Much, much worse. The little boy bore false witness directly against God. There would be no recovery on this day for the day got worse. It was only the beginning.

Back in the day, one might say it all scared the bejesus out of him. But it didn't. Might be appropriate at this point to explain the terms "scared the bejeezus out of him" and remove Be-Jesus. Both terms are extremely similar. "Scared the bejeezus" is slang for a "knock off from an era gone by." Something so terrifying as to forever remove the potential for one to be like Jesus. The term *Be-Jesus* is a conveyance of very deep respect that a person could ever be like Jesus. "Remove the Be-Jesus" conveys the highest and utmost possibility of becoming one with Jesus is gone, no longer accessible, or achievable. You should know. That is not ever possible. Everyone has the availability and potential to *be like Jesus,* no matter what. There being only two obstacles: belief and wisdom. Both are your choice.

What he saw were definitely three people. An older, seemingly much larger and more mature gentleman. Bigger in stature than the other two. He was tough and forbearing. His intent look at the boy as he seemingly came closer and became larger in size was as intended by God, and it was startling and fearful to the little boy. His demeanor obviously not intended to strike terror or horror but merely meant to demonstrate seriousness and firmness. But today, the boy who grew to manhood knows two very important observations and clear understandings of this encounter. One: God never gives more than the recipient can handle. Two: God turned His face toward the little boy. Once God turns His face toward you, he never turns His back on you. It was this day, seeking God, which was the beginning of wisdom. The little boy may have always seemed different to others, and that may have been because many things were clearer to him than others might be able to see. There were many occasions he just plain knew.

It might be important to note here the word *inspire, inspirare,* originates from its Latin root, *theopneustos,* or "God breathed." In other words, revelations and inspirations from deep within are from God's breath. Many who influence the air today have coined the phrase "follow your dreams." A special note of caution: As the body rests, the brain entertains many uncontrolled activities which leave a human very vulnerable and susceptible to other influences. There are many worldly influences which directly affect our dreams. It would be critical to follow internal inspiration as intended from its original meaning. And there is a way to identify divine inspiration from other influences. It's a practice taught long ago that will be addressed later.

Of course he didn't see a black pot with a fire; he lied to get the pressure off him. It worked; she left him. She told him to stay there alone but with the other children. She told him to stay with the other children until she came back. The other children wouldn't even get near him or look at him. She left in a huff. She came back with the man in charge. Although he knew the man was in charge, in no way would that man able to change what the little boy had seen. The man always wore black with a white collar. Maybe that man might believe him. Would he be nice? The anticipation was hard. Once they entered, the teacher called the little boy over. To once again stand with a firm, erect back. So he stood erect, but the back, of course, curved to look up at the man in all black. From shoes to round white collar. The boy's eyes started from the floor. From shiny black shoes. Sharply creased black pants. So sharp a crease as to cut a finger. But this time, as his eyes slowly went up, the little boy relaxed his posture. Somehow because the little boy knew what was about to happen. The man smiled very kindly. Oh, some relief? Then came the teacher's "Tell him what you said." The relief snatched away. Gone immediately. This time there would be less patience. Not from the two adults. The little boy would have less patience. The little boy started again boldly, He saw God. The man's response was calm at first, but clearly, the imposing figure was shocked and surprised by the declaration of a little boy. More questions. Soft at first. Then escalating firmly. *That's enough*, the boy thought. The little boy knew how to get him to stop. Out it came again: It was a black pot, with a fire under it. Again, the boy spoke with a grimacing face to make the point of something the two adults would believe. Then the opposing, scary, mean man in black revealed his true identity. The boy's face was merely a more animated mocking reflection of the faces glaring down at him. Right back at'cha? What was calm at first then suddenly demanding that when the little boy got home to tell his mom and dad exactly what had happened that day. This was all so perplexing, even worrisome. More trouble than it was worth? The little boy wondered, should he ever tell anyone again? Best just to forget about it? All he knew and understood was everyone was mad at him, did not like him anymore, and did not even want him around. Didn't remember if he told his mom or dad. Maybe, but certainly not the whole story. Maybe just a fraction of something like "I told 'em in church I saw God." And that would have been that. They probably would've just looked at each other a little puzzled then at their son as he ran out of the room, shrugging shoulders, Dad getting back to reading a newspaper.

A few weeks later, his brothers were at school, himself too young for school. His father at work. He was out front playing when a very big, black shiny new car pulled up. He guessed those kinds of cars were called Cadillacs. It was the man in black with a white collar. A long black overcoat. The little boy ducked behind a tree hoping he wasn't seen. As the man in black glared over his way, he simply continued a long stride with the tails of his coat lifting in the wind. The man strove as if on a mission toward the front door. Of the boy's house? Most friends of the family went to the back door. *Uh-oh*, he thought. This ain't good. He peeked from where he hid in the yard. After speaking with his mom at the front door, they both looked over at him. The boy couldn't hear them but could tell they were talking about him. They continued to talk while looking in his direction. He ducked to hide even though he thought they saw him when they looked his way. After their short discussion and as the man in black was leaving, he glared over at the little boy before getting into his car and speeding off. The boy was a little worried but was relieved by knowing that man was gone. Sure glad he didn't have to talk to him. He went in the house, worried but acting as happy as he could. He knew things went better when he would seem like he was happy and having fun. Never a recollection of his mom ever saying anything to him about it. Did his dad understand? The drive home from his last day at Sunday school with his dad and mom was yet to come. This ride was an unusually long ride to get to church. Just the three of them, though? Not his brothers too?

He remembered as a boy the three—he, his mom, and his dad—riding the long ride. His mom was crying while sitting in the front seat on the ride, but he didn't know why. The three parked and walked into the large structure. As they entered the stone foyer, the boy attempted to go in, but his dad stopped him. A lady met them. She left, and the preacher came and extended cordial greetings to his mom and dad then glared down toward the boy. The conversation seemed intense. The preacher turned and went back in, and they left. The drive home was memorable, but not for good reasons. The child really didn't understand why his dad was angry and his mom sad. He remained inquisitive but had to just let go of what happened. Never got or understood a clear explanation of what happened from the adults. Later, his brothers explained the man in black was a preacher and told Mom her little boy was the devil's spawn or a demon sent from hell. The little boy never talked about his side of the story. Never defended himself. Nobody believed him, and it just seemed saying anything would get him in predicaments with the big people, so he stayed away from it. But it was always there. It happened. What they told him the preacher said did make him wonder though sometimes. Was he bad? He learned the big people, adults, were hard to trust. Adults could be very mean. The little boy had a hard time ever trusting adults again. There would be very few.

He also knew there was no truth in him being a devil. Well? If he was, wouldn't he know? He was sure he wasn't bad, he liked being good. And all of this did bother him. A lot. When he asked to go to church, he was told "No." Maybe a different church, maybe another time down the road, he was told. It saddened him. He had loved going to church. Learning about a man and a God who was extremely kind. He found that many people, adults especially, were not kind. Not at all. And most adults were not honest. It was as if they all were hiding something. This was about the time in his life he started wetting the bed at night and sucking his thumb. Thumb sucking didn't cause too much trouble as he twirled the soft corner of the blanket in his ear, just embarrassing within his family as he got older. But wetting the bed caused many, many problems. His mom and dad took turns after everyone fell asleep, trying to wake him up prior to the mess. Didn't work. After he'd awaken, he noticed their frustration when Mom or Dad discovered he had already wet the bed. Sucking his thumb lasted many years. Didn't stop until the threat of girls in elementary school possibly finding out. Yea, thumb sucking probably wouldn't have gone over really good with his fifth-grade elementary school girlfriend. One time, his mom put hot sauce on his fingers. Ha! That added flavor. And why did she make all the brothers drink castor oil sometimes? Gross. Didn't figure that one out until his own children had fully grown and the remedy when his own kids couldn't pass stool would've been a dose of good ole castor oil. He stopped by himself. Sure loved that satin portion of the blanket though. Yes, that faded too.

Although wetting the bed grew to a huge embarrassment, this, it seemed to him, he had no control over. As he got older, regrets built. All the problems he caused his mom troubled him, especially the difficulties she went through when trying to provide him with clean sheets. The washing machine was in the basement. Very steep steps. No dryer. Everything and the sheets had to hang dry. Of course, being young and trying to alleviate his mom's troubles by not telling her he wet the bed again only ended in more trouble. One time, the elementary school teacher pulled him from class and called his mom to come get him because he stunk. He couldn't spend the night with friends. He did because some of his friends really liked him. Even they would get in trouble trying to take up for him. Some of his friends got in fist fights with their older brothers over it. Over him. The turmoil and embarrassment from that one was hard to avoid and was quite heavy to bear. Especially for his mom. He became very sad that he had burdened his mom and dad. Very sad, indeed!

After episodes at friends' houses, it was on many occasions he would hang his head and walk home. Sometimes ten to fifteen miles. It seemed the long walks alone would help. Sometimes kind people would stop and offer rides. Sure he'd hop in. Happy and glad to meet someone who didn't know about him and seemed kind. There were times when evil or meanness came. Sometimes a car would stop, and as he jogged closer, it sped up and took off. Sometimes objects were thrown from passing cars. Sometimes he got in the back, sometimes in front. This proved to probably help a lot. From the back seat, he could observe the actions of the individual. He also kept his hand very near even on the door handle. In school, he did pretty well on parallel bars, rings, horse, and tumbling mats. He learned how to take a fall: bend knees, cover, and roll. If he had too, he would easily and gladly jump from a moving car. The thrill, excitement, and skill of escape he practiced on his own in the woods, jumping logs and ditches just like gymnastics but in a world of unpredictable obstacles on a dead run. Even diving off treacherous cliffs into unknown depths of ponds and lakes. Some dug by building contractors to extract clay only to have to cease operations because they would hit the many unmapped underground rivers of the lower eastern shore. These would turn out to be great gathering and party places for high schoolers because locations were normally remote and in wooded areas. It was easy to discern that the water was from underground rivers because of the pureness of smell and the water was turquoise in color. Some good swimmers had been known to disappear in these large ponds or lakes, assumed drowned but their bodies never found. Families and kids were told it was because the pond or lake was bottomless. He understood that underground currents would carry the body to unexplored and unknown parts of the earth. After a death, of course, the waters would be off limits and patrolled. Really wouldn't stop everyone. Just slowed the pace. Until a generation passed.

When his little brother was born and came home from the hospital, he saw the beautiful baby boy had something different. He noticed he only had four fingers on one hand, and that same arm was fixed, bent at the elbow. The little baby boy, especially beautiful in blue, but his arm hadn't developed a joint and was missing a thumb. His brother's arm would never bend. So he asked, "Are you sure he's yours, Mommy?"

His mom seemed sad but smiled gently, came close with both of them touching his new brothers arm saying: "Yes, he is your brother." The little boy asked if there was anything that doctors could do.

His mom started to cry, and his dad helped by saying, "He will be fine, he is fine."

The little boy said, "But?" Then his mom told him and explained his brother would adapt and overcome, probably won't even notice if you don't. They were right.

The whole family never noticed, swimming, playing baseball, push-ups, didn't matter. Only when at the beach when others would stare. Sometimes his little brother would notice other's staring, then his brother would notice and withdraw. If and when he would notice people's unwitting ignorance, he would intervene by intentionally catching the persons attention with a very stern-like "What's the problem?" Look then punch his brother or tackle him and get him to chase him down to the water, and they'd both dive in. Sometimes he'd look back to make the point: See? And he would actually see a parent disciplining an immature child. This would sometimes give feeling of hope for others and his brother's future. It was on many occasions people still stared or even pointed in their direction. He would strive harder to get his brother to shake it while simultaneously getting his brother to catch a wave and body-surf it, seeing who could ride it farther. Whenever his little brother might say he couldn't participate in some activity, his brothers wouldn't let him back down from challenges. Even fights!

On one occasion, the young boy overheard his mom tell his older brother of a very strange encounter one night during her pregnancy carrying his little brother. It seems there was a "man with a hat" that was in her bedroom in the middle of the night. She told his oldest brother she awoke to see a man sitting in the chair by her vanity. The man sat looking at her in an unlit room. His mom had no clue who, and she never figured out who it was. Even though he was not supposed to know, one day, he asked his dad about "the man with the hat" in their bedroom. Was that why his little brother's arm was like that? "Why didn't you wake up Dad, so you could beat that man up or make him leave? Surely Dad would've thrown a stranger out of the house."

His mom said she was frightened and just did not understand why or what was happening. She said, "Stop worrying, nothing happened." His dad overheard their discussion or more technically what was escalating to actually an argument. His parents didn't realize why the boy was becoming very upset at learning this. The little boy was becoming upset because he knew things existed that others didn't. His dad was becoming very puzzled but brought an end to the discussion, saying it was probably a dream. Then brushed off any more concerns by saying there really couldn't have been anything his dad could've done anyway. As the little boy retreated from their room, he turned and said, "Well, how did the 'man in the hat' leave then? Did the man jump out of the window?"

Staring out into the great void outside of her bedroom window, his mom sadly and very contritely stated, "No. After the man uncrossed his legs, the man stood up." Then he made eye contact with her and tipped the brim of the hat at her. Then walked out of the bedroom and then out the back door. And that she had heard the back door quietly open and heard the door close behind, as the man in the hat left.

Asthma is horrible for the parents of children who go through serious bouts of struggling to breathe. As the airway closes, the burning and pain for each breath becomes terminally frustrating. Noisy too. Yes, bronchial asthma has caused death. In most cases, asthma causes death in the young verses an older person because the strength of the lung to intake air is not matured through exercise and age. Not even necessarily exercise. Just the increase in activity as one grows strengthens the lung. Like a muscle improves with activity or becomes stronger with activity or exercise. In many cases, growth combined with exercise strengthens the lung's ability to forcefully intake air even if the airway becomes the size of a small straw. Know this. A serious bronchial asthma attack is very painful and extremely worrisome, disturbing, and can be very frightening. Deadly for the elderly too. Since he was very young, his severe bouts with asthma caused great discomfort, pain and much fear. During asthma attacks, however, his mom and dad would have no part of him excusing seemingly lackadaisical behavior on asthma or use his asthma as an excuse not to go to school. In his defense, he would exclaim, "Remember when the doctor came to the house, held me in his arms, and told you two never let this little boy get to this point again, to call the doctor or to take this little boy to the hospital right away."

Both were shocked. His parents told him, "You were too young to remember that!"

He said proudly and adamantly, "No, the doctor was holding me in his arms when he told you two!"

Silence entered the room, accompanied by a quiet stillness, as he continued that's when the doctor gently laid him back down, gently brushing the little boy's head and hair with his hand. Then the doctor put his coat on, picked up his black bag off the kitchen table, then put a derby-style black hat on, and left. His parents in disbelief as he recalled the details of the man that held him. There was no need to say anything else. That day, he stayed home from school. That was just too hard. Sometimes, after not sleeping all night and feeling flat-out horrible in the morning, while sitting on the toilet, he would lay his head on the radiator. Then he would come out and go right to his mom asking her to check and see if he had a fever. Some older houses had a furnace in the basement. The furnace combined with a broiler connected with steam pipes sent hot water into radiators positioned throughout the house for heat. Sometimes these radiators were very hot, and this technique to warm a forehead for faking fevers had to be done with skill. It could actually leave burn marks on the forehead. Eventually his brothers became jealous and told on him. Look, nobody should blame his parents for being firm with a youngster. Today he is grateful for their sternness, which toughened and strengthened him for a world full of unknowns. School days were very rough until he got older and could run more. Combined with freedom and ability for more activities, the frequency of his asthma attacks digressed and the severity regressed. The flu (influenza, infection and fluid in the lungs) or a bad cold would be a major setback.

He loved the swimming pool at the Elks Club in the summer. Girls in swimsuits! But the drawback of girls in swimsuits, being on the swim team at nine, he had to wear these really tight little stretchy blue trunks. Yuck. His underwear wasn't even that small and tight. Didn't like that at all. Nope. His mom was always making sure they were tied and stuff prior to a race. That fussing, lovey-dovey, and all was really embarrassing. His mom probably fidgeted with his drawstrings because of what caused him to not come in first, once. He didn't do well in butterfly and didn't like backstroke, but in other strokes he was competitive. Always first place in freestyle. Except for that one time. On one occasion, just after a well-timed racing dive broaching the water with an awesome stroke, he noticed the water was quite cold in places normally not noticeable. It was becoming difficult to kick because his trunks were at his knees and almost coming off! He figured he had two choices: kick 'em the rest of the way off or stop and pull them up. The water was clear, though? He stopped and quickly pulled the tiny trunks up. Locating the pack, he thought, *I can catch 'em.* Furiously smacking the water with smooth, strong, deep, strokes, it was not long before he caught the pack. Knowing he was passing many made him smile under water. Passing many, he touched the wall near the front. He gave them all a head start and caught the leaders from a dead stop. Sure was happy about that. To come from that far behind was very exciting and had everyone screaming and shaking fists. Shaking the water off at the wall he saw his mom arguing with the judges that he came in second. It was close—worst case was a tie. His mom said the judge didn't notice and had ignored him, figured he had dropped out or something, and was so surprised that he came from nowhere. The judge was in disbelief and just assumed there was no way he could've touched the wall second. He didn't care. He did what he tried to do; he caught the leaders.

He was too young to understand why he had to spend the summer with his grandmother. It was so boring and not fun at all. She would get mad at him for wetting the bed. She was not kind to him. She was old, and he was genuinely an annoyance and disappointment for a proud older grandmother who lived alone. Why was he there? She didn't like him. Easy enough to see, he surely caught on and didn't like her. The last place he wanted to be all summer. No one his age around. She had this little noisy, annoying parrot, which she seemed to love and was overly devoted to. She talked to it then glared at him. She cared more about feeding the bird and cleaning the cage than slapping some bologna on some white bread with a drop of mustard for him.

Once, he tried to be friendly with the parrot and stuck his finger close to it while it was out of the cage by a mirror singing to its reflection, and it bit him. It hurt and drew blood and a deep small bruise. When he reached for acknowledgment, empathy, or sympathy with fake tears, Mom-mom gruffly explained how it was his own fault. She frustratingly, begrudgingly, and roughly treated his wound. This puzzled him, and he even told Mom-mom he'd rather just put a Band-Aid on himself. He told Mom-mom he didn't need it anyway. She would let that bird out of the cage, and it would fly through the house, ending up hanging by mirrors or especially the bathroom mirror when Mom-mom was in the bathroom. One time, he opened the back door to go play outside and her exotic parrot flew right past his head. At first, he thought it was attacking him. Immediately, his grandmother went ballistic. Accusing him of opening the door and letting it go on purpose. She was so mad she cried. He took off to go after it. Thought maybe he could catch it. He had noticed on many occasions, he could achieve what others thought impossible. Or what others wouldn't even try. He really thought he could bring it back to her, proving he cared. That it wasn't on purpose. As he chased, the bright green and yellow parrot flew tree to tree. He thought, *Try to outsmart it. Approach slowly, then either call it with whistles or climb the tree.* Now his grandmother was doubly upset because he ignored her hollers for him to come back. With a positive attitude, he exclaimed loudly, "Don't worry," that he could catch the bird and return it to Mom-mom. After a long pursuit of about three blocks, not of neighborhood blocks made up of houses, the distance he and the bird had covered was of overgrown shrubbery, briars, and wooded areas he slowly began to realize; he could barely see Mom-mom's house. Noticed also in unfamiliar territory. Then came the point he and the bird made eye contact and the bird flew out of sight. That's when the realization sank in, he was never to catch this bird. As he returned, Mom-mom was on the phone. After she hung up, still crying and unable to look at him, he said, "Maybe it will come back to eat."

She looked at him through tears and very angrily stated it would never come back and die when winter came. Stating he "killed her bird on purpose." His dad's mother called his aunt and uncle, his dad's brother by phone about the disaster that he caused. His aunt and uncle came over that evening to console his grandmother. She wanted him gone. Then call my mom and dad, he said. The big people staring at him, questioning him, of course wondering if he would do something like that on purpose. His dad's brother spoke to him alone. His uncle seemed to understand although there seemed to be doubt, his uncle finally told him not to worry it wasn't his fault. The adults gathered and talked, constantly looking in his direction. Boy, he sure did not want to be there. The next week would surely be uncomfortable days. Then he found out from his cousins his brothers were spread out at different relatives in Delaware, not really too far away. He wondered if they were having fun; he wasn't. He was told he might be able to see them, but it would be difficult. He was able to visit a little. Very restricted. They seemed much happier than him. He asked why he couldn't go home. They didn't know.

His mom must've heard how hard it was on her little boy. His mom called. It was weird. It seemed arranged and timed. He remembered crying to come home on the phone with his mom. Begging. Pleading. Impossible to explain how horrible it was. He tried, but what came out was just gibberish pleading, begging, and crying. It must've been extremely difficult to hear her little boy pleading and not be able to fully respond appropriate enough to solve his concerns. She couldn't handle the phone call, although she tried. His dad took over the phone call and had to be abrupt. Telling him he could not come home now. Soon though. A couple more weeks. There was nothing anyone could do. He had overheard conversations from relatives in the other room. She had been in the hospital with a nervous breakdown, they all said.

"What's that? Why?" He really didn't understand what that meant. He asked often, "What broke?" Then he had to clarify his questions: "What in the world did 'broke down' mean?" No one ever explained in a way he could understand. It did seem some of his older cousins cared. Some cried a little when telling him. She seemed upset to him but not crazy or mentally unstable. He loved her. He just wanted to be with her. They all said she would be okay though, but boy was staying with his Mom-mom horribly boring and difficult. As he grew older, he came to the understanding that having a disabled child led to depression and alcohol. His mom had spent most of a summer in Cambridge Mental Hospital, a State Hospital in Maryland. Whether this stay in a state mental hospital truly helped his mother was debatable. Make no mistake, his dad removed his mom from that hospital because of questionable treatment, questionable treatment philosophies and techniques.

After his own children reached adulthood, he thought back, could him getting thrown out of church have caused some of his mother's issues and also directly contributed to his dad's adamant disbelief in Church and God? Was it the combination of his little brother's disability and him getting tossed from church? It was something never discussed with him by his parents. As probably with many families, very commonly, what is not discussed is already known. Discussion of such topics can bring pain without solution. His older brother had a birthmark removed from his face when he was an infant? His oldest brother ended up with a small noticeable scar probably the size of a fifty-cent piece in his early years. The little scar dissipated as he got older never to bother his brother's two wives or three kids, or anyone else for that matter. To a young Mother, the first thing she looks at then sees? The nine months of carrying and anticipation to immediately discover a birthmark on the newborn child's face is most unsettling and worrisome for the child's welfare for a mother. Was it Dad's family never accepting their marriage? Trying to manage raising five rebellious sons? Only two sons finished high school. He would've drank too. He became her only son to earn a college degree but long after she had passed away. His changes and efforts came too late. It wasn't until fifteen years after his Mom passed. He wished he could've showed her his degree. He would've handed it to her without saying anything. Just to try give her the smallest token that her caring, love, and compassion was a gift to him that he would try to share with others throughout his life. Just silently smile and look into her eyes, hopefully accepting his apologies of all he did wrong, with a long, loving hug. That would've been all his mom needed. She was the best ever.

You see, early on, his mother sat him down alone and told him, as probably most mothers do, that he was special. But he believed her. No, not at first. Of course not! After all that's happened? After some internal soul searching her loving, convincing sincerity caused him to believe. Was it because all that had happened to him? Some interventions which were undeniably real. Probably not, she didn't know that stuff. But she was very loving, sincere, and convincing. She said he could do whatever he wanted. He knew that. Wait, anything though? His mom convinced him. Washed away doubts. She told him, when he grew up, he could do whatever he wanted to do and be whatever he wanted to be, because he was special. He believed her. She told him as she held him, "You are special. All you have to do is want it, believe you can do it, and you will." So he did. He believed. What he would come to know much later in life is something that would seem most unbelievably impossible. But it's true. There is One whose love is even greater than a Mother's love for her child. And that love can cause even greater impossibilities to be true. Even the greatest of impossibilities can be overcome if we would only believe in the love of our Father.

While he was young, he also became aware of some attributes he felt he needed to exculpate himself from. His keenness in observations seemed an ability others didn't have. Convincing others of what they couldn't see became very challenging. For the most part, he stayed aloof from accepting advantages with intangible skills he seemed to have. One might say he didn't believe in himself, but he did. If others would say, he wasted his gifts all his life, they would be right. Events in his life gave him an inner turmoil of not being worthy. There were so many around him poor and less fortunate than others. He would remain at their side. They were the ones he was closest with. Those were the people he could somehow help sometimes. The rich and elite were in their own worlds. He could be friends with anyone, but their behavior he found great disdain for. He wanted no part of it because on many occasions, he found himself challenging their selfish behaviors. He found later, in life, one of the greatest difficulties against a person's growth and success is how not to become a product of your environment.

He became very slow to mature. Staying naïve, he found himself vulnerable to those who thought themselves better than others. At times, his sincerity and social skills were used by others. Remember, he really didn't even care to match clothes as he trudged off to school. As for how he felt, if these capabilities were real, he felt he wasn't worthy and should not tap into them or use them for his own gains. He didn't want to use these skills he might have for his own gains. Even to the extent he could become rich, he'd rather not. Wealth was in what he knew. He found wealth in feelings. Feelings of joy. He found happiness in life, mainly in intangibles, not in having things.

Things of most value to him were things one could not hold in their hands. Really didn't want what others had. He found most that were attracted to others for what they had or what they owned weren't the kind of people he wanted to be with or around. Not for long anyway.

Always being one of the last to show at the bus stop each day for junior high, the senior high girls would make fun or tease him. His brothers couldn't stand him getting picked on, but they agreed, he looked ridiculous. His mom overheard his brothers making fun of him about what he was wearing to school. His mom worked at a record store and knowing the trends, she came home with some loud seventies clothes for him. So he wore the pink- and blue-striped bell bottoms, with big white buttons instead of zipper to school. Actually, he was excited to wear something people would make fun of in a different way now. It worked out quite different than he thought it would, though. That was the day he was passed a note by one of the hottest girls in school. He started seeing her. They were together in the mall one Saturday and her older boyfriend walked in the door. She got up and ran away. Wow, he thought they were broken up. He didn't care, he would've stood up to him for her. She was too scared though. She didn't believe he could. He probably didn't seem tough enough. It didn't matter; it seemed like more notes started coming his way. Even though the kids at the bus stop were still making fun of him, now it was different. School became a little more interesting for different reasons than education now. He made sure to tell his mom the difference she made. He thought he saw his mom change a little after that, like she became a little happier and proud of him, in a way.

It was after several unique occasions he learned he couldn't throw things at people. Everyone knows this. If he threw something to hit another, he would, especially at his limits or at the boundaries of his physical abilities. Uncanny? Look, everybody knows you can't throw rocks at another, but don't most people miss? Not him. Pretty difficult to stop a little boy first learning to throw though. Many boys got in trouble throwing rocks because a young boy has to learn basic skills and his own limitations. He found out he had an uncanny ability to hit something stationary or on the fly. He learned he couldn't throw things at people because he would always hit them even without serious aim. Basically just lining it up and throwing as far and as hard as he possible could. Growing up became a struggle of confusion. Try to be normal or withdrawal from social pressures. Stay kind or harden from building defenses from people's unkindness. Didn't care about clothes matching. What was the big deal anyway? Because we're in school? He'd rather not have been in the social pressures of school anyway. He did find out later he liked learning. And for him, girls got in the way of learning in school. Cultural differences caused disruptions in school too. As long as he was away with friends, there were no social disparities or cultural problems as he could get along with anyone. If he was alone, he could get along with almost anybody, and he did. Most of his friendships started blooming from other school districts and other neighborhoods.

Around fifth grade in elementary school, they had "show-and-tell" after Christmas. He brought in a GI Joe; that would be cool to show everyone. That backfired. Many of his classmates laughed and said he brought a doll in. Shocked, he couldn't imagine they ridiculed and compared an army soldier with rifles to a Barbie doll? Quite different, he thought. What appeared to make things worse was his girlfriend, Julie Holiday, walked up to him on a school break the next day and broke up with him. When he asked why, she said she liked Stevin. She had braces, was skinny, had glasses and was a little cute, but he thought Stevin was a dork, big head with glasses and clothes always matched with shinny shoes. He was a punk, he thought. Certainly he could beat Stevin up. He didn't care; Julie wasn't a great loss, although the breakup hurt his pride. Julie sat with Stevin at lunch. Still didn't care. He couldn't believe it, though. Stevin was scrawny. For real? After lunch on the playground, everyone was busy playing, he noticed Stevin and Julie walking and holding hands, way over on the football field, away from everybody. So he picked up a nice throwing rock, small but with good weight, and heaved it hard as he could, toward Julie and Stevin with all his might, quickly turning to climb the monkey bars like nothing occurred. Then the impossible happened. He heard a scream. Looked way out on the football field and saw Julie on the ground with Stevin raising her head looking at her. What happened? Impossible? He saw a teacher run over to the two. Then everyone else followed. So he ran out there too. Something had hit her in the head. She had to go to the hospital and get stitches. He couldn't believe it. He absolutely could not have made that throw, no way. It was a big deal. Someone must've hit Julie in the head with a rock, but no one saw or knew who did it. One teacher did suspect him. The teacher came to him and asked. He pointed to where he had been by the monkey bars, and he said to the teacher no one can make a throw from that far away. He then said he didn't do it. He lied. Still to this day he could not believe it, and if he tried to explain it, no one would believe it was a Hail Mary that nailed her right in the head. He hadn't meant to hit her. He just heaved as hard as he could in their direction. No one would believe he never specifically aimed at her. But it was still wrong, and he was therefore guilty. He could not ever tell anyone.

It happened again. He and his younger brother were playing in the backyard. Mom called from the bathroom window to come in the house. His brother stayed, ignoring the call. He called out to his brother, noticing his brother was now misbehaving, still ignoring him. When he got to the house, he saw his brother all the way at the other end of the yard by the apple tree. He called his brother because it was time to come in. He couldn't throw a football that far, let alone a baseball. As he walked, he saw a battery on the ground, turned and heaved it as hard as he could into the air as far as he could, generally in his brother's direction. Wasn't even trying to aim. It was a size C or D but no way it would hit him. It did right in the face. This was bad. Oh my God, he hit his little brother in the mouth. Saying he didn't do it wasn't going to work, so he tried to explain. He thought the throw impossible and never in a million years would've thrown it if he remotely thought it would hit him. After his brother came home from the hospital with stitches, his brother almost forgave him immediately. He was so sincerely sorry and apologetic. He was sorry; it was a truly horrible thing to do. So never again did he throw what would hurt someone again, even if it would be an impossible throw. One might think it was the beating he deserved and got which changed that particular behavior. No, it wasn't that. There was something else.

Something that no one would ever believe. It would never do any good to try and explain it to someone else. There was something very strange and uncanny demonstrated in numerous various ongoings. It was when the impossible was attempted with all his strength, skill, and ability the impossible was conquered. He came to the conclusion that those efforts could never be used to do harm.

Nope, absolutely not—it wasn't the beating with the belt he would've got for hitting his brother that would change behavior. Nope, you would have to understand. He did not fear the beatings with a belt or whatever beating he got from his dad. He didn't fear pain from beatings. He did fear his dad's disappointment. Most of all, he feared and was most troubled mostly by disappointment in himself. Stopping to throw things at people came from the discovery he could hurt people. He could really hurt them even in seemingly impossible circumstances. He feared this most. He learned he would have to be more careful. He never wanted to hurt anyone.

Then came another type of learning as he matured. Girls. And competition for girls. He was slow to learn. He could date almost any girl he really desired. Being very slow to learn about girls, his insecurities and self-doubts and sometimes apparent difficulty with "cleanliness" caused awkwardness, embarrassment, and self-induced heartache. With all the extra baggage he carried, he thought he had to impress this one well-to-do girl, to possibly go steady with her. She lived in another neighborhood about five miles away. Her family, being affluent, had a very large home accompanied with a very large open front yard. He came up with a plan to impress the girl. He organized a very large neighborhood boys vs neighborhood boys football game, right in the girl's front yard. These types of tackle football games offered audacious opportunity for guys to build reputations. Or to display character, competitive spirit, and genuine camaraderie. Even to extend friendships outside the neighborhood. That was the part he enjoyed. He was genuinely longing for the possibility of friendship and relationships outside his own neighborhood. Personally, he carried the football well, didn't fumble, and never dropped a pass, plus he was a great tackler. Learning came about by playing with and against friends of his older brothers and other older guys in his neighborhood.

He thought a football game a good opportunity to impress the girl of his interest. He noticed the girl had been giving extra attention to one guy in particular. When she talked with the other guy, she displayed extra femininity, seemingly flirtatious with him even though the girl and he had agreed to see each other that day. Yes, a date. From what he could see, the girl displayed more than friendship. On purpose? Were the two just friends? It didn't seem like it.

During the chaos of a kickoff return, some block, but most avoid contact, while many make serious attempts to tackle the ball carrier. He went out of his way to catch the kickoff, made enough moves to avoid some tackles straight in to the chaos. Suddenly bursting into full steam, he veered straight for the guy of her attention. At first the guy seemed to try to prepare for a sly tackle of the ball carrier but then came wide-eyed amazement as the unsuspecting tackler that the tackler was now going to be plowed into. Quite the opposite of how the game of football is intended to be played. Now on top of Johnny, he set the ball down and hit Johnny in the face. He knew the girl was watching. But the guy didn't fight back. He let the guy up. As the guy walked away, he watched the guy with a growing sense of regret and guilt. Now with an overwhelming sense of ignorance, he looked over at the girl. She didn't seem to care. He looked back at the guy, gaining more respect for the guy than the girl. The girl now didn't seem to care about her friend. He felt awful. He knew almost immediately and from that precise moment, he personally saw the guy leaving as the better man. Much better than him. Maybe the girl was impressed. Didn't matter—the game was finished; everyone left. They sat alone on the girl's giant porch. The girl was really pretty. They were close. He almost came in for a kiss. The girl seemed receptive. He stopped. He asked if that guy earlier in the day had been a boyfriend. Then he asked if the guy was a friend. Then out came some honesty. It got a little testy. He was surprised when the light flipped on and the girls' mom opened the door, saying it was time to come in and that it was time for him to leave. He thought, *Was the mom listening?* He knew the answer but boldly said it anyway: "Since he lived ten to twelve miles away, would it be possible for a ride?" The mom glared at him, ushering the girl inside, slammed the door, and shut out the light. Slowly he stepped off the porch and walked to the middle of the front yard. Then he remembered deep regret and remorse wondering if he would ever be able to make it up to the guy. One day, he saw the two holding hands in school. He thought, *Good. Either the guy forgave her or just let it go.* He knew that guy was definitely way better than he.

Then came his turn. Some tough guy overhead him talking on the school bus on their way home from school. Evidently the guy needed to demonstrate bravado and did not like the sounds of his words and conversation. The guy challenged him to fight as soon as they got off the bus. With apparently no immediate way for him to back down, they both got off the bus at the wrong stop. The guy tried everything verbally possible. But he wouldn't fight. Nope, not a reasonless fight was he going to participate in. The tough guy, bristling with testosterone, threw him to the ground. He got up. Stood firm. Again, the guy knocked him down, accompanied with verbal stabs of ungentlemanly name-calling, let's say like "chicken." He was extremely mad and on the verge of breaking, preparing for a fight. A battle bringing overwhelming force? Again, he got up. No! For some odd reason, something inside him prevented that type response. He thought, only reciprocate with force and skill necessary to end the fight. Suddenly, people came out of houses who had been witnessing a one-sided bullying and his unwillingness to fight. The people, some his age, some older, and some adults, many came charging to his defense. But he himself had bullied before. He felt worthless. He felt deserving of the beating. On the verge of being able to take no more. No. The point was reached, and he was almost ready to snap. All these mixed emotions overwhelmed him. It was too much. On the verge of tears. His eyes now filled with water. No one would ever understand. The tears were from something else. Something inside that was not generated from being scared or intimidated. He hung his head, turned, and slowly walked toward home. So many witnessed it. His opponent hollered "sissy," "chicken," and many other words which shouldn't be repeated. But many wanted to help him? He definitely wasn't worth it. He quite possibly could've won the fight or definitely made the aggressor regret ever trying but now completely and clearly understood what the guy at the football game might have felt. Maybe someone told his dad what happened.

One day shortly after, out of the blue, his dad told him, "It takes a better man to walk away from a fight than it does to start one." This "man rule" his dad taught him stuck. This "man rule" he believed and learned from life experiences to be true. These life lessons were extremely difficult to go through. These lessons were reinforced by his dad. Many respected his dad greatly. He really didn't know how highly others thought of his dad's ethics and intelligence until much later in his own life. Honestly, when he was young, he was too busy treading in a lake of fire, keeping his head just high enough above the sulfur fumes to gasp for clean air.

Later in life came clearer a far greater truth, a deeper message. Truthfully, he had longed for it when he was young. But by his own actions, especially his very first lie, he had jumped off a cliff, and it would be a long climb up. As he climbed back up over the many years, he had no clue of the knotted rope which had been prepared for him. It may've never seemed like it, but it sure was a blessing. If only he had known that beside the knotted rope was a ladder. A ladder right beside his tough climb. It had been there all along. All he had to do was gently reach over and step on the ladder to easily climb out of this pit he had jumped into.

He came to know his life lessons were matching messages and lessons from the greatest teacher in history. He came to know this deeper lesson of love for his fellow man. Some of this message can be found in the Book of Matthew 5:38–42, where the Son of Man attempted to explain lessons of love and forgiveness by explaining "turn the other cheek." The greater expectation of wisdom, love, forgiveness, and understanding would be gained from reading His Word in all of Chapter 5 from the Book of Matthew. Then understanding that the Son of Man was simply trying to explain and expound for clarity to those whom did not have the Word available to them. The Word was being blocked by many forces, governed by a foreign military occupation force, the Romans. A divided nation led by elite political religious groups: Sadducees, Pharisees, and other Rabbis who were greatly concerned with their own well-being. Plus a ruling monarchy, a king and his entire court with a small army, all which much be sustained from the efforts of the poor working class. The Son of Man came at a time when people were being blocked or excluded from the Word of God. But more importantly, the people were excluded from forgiveness. The people were living as 'unforgiven by man's law'. If you, the reader would ever take the time to read the Book of Matthew Chapter 5, try to understand how difficult it would be for one to speak on the side of mountain, without a speaker system so that everyone might hear. Son of Man speaking in a clear, compassionate, and loving way to those excluded from forgiveness that they can be forgiven by the greatest of all. Their Creator. Their Lord. Your Father.

The people in the region had heard of the powerful message this man brought. The people came out to the streets from the towns He passed. The great crowds built as they followed Him from Galilee and Decapolis. From the capital Jerusalem and from the region of royalty, Judea, even from beyond the Jordan (Matthew 4:25), probably stopping to rest. He was able to gain some advantage that the sound of his voice might carry as He spoke softly and sincerely to thousands from the side of a mountain near Capernaum. The people longed for a message of forgiveness.

How far has this generation drifted from the message of forgiveness and love? On June 18, 2018, Charleston, South Carolina, the City Council passed by a vote of 7–5, a resolution apologizing for its role in slavery. As anyone walks through the streets of Charleston, South Carolina, try listening for the sounds of the brick and mortar buildings whispering, "We're sorry." City buildings, monuments, churches, and streets apologizing for what the city did? It is not going to happen. Now try to reach inside for inspiration of God's Word. When Jesus explained the love of which God wished to reciprocate with all men and woman: the apostles became perplexed about how to pray to the One who was to be revered and feared. Matthew tells of how Jesus explained how to simply pray with God who wants you to know of Him as your Father. Jesus wrapped up the prayer in Matthew 6:9–13 once it was complete by saying "Amen." Then Jesus followed up by explaining, expounding upon, or edifying the prayer in

Matthew 6:14–15 (KJV): "For if ye forgive men their trespasses, your heavenly father will also forgive you." It is remembered slightly differently in the Book of Luke but clearly stating the same importance of forgiveness. Luke 10:4 (KJV) states, "And forgive us our sins, for we forgive everyone that is indebted to us." This generation must come to internally know and outwardly express it is not only the people today which offend you which must be forgiven: And it is especially not only the people of the past who require forgiveness for surely they too must be forgiven, but this nation is not long to survive if its people cannot forgive its nation's past trespasses too. But know this, survival also requires not only forgiveness; this nation requires reconciliation and unification. Know that today, for this generation, there is a way.

Just a recommendation from personal experiences, though, about arguing with your father. Sure, disagreements arise. Mainly from directions which seem impossible, infeasible, even totally out of mainstream society, so how or why would anyone listen to a father leading you in that direction? Yes, disagreements arise. Another recommendation: a little caution for those "discussions." Although he never really feared his dad's beatings with the belt, fearing more his disappointment or letting his dad down. Your Father, God, doesn't really have to use a strap, belt, or whip. Your Father, God, prefers using nature. And personally, he'd rather choose his switch to be beat with any day over a crack of lightning snapped just right on one's butt or back. For this generation to understand, just as your dad sometimes longs for a call, just to hear from you, good or bad; know your Father would love for you to call out to Him. Even if it were just to talk with Him. He truly longs to hear your voice and misses hearing you. Truly He cares. Just ask. Ask Him anything. Jesus showed you the door is open. No matter what you feel you can't be forgiven for. And no matter what others don't forgive you for either.

He learned many things through the reality of experiencing these internal conflicts. Mainly his own mistakes. But he witnessed many brutalities too. He witnessed many trying to impress. Many that would gain their personal successes and attain social status in "cliques." They would feel secure in feelings of grandeur, only to personally lead others in wrong directions. And with wrong ideologies.

Many of these ideologies, the so-called leaders, didn't even believe in themselves. But that did not matter to the "leaders." To them, what mattered was a feeling of power. The feeling of being a leader. So they would say things purposely that groups could identify with to simply maintain their connection or to maintain their group status. Many of them felt a small sense of responsibility to their followers. That responsibility would quickly dissipate if trouble was ever traced back to the leader. These clicks quickly fell apart if actions caused angry parents to unite or prosecutable trouble reared. Quite simply. He purposely alienated himself from these cliques. Although he would easily make friendships or bond with individuals. On occasion, some he befriended would act different towards him once around their group. On other occasions, some he befriended stood for the difference between right and wrong and would try to take a stance in the group on his behalf. He would quickly observe that it would be best for the new friend if he were to leave and keep distance. He also noticed as he grew older, there were not many changes except the trends they went through, appearances, and wrinkles. There are people who make it their purpose to extend power by influence or even by any means necessary to quench their inner thirsts. To satisfy self-insecurities. This pattern is seen in today's politics, today's government, today's news entertainment industry and even today's social media. Twitter and Instagram "leaders and followers." Movie and TV actors and entertainers long and strive to be leaders and have followers. All those previously mentioned require followers to fulfill mental deficiencies and procure monetary success. Many of these so-called leaders have an identifiable social disorder. In many cases, these with social disorders seeking power, attention, social status, and fame attain great monetary successes. Mansions, extremely expensive cars, yachts, personal planes or jets, four-wheelers, jet skis, all the most fantastic material things the world offers. Many become idolized. Let him be clear, there is no harm in providing for a family, success, and sharing success. But there is a distinct disorder in idolizing and in seeking success from idolization. Much of this generation's divisions and deadly problems stem from these very distinct social disorders at very early ages.

The writer must apologize for seemingly sidestepping from the flow of a good story of the truth of a little boy who saw God. But hopefully, the reader can at this point try to understand the story is not entirely of his own doing. You see, there are many stories or books written, provided as a gift that the artist or writer is providing a route to stir the imagination. What one reader might gain from the reading is quite often different than that which other readers might gain. So in an attempt to make some messages of this little boy's story clear, provided is a correlation to certain truths. Truths that have been passed on generation to generation. But these truths are successfully being distorted and blocked. Some efforts are unintentional; some are intentional. Still the truth is, even the little boys' message will not be for all. But every once in a while, the Son of Man is brought to a generation to explain to that generation in a manner by which those chosen or elect are given opportunity to see God. There are those who should know, all which was brought forth to this day is for them to know a life of enjoying heaven while they are alive on Earth.

While very young, he was able to understand life's learning and experiences meant more to him than money. These life character observations, memories, and lessons began within his family. In many cases, foundations of his moral character began with or were solidified by his mom and dad. Even his older brothers and younger brothers contributed to his character. He was probably eleven or twelve years old when he believed his abilities were certain, the day that he shot a blackbird in flight with a bb gun. He took aim, leading, adjusting for of the bird's in-flight speed. The bird was weaving. Anticipation of the sloping curvature as the bird swooped. He also took into account the drop of the bb over such distance. He took the shot; the bird fell. Being only wounded, the bird hobbled in moderately tall grass, trying to get away as best it could from two seemingly bloodthirsty kids. At a dead run, he pulled his six-inch hunting knife. He had practiced throwing it a little learning its balance when held in his hand. With a quick flip from holder to hand, while running and jumping over logs, bobbing and weaving, he threw his hunting knife. With the most amazing accuracy, he stuck the knife through the wounded bird's head and buried it to the hilt. Dead center in line, starting from the back of its beak to the back of its skull. He pinned it to the ground, killing it instantly. It did not flutter, move, or twitch. Death was instantaneous. He thought, *Great!*

He put the wounded animal out of its misery swiftly and as least painfully as possible. It happened so fast. His friend's shock and amazement quickly turned to grizzly disdain for such a barbaric act. He was puzzled. His friend was seemingly so aghast and shocked at the accused cruelty. His friend, who never seemed religious before, all of a sudden demanded they pray. He said, "No." No animal, any animal, even a blackbird, if wounded, should be left in pain. His friend stated disbelief in what he did and that it was so mean. He paused. His friend was right. He shot and killed the bird merely testing skills and having fun. It was wrong. Dead wrong. But he had seen his friend shoot a squirrel from inside its nest then pick it up out of the creek screaming and shove it in his hunting jacket pouch, but this, his friend could not understand putting this blackbird out of its misery so quickly. Sure, absolutely, he knew he was wrong to kill an animal he was not going to eat. Once again, attempting something seemingly impossible, the impossible happened. He relented. They both prayed for the bird and each other. His friend, who had never displayed any leaning toward religion, now had him praying for a bird. Seemed like the right thing to do anyway. As far as he knew, the bird never knew the difference between right and wrong. Although even being so young, he knew in all seriousness there was nothing wrong with a young lad honing skills. But by killing a blackbird, was there? How else could one measure, taking into account all those different aspects with a shot like that unless he tried it? That situation could not be duplicated with clay pigeons. But again, it was amplification to him. Once again, somehow, it seemed word got out. His dad, out of the blue, told him he shouldn't shoot birds with the bb gun. He seemed to be held to higher standards than others. By others. But by himself too. He definitely agreed. He absolutely knew with all his heart and soul it was wrong to hurt and end innocent life. Any life. It was for some odd reason he debated or argued the point internally. At the time, he did not know that; yes, man was to have dominion over animals, but animals had no sin. Many animals see, hear, or smell what we cannot. It is safe to say, unless the animal has been plagued or was with sickness, many animals know and can hear God. They can see the unseen. Since animals bear no sin, man is not to abuse animals. If he does, he will be judged just as he would any other sin on his day of judgment. There would be another time he did not learn how to have dominion, and after unintelligent training techniques lacking wisdom, he turned the pet over to an organization that found it a good home. His skills in hunting and fighting would only be when absolutely needed. When hungry, he did help in the hunt and eat deer. He understood there were laws governing hunting. Honestly, when he killed deer, he wasn't hunting. He was procuring food. And given no other choice available, he did fight. He was shot at, stabbed twice, and there were many occasions when he was outnumbered by aggressors or cornered by oversized and overbearing aggressors he was forced to defend himself. But after he had pinned the fellow during the football game, he made an oath to himself. He would never again fight someone whom he knew he could win the fight against. On numerous occasions, his quick wittedness prevented disaster. He much preferred getting someone to agree not to fight. Actually, it seemed convincing others not to fight took more skill. Calling him chicken about that mattered absolutely not. People he knew had put someone's face on a curb and stomped the back of their heads, knocking all their opponents' teeth out. On many occasions, once a fight started, it didn't stop until someone did not move. Mostly because of a refusal to accept defeat.

On one occasion, one of his dearest friends tried to get him to fight over a disagreement. His friend happened to be older and a state wrestling champ. Which if it was game on, that wouldn't matter. This friend had actually given him a personally autographed black-and-white picture of President Truman. It was said the president came in to work (Oval Office) early one morning and saw a stack of pictures, grabbed a pencil, and started signing them. Until the president's assistant came in and said, "Mr. President, stop. We do that for you."

Mr. Truman was noted as saying, "Sure, okay. But let me finish just these." And so the president signed one hundred black-and-white photos of himself in pencil.

Now completely encircled, the two stood face to face. Then came, of course, every name in the book to fight from his friend and those mongering for a fight. He refused. His friend spit in his face. That almost did it. But just then, this came out of his mouth: "If we do this today, you will regret it the rest of your life." He liked him a lot and thought they were really good friends. Today he was not going to let whatever just happened during the foosball game ruin that friendship.

He wiped the spit from his face. Then he said, "Oh my god, and your breath and spit stinks something awful." They laughed. Truthfully, it meant so much to lose the friendship at that moment tears were welling in his eyes. Probably the water in his eyes misread by others but not his friend. His friend brushed it off, and the crowd followed his friend. He watched them. Then he walked away too. Alone. The other way. He learned later from another friend that was present, that Jack had a .38 caliber revolver pointed at the back of his head. Held in a manner with very few seeing it. But if he had fought, he would've been killed. Would Jack have killed him in broad daylight that day? Within a week or two, in 1975, Jack Truitt and another were arrested for murdering two people with a .38-caliber revolver and shotgun. His defense was a first in Maryland, which claimed lack of culpability because Jack was high on PCP (Phencyclidine). Jack Truitt for his role in the double murder was sentenced to "Life Plus 30 Years" (https://newspaperarchive.com/salisbury-times-jan-03-1975-p-1/. Publication: *Salisbury Times*, Salisbury, Maryland, January 3, 1975; ret 4/3/2019 Newspaper ARCHIVE.com).

Jack Truitt's sentenced was originally to be at Jessup Prison established in 1878. Today, Jessup Maryland House of Corrections boasts of five prisons near Jessup Maryland. These Maryland prisons originally had their beginning simply because of location. Jessup Maryland grew as a hub because of the convergence of three main railroads of the northeast connecting with Ohio at the beginning of the Civil War. Because of its location, Jessup Army Camp 1860–1865 was assigned to imprison the many Union deserters. Since already being converted and purposed to house prisoners, Jessup Army Camp also became a prime location to imprison the Rebels of the Confederacy.

When the war was over, the prison with brick walls, bars over windows, doors with locks, even a creek running through its center as a latrine was quickly and easily established to house felons. Not much had changed in about a hundred years when Jack was sent to die there. (http://thecommunityofjessup.homestead.com/History.html, "The Community of Jessup, The History of Jessup Discovering Our Community," Jessup Improvement Association, ret 4/3/2019).

Would Jack have killed him that day if he had fought his friend possibly gaining an advantage with an apparent victory at hand? What is only known is that he was capable and prepared. What prevented his death that day? There seemed to be an internal "inspiration" that he himself was not aware his was capable of. One thing for sure. It was not because he was afraid to fight. After what he had seen when he was very young there wasn't much in life that made him afraid. Sense of urgency for survival? Absolutely! Instincts to survive and prevent self-harm? Yes! Truthfully, there came later in life, a type of indescribable fear. It was the fear of an evil that exist which lives yet remains unseen. Fear came for him when it began to manifest. He was very slow to realize there is a war. At the time of his first realizations: yes, evil can be horrifying. And it was.

He came to the conclusion it was not for others to believe he saw God. He learned it was because of man's own limitations, doubts, and disbelief that create boundaries. Besides believing seems to become a major investment. And it does! He learned it very difficult in submitting one's free will elsewhere and so it should be. Submitting to an unknown or submission to only a possibility of divinity is way risky for human frailty. Plus, the commitment has to override the perception of what if they die and find death to be final. Well, if you committed and lived your entire life to a greater good of love and righteousness, and death became final you really didn't waste your life. Well, to him you wouldn't have. It's understandably hard even if evidence is all abound the claim remains there is no proof for them rendering them incapable of going beyond their own limitations. So being just another guy, why would he be special and have seen God? Especially since everyone has been told they can't! Even every church knows no one can see God. So why would've he been able to? Seems there is a misunderstanding of teachings and words communicated. He learned it was the sincerity of really wanting to see, combined with an innocent mind which knows no doubt or disbelief. Purity combined with confidence. The mind not corrupted from others with reasoning or caution. A genuine and pure request, accompanied with pristine truth and purity. Almost a demand to see what he knew existed. No confusions. With clear confidence only an uncorrupted mind, body, and soul can have. A mind as yet that has been introduced to any of life's smallest of corruptible nuances (sins) let alone an important occurrence that causes the brain to store such event for recall the rest of one's life.

If an innocent child asked to see his father, if the father knew seeing him at that moment as he was would damage the child's health, might not the father cover himself? Cover himself enough, change his clothes, or at least make sure his appearance was appropriate that the child at that moment in time might have a word with his father?

Maybe once the question is answered or the child is given the best possible answer at the time, might not the father explain that there are more appropriate times for this type of discussion. In this case, he did. With just one look. Face-to-face. And making eye contact. There was much more to the "look"—deep stuff. The realization of the many things that can come from one look would not come till much later in life. Much was needed first—experience, lessons, training, discipline, punishment, wisdom, and so much more. Just from one look? Yup, just from one look. Much more.

Besides, there seems to be a very relevant misunderstanding of the teachings of Jesus Christ. What the Apostles explained has not been clearly transferred. To stand in the presence of God required sacrifice. The particular smell of smoke and blood combined with atmospheric water (rain) and water produced or filtered by the earth (underground springs or rivers) provided for a filter or translucent barrier. Kind of like the earth's atmosphere blocks some harmful rays from the sun. This barrier or filter prevented the energy emitted from God's radiance of pure righteousness from the molecular anti-bonding, disassembly, or dissolving of human flesh. These requirements began being met with the sacrifice of Son of Man, the Christ, Jesus. Then it took three days for complete transference of his spirit to change His Spirit to be part of the filter or translucent filter to prevent the annihilation of human flesh when standing in God's presence. But still there is another step. The flesh, mind, and spirit which stands in the presence of God cannot be corrupted or contain sin. All three for consumption preparing its time made clear to this generation. And there is a reason. It's becoming critical. Could the little boy have seen God without the Jesus Christ? Yes and no. Yes, because God can do anything! Or God can make anything happen. No, because each event that happens on earth in earth's time happens for a reason. So no, this little boy in particular would not have seen God without the presence of our Lord and Savior, Jesus.

Belief? Why won't people believe?

He was twelve to thirteen years old, playing sand lot football with the Chesapeake Heights neighborhood boys. Most were much older, sixteen or seventeen, and some were eighteen or nineteen. Only a few his age. But those few would quit when they saw the game as to rough or have to quit when they got hurt. Only two others his age would try. Even they would get hurt too though. Because the game was tackle football. He wasn't afraid playing with older, larger, and tough guys. Even though he was of much smaller stature, he knew if he hit hard enough or leaned in with full body weight on a full sprint, simultaneously wrapping his arms totally around and near waist level, everyone bends, goes off balance and down. Sometimes he surprised the crap out of the big guys. And they'd come after him. You needed to keep your head on swivel. If they didn't go down, he could knock them off balance enough, and if he could hold on long enough, someone else could come pile on or help with the tackle. He could catch. He focused on skills required to catch a football and tuck it tightly away. Don't be distracted by the hit that's coming. Lock the ball to hands. If anyone would ever trust enough to throw him the ball, he made some fantastic catches. Never fumbled.

Thanksgiving was the best time of year. Four days off from school. All that time off. Just show up to the field, and within an hour or so, there was a full-blown game. Word spread fast. And not by phone. Sometimes he might get a landline ring. But he was never home to answer a phone anyway. November was cool weather. Peeling off coats in the chill and seeing the moisture of warm breath meeting cool air was awesome. Oh my! If it snowed, that was the best bonus ever! Rain was fun. Slipping evened odds for the smaller in stature. But tackling a big, tough guy, forcing that mean face in snow was the best. Everybody would get a laugh when someone spit grass and mud, wiping their eyes 'cause they couldn't see through the snow and mud. Especially when a little guy got 'em. And cold hands. Oh, that hurt so much, catching the football and tackling. Still never dropped a ball!

He loved kick-offs. Maybe he would get the ball in error, and he did. He loved bobbing and weaving, avoiding the solid hits. If he saw a solid hit coming, he would turn straight into the tackler, usually surprising the tackler therefore avoiding injury. During a game, his strategies would only last for so long without physical bodily damage. He took his lumps and bruises well. Sometimes, if he walked away bloodied, it was even all the better. It would seem as the game wore on, the other guys respected him or at least a little bit anyway; even if it was temporary, it was a good feeling. He noticed how acceptance or fitting in seemed to matter to many. More important to him was the feelings of accomplishment and equality he gained from the ability to tackle larger, tougher, and older guys, at times surviving brutal tackles that were most assuredly meant to take him out. Getting up and walking back to the huddle after the most brutal intentional hit knowing the guy gave his best shot was a way to gain a least a tiny bit of respect. At least among the neighborhood crowd.

One Saturday's game, the same as any other, a single engine plane flew low overhead. Not so low as to gain attention but not much higher either. About 2,500 feet? It was in between plays, and as a young lad might, he watched as the plane flew overhead. The plane slowly banked toward the Wicomico County Airport. The airport was probably three to four miles away, as the crow flies. He had almost turned his attention back to the game. Suddenly, the nose of the aircraft dropped. The plane began to corkscrew toward the ground! Falling out of the sky! Now in a spiral, heading straight down! Like all of a sudden just dropped? *Oh my god*, he thought, *that's unrecoverable!* As young and inexperienced as he was, that was not a recoverable maneuver! The plane disappeared below the tree line about 1½ to 2 miles away. It crashed! Couldn't hear it, but it was obvious. Quickly, he scanned everyone else and no one else seemed to notice. They were exiting huddles and lining up for another play. What? Was he the only one to realize that a plane crashed? So he tried to tell others, and of course they just brushed him off. Out of eighteen to twenty-two teenage guys, why would they not believe? His brother was the only one seeming to care he wasn't in the play. Others noticed and looked his way but really didn't care.

So he ran over to the whole group, clearly announcing to all, "A plane just crashed!" They looked at him, but all seemed to ignore him. He thought, *There was somebody in it!* Now becoming more animated, clearly upset, he said, "A plane just crashed!" Nothing? He turned to his oldest brother, who had been born on the same month as he but was five years older. He pleaded, made sincere eye contact, searching for belief. Certainly his brother would believe him, especially in a case like this. Nope? His older brother cared and tried to calm him down, saying it was probably another crop duster doing stunts, spraying the local farm fields. No! It wasn't—those were biplanes. He'd seen them fly under the electrical lines, the height of telephone poles. Yes, absolute crazy, unbelievable stunts. Sometimes even showing off to young groups playing football. Not completely uncommon. But this was different. This was a plane with one wing. Although this was a single engine airplane it was not a biplane, like most crop dusters of those days. And it spiraled straight down behind the tree line without visible recovery. Actually, he knew there was absolutely no way to recover from that spiral. Had he seen a plane crash before? No. On TV? No. Didn't matter. That plane crashed!

Nah, his brother said, "You just didn't see it recover."

That was enough! *People could be dying*, he thought, *and nobody knows.* He ran into the house to tell his dad.

It was Saturday. His dad was home from work and happened to be reading the newspaper. Great, his dad would believe him. He didn't believe either! He about became so unglued and animated he decided to once again step out of bounds. In so many words, he reminded his dad that reading the newspaper wasn't really that important anyway and that someone could be dying! His dad, at first, got angry. He could tell by the way his dad was not gently folding the newspaper but kind of giving up on what little free time his dad had. His dad worked very long hours all week, and with five sons, coming home from work was never smooth sailing. Always something. On this day, his dad seemed to stare out the window with his head turned away, then came a softer look.

"Come on, Dad!" the young boy still pleaded but slightly changing tone. "It can't be that far. It was between here and the airport. We'll find it."

Maybe his dad thought a little drive with an odd son might afford some time together that normally wouldn't occur. Try to imagine the desperation and despair of a young one witnessing an air disaster, trying to tell others and no one believing in him. Something he knew to be true. He was desperately looking out the window, trying to figure out where it would've come down exactly. There would not be a road straight to the plane or even to the airport from his neighborhood. Around farm fields. Crossing a major dual lane highway at the closest road crossing nearest to where he thought the plane went down.

His dad followed directions. As expected, he lost a little patience once in a while as the young lad tried to gain his bearings. Kindly put, he patiently followed his young son's directions. Upon a young one's very eager commands and navigating the back roads must've been a little annoying to his dad. The young boy imagined a straight line from right here to the football field. To…here? There! There, stop! "Right here," he said.

His dad was puzzled but stopped the car. His dad didn't see anything. Neither did the young boy. But he knew. Behind that small hill. It had to be there. As the car was stopping, he opened the door, starting to jump and run. *People hurt and no one knows?* he thought.

His dad said, "Stop!" Wait! Maybe he was getting curious but also realizing some caution might be needed. Fuel? Fire? His dad said, "Wait, slow down, wait for me." The young boy did slow down, kind of understanding without spoken words the need for caution.

The silence was eerie. "Come on," he lamented. He knew. Moving cautiously yet briskly over the small crest, there it was. A farmer was walking away from the plane toward his house. They both looked at the farmer. They young boy looked at the farmer with anticipation and hope. The farmer stopped. Made eye contact with the Dad. The farmer turned saddened eyes toward the ground, shaking his head in the negative, then turned, continuing a slow walk toward the farmer's house. The farmer's property, he guessed. But why wasn't the farmer in a hurry to call for help? Maybe the farmer was wrong? He said, "Let's get closer, Dad."

His dad said, "Be careful, son. Stay back." The little boy moved in slowly with his dad. They were cautious and kept their distance, only seeing if they could render help. Realization was settling in for his dad much quicker, firmly stating again, "Be careful, son, stay back." He moved closer, his dad slightly behind, weakly reaching out an arm into empty air but close enough to grab his son if necessary. Realization began to sink in for the boy too. He stayed just out of arm's length from his dad. Anyone could see there was no need to get closer.

Then the little boy saw; there was no doubt. The "two-seater" single-engine plane's pilot and passenger's faces were buried in the instrument panel past their ears. The pilot's wedding band was broken in half and stuck back through his finger, arms extending out where the windshield used to be, hands almost touching the dirt on the ground. This was not what the boy wanted to see at all. His only previous thoughts were, *Did nobody else see or know?* and, *What if someone needed help?* He figured they must've braced for impact. Deeply saddened and in solace, he and his father traded looks without words then turned toward the car. He knew. They were both dead.

He was told the plane's propeller was never found. Must've became unstable and noisy, which is why they turned toward the airport. Then propeller disassembled (came off) from the engine in flight, as horrible as it was. And it was absolutely horrible and the sight extremely disturbing; it helped him that his dad had risked believing him. It helped the young boy. Walking beside his dad with a feeling that his dad knew that he had been right. Not something to be happy about at all. But some maturity occurred. Being right when no one else believed. Even being looked at and treated like a fool when something so serious as life and death was at stake. He spent a long time alone wondering, *Why is it so hard to convince other people when you know something you saw is true?* Was it punishment from the very first lie—from then on he was not to be believed? He saw people tell other people the craziest of things and others would believe. He saw people believe almost everything on TV, magazines and the newspaper.

He used to get great amusement watching his older brother trick people or tell stories they believed. His oldest brother was a very good fisherman. Like his grandfather. On occasion, his older brother took him fishing for striped bass (rock fish) from the Rt 50 Ocean City, Maryland, inlet drawbridge. It was night fishing. There were many streetlights on the bridge casting their glare on the street. The bridge lighting provided some light down on the water below. His older brother told him to cast the spoon out pretty far and let it drift back in with the current, near the rocks by the pilings. "As the line nears the point, it will become taut near the rocks. Snatch it," his older brother said. "The bass can't resist the flash and are just sitting here waiting by the rocks."

They waited for the current to bring some food by.

His brother said, "You could tie a hook to a tablespoon and the fish would bite that. It's the flash, glint, or reflection of light that gets their attention. The bass can't resist and will strike it. Then set the hook."

On this particular occasion, there must've been thirty-five to forty other fishermen spread out on the bridge. His brother and he were the only ones catching striped bass. Some would walk over after a catch and ask, "Hey, whatcha using?" His older brother would pull out a tiny dark jar, unscrew the lid, and drop a few drops on the silver spoon. Then his brother would say some made up word like: "Strom Juice." They'd ask where he got it. He'd say something like the sixty-fifth bait store. They'd walk away, and his brother would put it back in his pocket.

After the other fishers left, he asked his brother, "So what is that stuff?"

His brother said, "A little dye and a little water." His brother added that our grandfather showed him that one. Needing leads, they went to the bait store his brother had said carried the "secret sauce" for catching fish. As soon as the owner saw his brother, they would laugh together.

His brother would say, "How many?"

The owner's head shaking and laughing would say, "More than a few."

He interjected, "So what'd ya sell 'em then?"

"That stuff over there," came the reply.

"Does it work?" he asked.

"Sure, absolutely," the owner said. Shook his head, thinking, *What a world.* Once they got back in the car, he was way more interested in the time his older brother spent with Pop-Pop. Maybe even jealous of the time his brother had spent with Pop-Pop. Both grandfathers had passed when he was very young.

It was after his dad died that his dad's sister revealed Pop-Pop was a pastor. His dad never, ever talked about Pop-Pop. After his dad died, his aunt told him his pop-pop was an alcoholic. But one day, Pop-Pop quit drinking and became a pastor in a local church in Delaware. His aunt said that the congregation absolutely loved his pop-pop. That Pop-Pop would prepare most the week for Sunday's sermon. The congregation loved the sermons and his pop-pop.

His dad was a hard worker and got straight A's in every grade, every class, every semester. Although his aunt said his dad got one B, she said the teacher didn't like his dad. That the family went to the teacher, and it was extremely evident something had happened between the teacher and his dad. And that the teacher had it out for his dad. He never heard his dad cuss much. He knew his dad did not believe in God. His aunt told him that his dad used every foul cuss words to describe church. To this day, he does not know why. The reason might lie somewhere in the relationship between his dad and pop-pop. Maybe if his dad had known in Mark 8:34–35 (KJV), "Whosoever will come after me, let him deny himself, and take up his cross and follow me. For whosoever will save his life shall lose it: but whosoever shall lose his life for my sake and the gospel's the same shall save it."

Would this have consoled Dad? Maybe not. But it seemed it mattered to his dad's father. But his dad was very intelligent, and had he told his dad this, he would like to think his dad would pause for some consideration. After his dad died, his aunt told him Pop-Pop had a brain aneurysm in the stairwell at church, never regained consciousness, and died on the way to the hospital.

On the bus ride home from school, he knew the punishment would be severe and ruin the weekend, not to mention the weeks ahead. The four E's on his report card did not mean excellent. He decided to change the four E's to B's. Why did they issue report cards on Fridays? Report cards have ruined numerous weekends for many. He thought, *It's in ink, just get the same color and turn the E's into B's!* His older brother and some others warned him, told him not to. When the carbon copy came next semester, there would be nothing he could do. The punishment would be far greater once his dad found out he had changed the grades from E's to B's. He told his well-meaning brother and others he would bring the grades up by then. That would reduce the severity of trouble. They tried to warn him. He figured he'd cross that bridge when he got there; this was just too awful to turn over to his parents. Plus, he knew he could get good grades if he tried. He would have to do homework and win the teachers over, though. Prove he cared and stay out of trouble. Trouble proved very difficult for him to stay away from. Boundaries, limits, and challenges of all kinds were tested. All was smooth and forgotten until on the bus ride home from school. Wouldn't you know on a Friday again! He had one B, an A in Gym that didn't matter, C's and D's, but still one E. Failed English again. *English sure is a messed-up language*, he thought. Something was a little strange, though. Even he couldn't figure out what was wrong. He never did figure out the ABCs. The memorization of the few letters, twenty-six? And multiplication tables didn't come till much later in life. It was all confusing and extremely hard for him. It was frustrating, even embarrassing, when the early grade teachers would make a fool out of him for pour work with easy letters and multiplication.

Now he presented a bad report card on top of a terrible lie. A devious cover-up. He didn't completely understand. There were many things happening in school that were just plain wrong. Unfairness. Fights. Riots. Martin Luther King Jr. was assassinated on Thursday, April 4, 1968. While he was in junior high school, there was a lot of tension and fights. He tried to explain but to no avail. He could never explain exact details of some of the daily distractions. To his mom and dad, the distractions shouldn't matter. Challenges must be overcome.

When he entered junior high school. The senior high teenagers from his neighborhood told him to never back down from a fight no matter what. If he were to back down from his first fight in school, he would be labeled, and from then on, he would be bullied and attacked. He would never live it down, and survival would be precarious at best. Win or lose would not matter. Just don't back down. His day came quick.

After lunch, all students were forced outside. Doors were locked, waiting for the door to open. He acted up and started to mess with a neighborhood friend. He liked John a lot, but John was slower than the rest. They were friends.

Sometimes he spent time with John when others wouldn't have anything to do with John. John and he actually had bonded a little before. But on this day, after lunch recess, he messed with John's head a little. He was just playing, but it was wrong. Given the chance, he would've had apologized to John later either alone or in front of others; it wouldn't have mattered. That's the way he was. He did feel relationships were built better one-on-one, though. Proof might later appear in front of others. After the lunch break in the cafeteria, some gathered at a door to enter a different school wing for afternoon classes. It was on this day and at this door he let his friend down. Was it bullying? Not really. He was probably making fun of John carrying all his books at once. Would it be called bullying today? Oh yes! Could the event have possibly revealed realities of life with younger friends, ultimately strengthening both of them once rebonded? Might it have come around to him helping John at his locker or something? Maybe. Who knows, because what happened next added to the mix.

Other's witnessed. He really wasn't paying attention to the others around because he and John both knew there was no seriousness to his seemingly unkind playfulness. A group did not like the way he was treating another at school. He was wrong to talk to his neighbor this way, and he knew it. Today, he was doing what he would never let anyone else do. Four black kids his age, led by an albino with rose-colored glasses, pink eyes, and pinkish-white hair decided they were going to teach him a lesson. Did the color of skin matter? No! Of course not. It was just a description of those involved. By the way, John looked Jewish—short in height, thick glasses, and wavy over-the-ear-length hair. He formed his words deep and in an animated way and dressed oddly—plaid shirt, khaki pants, and street shoes—but dressed far better than himself. And as far as he recalled, his family wasn't Jewish. Who knows? Who cares? He didn't care about any of that. But he did care about people and relationships. On this day, the five were right, and he was in the wrong. Seemed this was not an occasion to explain. Really wasn't a good explanation anyway. Although John was his friend, he was wrong. He remembered what he was told, couldn't back down. His first real school fight, and it was going to be five on one? *Oh well*, he thought as he dropped his books calmly.

His books landed in somewhat of a neat stack. He squared up his shoulders, stepped in closest to the albino. Only because he was center of the five and he seemed to be the leader. Smiling at first slowly changing to a businesslike expression. Interestingly enough, the five seemed excited to get to work too. Then he heard a deep voice coming from behind and over his right shoulder: "You're messing with him, you're messing with me." Very surprised. He twisted his head to look.

Wow, he thought. *Robert?* Barely knew him. Bob was taller, well-built, and on the basketball team. He thought it strange at first because why would Bob help him against people of his own color? He turned back to the five with much greater confidence. Five to two? Okay. Much better than before. The bell rang. The doors opened.

Most students ran. A few stayed back to watch. The five seemed to start a debate? He noticed a couple of heads shaking side to side. Returning to class suddenly became more important for the five as they hurried off to class. Picking up his books, he watched them and Robert leave.

For some reason, he didn't care about being late and stopped in the men's room. Walked in and noticed Robert. What were the odds, he happened into the same bathroom? So he asked Bob, "What made you want to help me?"

Robert said, "Didn't seem like a fair fight, so I decided to even the odds." He was impressed, didn't even know Robert. Except for loaning Robert a pencil one day in class. Just like the gratitude shown after being given a pencil. "Thanks. Thanks a lot, Robert," he said.

Robert said, "No problem. Don't worry about it." He learned that day what many never get the opportunity to. He learned the color of one's skin doesn't matter. It is one's deeds, character, and behavior which matter most. He would grow to ensure his sons were raised color blind. Both his sons grew up having friends built upon relationships, not color or ethnicity. Both his sons had and have a variety of friends. He could attest, "Those who refuse to see, miss some fabulous opportunities. Life's education is planned but one has a choice whether to participate in the schooling or not."

Everything he did in school seemed to come harder to him than other students. All that really didn't matter. He still should've gotten better grades. It seemed he was certainly capable. Plus some teachers simply did not like him. His appearance brought judgment. He would pull away and retreat from inequity. He had brought almost all the grades up. For him to completely grasp the moment of shock and hurt his parents felt was very difficult. It wasn't just his grades that were disappointing, it was the dishonesty, unscrupulous behavior, and deceptiveness which broke his mom's and dad's hearts. He could tell. His dad couldn't even muster the strength to punish him. His mom looked at him through watery eyes and walked away. He learned about punishment that weekend. He learned punishment is to correct bad behavior. To give meaning toward improving something wrong in character. Even though his mom and dad were highly intelligent, these actions proved too much pain for any mother and father. They did not know how to discipline this type of severe deficiency. Something was wrong besides bad behavior? No way to correct this one. They tried. He noticed reciprocal pain change to indifference between he and his parents for a short while after that and it was all his fault. But with conviction and forgiveness love endured stronger than ever. After all, they were family. No turning back. He would have to continue forward.

His mom helped him get into summer school. Before he could leave junior high school and get into senior high (ninth to tenth grade), he had to make up at least two of the core classes he failed, some of the ones he got the four E's in. He couldn't recover completely from how far he fallen behind. Summer school actually wasn't that bad. He did really well. He and the teacher clicked. He actually learned from this teacher. The teacher seemed to care. The summer school teacher didn't really have to be there. The teacher wasn't making that much money over the summer when everyone else was on vacation. The teacher was genuinely trying to help students who had problems and were in summer school trying to get help. He was getting B's. Face it. It was summer. Couldn't be all in. Come on.

It was on one occasion in math class the teacher called him up to the desk after a test. *Uh-oh*, he thought.

The teacher said, "Look. He was doing great. But some other students were copying off him. He settled in to defend himself. The teacher said, "No. Look I've been watching." The teacher explained that the teacher had been watching and knew that he had no clue anyone one was copying off him.

Well, what's the deal then? he was thinking.

The teacher said, "Look, there's another test tomorrow," but this time he wanted him to write bogus answers like 48 × 12 = dog. Just way off the wall answers on the whole test. Right away, he backed up, shaking his head. "Set people up? Unh, ain't gonna happen." The teacher grabbed his arm and explained that the teacher needed to let those cheating know that the teacher knew they were copying and to stop. Because if they didn't get the ones wrong that they didn't understand, that the teacher couldn't help them learn. This guy seemed to really care. Problem was he had all night to think about. He knew the teacher cared. But could the teacher be trusted?

Next day was test time. The teacher handed him the test and smiled. He couldn't do it. Well, he could and he couldn't. He would put enough blatantly wrong answers that it could be obvious. But not enough wrong answers that anyone copying would fail. They all turned in the test. At first, he could see the teacher comparing answers and getting mad, but then it was like a light went off inside the teacher. The teacher's eyes lit up. The teacher had enough proof. He looked at him and smiled then went into the act. The teacher called them out, not by name, just held up all the tests in the air and explained. He walked over and put the hand of a good teacher on his shoulder, continuing to lecture the class. Even though he had not wanted to go along, he had put enough wrong answers so the teacher could actually help those who needed help. The teacher went on to explain for them not to worry. Nobody would know, and the teacher would just help them if the students would only allow it. Wow, finally he had met an awesome guy. A teacher who cared and was really willing to go out of his way to help people. He would never forget.

Sitting next to windows in one of his seventh-grade classes provided an excellent view from the second-floor wing out over open fields that were used for physical education (gym classes) and practice fields for school sports. In other words, his seat proved to be a great vantage point for daydreaming.

One day, he noticed a crowd gathering around an eighteen-wheeler under an overpass just beyond the fields on Route 50. The large truck and trailer was only partly visible. Most of the tractor trailer seemed to be under the overpass with only the back end sticking out where most of the commotion happened to be, hand waving, pointing, and talking was. Traffic on the dual-lane highway was greatly hindered and slowed to a crawl. Then he noticed a young kid. Was the kid out of place? He didn't fit in the picture. Riding a banana seat bicycle along the side of highway toward the scene. From a distance, he wasn't sure, but the kid looked around his age or most likely younger. All very curious. What was happening? And hey, why wasn't that kid in school? That didn't seem right. It left him a little jealous. Then the kid stopped near the men gathered near the trailer. They seemed to exchange a few words, and he noticed the kid pointed at the trailer, maybe said something, then returned to his cycling position, and meandered on his way. They seemed to stop talking, seemingly in agreement, all dispatched forward for the task about the trailer. Just then, he heard a bloodcurdling scream, seemingly right in his ear, right next to him.

Leaning away from the continued screaming, he turned to see the girl seated next to him screaming and pointing at him. He looked toward the teacher. The teacher seemed frightened and too scared to even move. Not sure what was wrong with the girl, he looked back at the girl now resolved to get answers. This was disturbing. The girl kept screaming, pausing only long enough to get out the word: "Rat!" She continued screaming and pointing at him.

Somewhat alarmed, he looked down and then saw the white mouse with a pink nose sticking almost halfway out of his shirt pocket. Oh, he had forgotten. His first thought was, *Wow, silly girl. It's not a rat. It's a mouse.* It was his. He had brought a pet mouse to school, putting the mouse into his shirt pocket, and had forgotten all about it. It was almost lunchtime, and the li'l fella was probably starting to get hungry. At first, he tried to explain. But everyone seemed in some kind of shock, unable to relate to his reasonable and harmless explanation. Surrounded by an atmosphere of utter disdain, he was ushered to the principal's office. They called his mom. Now he felt bad because his mom would be troubled by his interactions with others. He always felt great sorrow in disappointing his mom. Once his mom came, his offenses were made clear. Germs, disease, filth on his person, suspension. Once his mom seemed in agreement with all the school's admonishments, she said, "We can go now."

In the car, on the way home, the mouse stuck his head out, twitching its nose as it looked around and smelled. Helping the mouse out of his shirt pocket into his palm, beginning to think about some lunch, he looked over at his mom. It is very difficult to explain the peacefulness and ease he felt seeing his mom's glow and demeanor. The seriousness and authoritative mother back in the office had dissipated and transformed into the loving and caring mother he always longed to feel. He was troubled and confused. His reasoning, position, and claims of innocence were so easily ignored and dismissed, but his mother seemed to understand. Once home, it made him aware of not looking forward to his dad coming home, for now though he had half the day off. Just like the kid he had seen on the bicycle.

Later in the evening, he saw his dad pull into the driveway. Deciding his mom's explanation would be better than his, he retreated to his room. It wasn't long before his mom and dad came into his room. "Where is it?"

Trying to convey the harmlessness, he took it from its box, presenting it to his dad. He said, "Want to hold it?"

His dad responded with an authoritative "No." Then came all the rules. "Now go wash your hands before we eat. Always wash your hands after you handle it."

"Okay, Dad. Okay, Mom." Dinner seemed unusually at ease that evening with all gathered in contentment. No problems, no arguments. Then came the story from Dad.

Since Dad was dispatch manager at a trucking company, he had heard an unusual story about a tractor trailer (eighteen-wheeler) stuck under the bypass on Route 50 downtown today. The truck driver didn't notice there wasn't enough clearance for the trailer and was driven to a grinding crushing halt, forcibly jammed or wedged under the bridge. No one could figure out how to free it. They couldn't lift the road and couldn't tow it free. Dad said, "Then a little boy came along on his bicycle, stopped, and said, "Why don't you let the air out of the tires?" After enough air was let out all of the tires to lower the truck five to six inches, the driver hopped in the cab and simply drove the trailer free. There it was. He actually saw it. The voice of reason from a little boy. It left him puzzled. Would he ever be heard when he spoke the truth? Why couldn't others see what he saw?

His teen years brought more bad behavior and more poor decisions. A good friend's parents invited him and several others in the neighborhood to their church. All his friends and he were in desperate need of mentoring. He did look forward in going to church.

Actually, he was a little excited. He was surprised. It was a newer red brick Jehovah Witness church. Not an old building. Inexplicably, there seemed an underlying sense among the others in his group of a "lesser" religion. He thought, *How would they know? They never go to any church*. The service started off well. All the teenagers felt a little odd but somewhat welcomed. Upon direction from the pastor or reverend, many—and it seemed like all—got up, exclaiming they had the Holy Spirit in them. He noticed all, but the half-dozen teenagers began running around the pews and church shouting, hollering, and waving their arms about wildly as almost everyone began running around the church. Except for he and his friends. The whole Church. Some crying. Some yelling with hands in the air. Some just very loudly exclaiming and exalting Christ. Some with eyes rolled, while others guided them. He was shocked. It seemed too much. It just seemed fake to him. To this day, he doesn't know if it was because he was too overwhelmed that people would act in such a manner or that he just didn't believe them. He walked out. As he walked outside to wait for his ride, he was content to wait while he was trying to figure out what just happened. Then his friends came out. Must've seen him step out.

They all stood outside in disbelief, asking each other what had just happened in there. Then a little toad hopped right up to him. He asked the rest if they should they let the toad go in church. He doesn't remember if he had actually picked up the toad and let it go in the church. It took two, one to open the door, the other to shoo it in. He was just as much at fault as any of the others. It was as if he had let the toad go inside the church himself. It wasn't long before there came horrific screams of the devil inside. Oh boy, were they all shocked. Wow! Such a commotion from inside the church? Sounded like a fight broke out. Slamming and banging. Sounded like women fainting? The screams from inside brought the small group of teens outside the church into slight shock. As they all stood with eyes wide open, some with mouths wide open too. The doors to the church swung open. Almost the whole congregation formed inside and outside the double doors. Some men from the congregation threw a dead frog out to the ground. All of the congregation told the teens to go away and never come back. They told the teens they had allowed the devil into their church. Quietly, the small group of teens started walking. It was going to be about an eight- to ten-mile walk back home to their neighborhood. This was the second church he had been accused of demon-like behavior, thrown out, and never allowed back. He couldn't argue with the decision in either case. Whether the toad that happened up was actually a demon or an unclean spirit, as one of the three "frogs" referred to in Revelation, will never be known until Judgment Day. Certainly, unknowing youngsters letting the frog go in a church turned out to be similar enough to the biblical metaphor. The mischievous behavior couldn't be accepted as a light-hearted prank. Another of his "unforgivens'" until he would eventually ask to be forgiven. There would be many more. Even worse. But as much as it sounds that this story is of a little boy bound for life in prison or a death sentence, it was quite the opposite. Although he remains unforgiven to this day, he has continuously sacrificed to this day. He has served. He has helped thousands. He learned that the large majority of people are misled to becoming people incapable of forgiveness.

Go it Alone?

The first time he was shot at was quite a surprise. He was about twelve years old, and he and a friend about three years older than himself were walking down a dirt road. There was a field with corn already harvested. Rows of the brown stalks cut to about three inches high with dirt furrows on each side of the row of stalks to their left. Immediately to their right a woods or forest. They both had done nothing wrong. Just walking. Being shot at really did come as a sudden deadly surprise. They were walking a slight uphill grade on dirt road between the corn field and the wooded area. As they crested the hill on the dirt road, the tree line curved back away from the road, a large enough area for a farmer to have had another acre of corn or so. Now there were stalks left and right. The two boys kept walking innocently and unsuspecting. Now they were exposed to open areas on the left and the right. The sound is, as they say, of a hornet or bee came buzzing by. Then the sound of the shot immediately followed. The first shot whizzed by really close to his head. *A .22-caliber rifle*, he thought. Even having never heard or experienced this before, he immediately dove down to one of the two ruts in the dirt road. To him, there was no mistaking what just happened. He was clearly hearing the zing before the bang sound from the rifle. There was a little grass between the two tire ruts, and he was noticing the grass and sand plucking or kicking up between six inches to two feet from his head. Extremely close. *Good thing the guy shooting is a bad shot*, he thought. Or the guy shooting was playing deadly and dangerous games with him and his friend. His friend? Feeling somewhat safe, he angled his head enough to look back. His friend behind him seemed dumbfounded and was quizzically looking into the woods toward the sound of the shots. He kicked at his friend's feet and legs, emphatically saying, "Get down!" His friend seemed ignorant to the command. Then he angrily kicked his friend so hard his older friend lost balance. Then his friend finally lay down. He guessed it was a good thing he was the one being shot at. Because if it was his friend that had been the one being shot at, he would've been hit by now. It was him that was the target! Why? Oh, he wanted to know why badly. But not yet. Once his friend finally lay down in a tire rut, his friend still seemed dumbfounded. So he kicked at his friend's head and commanded, "Back up! Stay on your belly. Crawl back. Get back to the tree line." His friend was mad at him for kicking him but reluctantly followed the younger boy's commands. All the while, the dirt plucked up within a few inches to a foot around his head and body. Especially when he had to lift his body maneuvering enough to kick his friend.

Whew! Must've been at least a ten-shot .22 semiautomatic. Sure seemed like all ten shots were fired. Maybe even reloaded and more fired as they backed up? After they backed up to the tree line, he stood up. The shooting ceased. He tried convincing his friend to venture into the woods. They needed to find out who took some shots at them. His friend would have absolutely none of that idea. Oh, he tried very hard to convince his older friend. To at least get close enough in the woods to see who it was. He needed to know. The issue needed to be addressed: why? His friend's only idea and obvious immediate solution: running home and telling Dad. One-track mind and scared. He knew calling the police wouldn't solve a random shooting. First they would have to be believed. The police never talked to him about it. How did he know the sound of a bullet whizzing by? How does someone explain at a very young age, no, it's not something he was experienced in. No, it was not something he had practiced. No, it was not something he had scientifically studied. He just knew. Lucky? No. For him, he knew immediately. He hit the ground immediately. Put his face in the soft sand. He could smell the dirt. Then came the second shot, plucking dirt inches away from his head. Even heard the slug hit the dirt. A kind of soft thud mixed with fluff. The dirt went in his hair and hit the side of his face. Good thing he instinctively had put his hands near his face and had squinted his eyes. He had needed to prevent the sand from getting in his eyes that he might see clearly the next move.

Once again, did others believe him? Reflecting back, he hadn't kicked his friend to get attention from projecting his own fear and panic. He had kicked his friend out of a clear sense of urgency, knowing it would be the only way the younger one would be taken more seriously in relaying how dangerous the situation was that they were in. The situation required immediate recognition and reaction. Today, it is referred to as situational awareness. There were many times his thoughts drifted to "what if." He needed to know who possibly, even if playfully, tried to kill him. He always wondered what if he had gone alone. Venturing into the woods to see who it was. Maybe he could've been much quieter than the two of them searching, walking noisily among leaves on the ground. Instead of going for it, his efforts were wasted trying to instill courage into a friend three years older than him. There could be no going back. It seemed his friend was intent on telling his dad, looking to an adult for remedy. Even at the moment of decision his older friend made, he knew that telling an adult wouldn't help. He always wondered if he had snuck through the woods alone, getting close enough to have seen who it was, at least he would've had known whom. But for him, it wasn't over.

He had that ability to make friends with people from other neighborhoods. At school, he met Raymond from a different neighborhood. He told Raymond he would like to come visit. A little bewildered, Raymond asked, "How?"

He boldly stated he would just ride on Raymond's bus and get off at Raymond's bus stop! Of course, this wasn't permitted. Getting on the bus after school, Raymond stepped back and watched amused at the bravado but also in disbelief. As people lined up to board the big yellow school bus. He kind of slipped in by a cute girl smiling and being as courteous as possible. The girl smiled in amusement of his silliness. The girl also seemed to understand he did not belong on her bus. He would pack in tightly as the other kids, and he boarded. He glanced at the bus driver. Careful not to make eye contact. The bus driver was busy scanning everything. Footsteps, hand on handle, scanning everyone and looking for oncoming traffic and checking the giant mirror made and positioned for watching kids. Once seated, he looked up and noticed a puzzled look in his direction by the bus driver. Off they went. Raymond was excited. Raymond witnessed and learning something of social order and social disorder, if you will.

On the bus ride, he was a little overly flirtatious with some girls that didn't know him. Then Raymond and he talked. Raymond became more comfortable, as they talked. Raymond and he actually would become good friends after this. He learned of the family there was three boys and a girl. Two boys and one older. He was clearly and in no uncertain terms warned to stay away from checking out the little sister. Too young anyway. Besides he was on a mission. The location of their neighborhood was prime location for whomever shot at him must've lived? Maybe no one will ever understand how he had laid in bed at night wanting to know who shot at him. He couldn't let it go. Doesn't matter. He was on his own. No one ever believed him anyway. The bus headed all the way down the street. Ending at the same woods. Dead at railroad tracks. Just opposite the side of the woods from which he was shot at, watching who got off the bus along the way. *Uh-um, prime location*, he thought.

"Hey, do you have a gun? Like a .22," he asked, stating he was a good shot.

Raymond said no.

Then he asked, "Does your older brother have guns?"

"Yeah," Raymond replied, acting excited and interested. "Does he let you shoot them? Nah, not unless the older brother is present." The bus came to a stop. When they got off. The bus driver grabbed his arm and obtusely asked for a note. He quickly told the driver that he was just visiting a friend and lived right over there, referencing over a mile away. The bus driver knew what he meant and said, "Don't ever try that again. Not without permission."

Acting startled, he said, "Okay." Didn't really matter. Mission complete. He was there!

Getting invited in wasn't difficult. Raymond made it clear to stay away from his little sister. "No problem," he said, "she's cute but too young." Raymond kind of did not like that. He could tell. Then he got serious and sincere with Raymond, making eye to eye. He made clear to Raymond that he would never mess with his little sister. And he wouldn't and never did. Inside, they eventually made way to his brother's room and curiosity about the guns came around again. Then Raymond's older brother came in the room, about three years their senior. It was at that moment he could tell. Then came the authority and establishment of the elder present in charge thing. Trying to act cool, he showed interest in particular to the .22 and claimed to be a good shot, asking if they could go out and shoot it. Out back, behind Raymond's house, was a small range with a target. A very large open field behind with the woods of interest to him to their right. No way was it an accident. The woods were very thick. Over a mile and a half to two miles thick at that point. If someone had walked a straight line from where they were standing, up to the tree line near the open area from which the previous shots came, they've could've easily taken clear shots at two unsuspecting targets. It was at that moment he knew. He didn't clearly understand at this point in his life, but he was being shown.

As best to his recollection, Raymond shot first and shot Okay. A car pulled in to the car port. *Uh oh*, he thought. The mom came home. Raymond's mom got out with questions, of course. Raymond went over to the car to cool things over with Mom. He waved hi to her. She waved back. Obviously, Raymond was explaining who the new kid was. Then the older brother shot. Somewhat better? Then the older brother loaded ten rounds in the 22. Of course then came the treatment like a novice showing him where the safety was. And then came the arrogant way of explaining: never point a gun, et cetera. In his state, he felt what were normal gun safety rules being explained as rules being explained by a smart aleck. Standing, he spread his feet shoulder width apart, turned his front foot toward the target, and snuggling the gun into his shoulder like it is was now a likable part of him. He closed his eyes and felt the gun, began breathing deep, felt its weight, its smooth pommel. He opened his eyes and steadied, took aim, and slowly fired four shots. Dead center. Adjacent placement. Some holes touching. Then fired four more simultaneously. *Pap-pap-pap-pap!* He stopped, lowered the barrel, then looked at Raymond's older brother. The older brother's eyes wide open. Then he changed. He looked the older brother in the eye and asked, "Two more left?"

"Uh, yeah, think so," came the reply. Keeping eye contact, he slowly pointed the gun toward the ground with finger beside the trigger.

The older brother pointed, saying, "Safety!" Then came the question: "Did you take a shot at him a couple weeks back?"

Then came a very odd and awkward smile from the older brother. Not answering though. Now he reached for the gun, saying, "Put the safety on."

He stepped back turning to one side, using his body weight against the older brother's half-hearted attempts, pushing the older brother's hand away, now becoming very animated, demanding, "*Did you shoot at him?*"

Raymond's mom saw something going wrong and became upset, walking their way, saying, "Stop! What's going on?"

Raymond came quickly too. He really could not and did not want to upset the mom. He turned the barrel up in the air on purpose to make his point. Clearly, he clicked on the safety and kind of shoved the gun into the older brother's open hand. But before he let go of the gun he said, "Don't ever shoot at him again!"

The mom demanded to know what was going on. Raymond was upset. The older brother, although still wearing an awkward, sly, curved smile, calmly pointed the gun down, saying nothing. They kept eye contact momentarily. The mom and older brother went inside. Raymond was now uncomfortable with him, stating homework had to be done. Probably felt a little used. He genuinely liked Raymond. He turned and headed down the railroad tracks alone toward home. At least he thought he was. He thought he was alone. He walked trying to stay on the rail, speeding up, sometimes running almost full speed on a rail but then would come a misstep or not having full placement of the foot on the rail. He painfully turned his ankle. Most others trip and fall at full speed turning a headfirst dive with arms extended to break the fall. Instead he turned and tucked his shoulder and arm rolled on large wooden railroad ties, large rocks and stones down the side of the raised railroad toward the briers of an unkept ditch. Tearing holes in jeans. Scraping elbows. Drawing blood. After examining wounds and blood, he calmed down a bit. Then just walked home.

As he entered the neighborhood from the end of the street, a friend noticed his unkempt appearance of what were once school clothes. Of course, he exaggerated greatly over the confrontation of someone whom had previously shot at him. It all fit. He did not hurt himself on purpose on the railroad tracks. To say he might have been in a reckless and excited state might be an understatement, but it was no validation to lie. Once again, he stretched the truth. Nope, once again, he had lied. He really didn't lie that often, but it became clear that no matter what, people either would not believe truth or were overly blatantly and so critical of truth. It seemed people found it much easier to believe lies than truth. Very puzzling indeed. Once he came to understand this, he found it so important to the point of critically deadly serious that he must tell the truth. Even the white lies which are claimed to be innocent. Even the little lies which many claim are important to the survival of a marriage. He wouldn't do it. Honestly, being truthful does make it harder on a marriage. But when you come to know and trust the love of your life, honesty is paramount! If you're not totally and completely honest, then husband and wife will never truly come to know who each other really are.

He really didn't lie or stretch the truth that much when he was young, just enough to learn most people had a harder time believing truth than lies. He learned to lean toward friendships and relationships whose foundation began and remained with trust and truth. He learned this very young. And he rarely trusted adults. Some seemed to have ulterior motives or goals and objectives that did not benefit others. Not all, just a lot. This observation's ratio of those with self-interest compared to those who genuinely cared about others seemed to grow over years. He observed an accelerated increase of "self over others" after the Vietnam War. Everyone believed the protest was to benefit the country and the greater good, saving lives and a nation's morality and ethics, and maybe the protest was. But actually, the generational movements somehow morphed the next generation into a self-grandiose generation, if you will, a self-absorbed generation of self-righteousness. Then the next generation pegged the needle to full self-absorption, magnifying ideological differences and social disorders into social rebellions and self-righteousness then into a desire to control others. Even thoughts and words would monitored and captured supposedly unto perpetuity. An apparent attempt by man to mock God's abilities. Who or what led this charge? Was it really just for profit? Foul language remained. Blasphemy of God grew. Religion became alienated and not allowed in schools. It became strange times. There became a progressive movement to block children from coming to know God in school. Children were openly taught how to have sex without getting pregnant during sexual orientation training classes. Eventually, by the year 2020, it seemed a climate of that which was bad was good and that which was good was bad was in the air. Since biblical edification declined, very few noticed the signs. Those chosen as experts announced the weather was changing, the polar ice caps were melting, and the oceans were rising, endangering coastal cities, regions, and life itself. The earth's changes were named global warming then climate change. The changes reached worldwide attention as an actually catastrophic event with an end time and date of doom. The year 2050 was declared the "or else" or "drop dead" date. The recognition of the end reached the level of worldwide unity toward preventative measures. But people just *could not read the signs.* Wars among nations continued to escalate on a global scale. The approach of the final battle against God at Armageddon would've been obvious to the most casual observer. But we're distracted, and events were prevented from being in the air.

A Turkey for Thanksgiving

At fourteen or fifteen, he ran away. Shouldn't have. Why? Seeking liberty from parental rules? No. His parents' rules weren't that strict. For some reason, he thought he didn't need boundaries. He wanted to experience liberty. Not yet knowing and understanding with freedom comes responsibility. He still went to school, though. Who does that? He ran away during the week of Thanksgiving. Who does that? As explained before, riding a different bus to school normally took coordination of parents and approval at school district administrative levels. Quite brazenly, he just boarded the other bus. What would they do, tell him no? He could handle that. So he went to school with a friend from a neighborhood several miles away from his. At first, just as he thought, using the same tactics as before, the bus driver didn't notice. He wondered at times, sometimes it appeared as if the bus driver did notice. It seemed many who noticed kind of liked him or just accepted as part of their own. No harm, no foul?

He was amusing to many. And it was easy for the girls to flirt with him. There seemed to be less barriers because this guy wasn't from around here. Some girls seemed to recognize an advantage of a certain anonymity he came with? Guess he could've figured that one out but, it really didn't matter to him why. As long as he knew it was real and it was a real social behavior with cause and effect. He had some fun with this one. Maybe too much. Some of the kids on the bus began to talk. Mainly because some of the guys were jealous and that he was gaining attention from their neighborhood girls. Of course the girls couldn't help it. Some were interested in his bold-ness and cavalier behavior. The bad boy thing, he guessed. Or, were they right? He genuinely enjoyed love and kindness. He did not enjoy fighting. Older teens on the bus tried to challenge him. He cared not. Now it seemed he found advantage in anonymity. What were they going to do, call his parents? Good luck with that one. He was on his own now. Really shouldn't have been. No job. Nowhere to stay.

Concern of the kids from the other neighborhood knowing the specifics mattered a little, but he kind of enjoyed that some of the hot girls from a different neighborhood were attracted to him? Wouldn't hurt anyone to take advantage of that. Maybe he could get a date. During the three days of school to and fro, the jealousy seemed to brew. Eventually, the bus driver figured something was going amiss. The driver said he would need a note next time. Discovery came on Wednesday afternoon just before Thanksgiving break. He thought, *Oh well, freedom.* Four more days of doing whatever he wanted. His brothers contacted him through the network of people, school, et cet-era and convinced him to call Mom. They said Mom was devastated. Crying because he left. He couldn't have that. That was wrong. He knew if he called her, that would be it. He would go home. He called his mom. He hated the hurt in her voice and knowing he was the one causing it, he decided to return home. But he asked these next four days, these four days, to be on his own. His mom was extremely intelligent. A forward-thinking woman. She relented to the boy who wanted to think he was a man. But he did wholeheartedly promise to return Sunday in time for school the next day. Monday.

The Lower Eastern Shore of farms and chicken houses every-where really had no jobs to speak off. Money was tight. Carding someone? Don't make him laugh. At one point, the drinking age was still twenty-one before they lowered it to eighteen. One of his friends, Eddie, while on a double date with Diane and Donna, took him to some back-country store. Store-home combos on the Lower Eastern Shore were really rather common and conveniently located places to get gas, goods, supplies and necessities accompanied with great customer service. There were no BP's, Sphinxes, Shell's Speedways, 7/11s, et cetera. This store-home combo happened to be between Chrisfield, Maryland, and Deal Island, Maryland, back in Oystermen country. Eddie was old enough to drive and had a Mustang. The girls were impressed with Eddie, but Donna loved him and he loved her. Donna was his true first love. Both were fifteen years old. They pulled up to the old country store, and Eddie told him to go in and buy a case of beer. At fifteen? Eddie said, "Go ahead, just tell them you're twenty-one."

He got out and went in, walked over to the cooler, and grabbed a case of Budweiser in the can. Someone was in front of him in line. The older couple behind the counter were working as a team. As they were finishing and helping the person in front of him bag, they both looked at him standing there with a case of beer. Blue jeans with a slight flare, boots, and denim jean coat. He looked down at the case. Then came his turn. Never taking his eyes off the case, he had to lift it seemingly high to set the case on the counter. He reached for his wallet, focusing on the money. Then came the question, "How old are you, boy?" Even the person that was leaving stopped, turned around, and waited. He was so nervous. They would never believe a fifteen-year-old was twenty-one.

Out came, "Eighteen?"

Everyone laughed, laughed pretty hard. They said, "You were supposed to say twenty-one, boy!" They held out the hand for the money. As he walked away, they said, "Remember, boy! Say twenty-one!"

The person in front held the door for him. His face, beet red, had to change immediately. They were all watching the door with anticipation. Jimmy kind of leaned over, two fingers on the wheel. Diane, smiling and somewhat proud of her twin sister's boyfriend, swung her door open quickly. Wearing a halter top without a bra, she had to lean way forward so she could pull the back of the seat way forward so he could get in. It was not easy to get in the back seat of an older two-door Ford Mustang, let alone with a case of beer. Donna was extremely eager to slide over and make extra room. Funny. Donna must have been at the car's small back window looking or watching to see if he would come out victorious. Donna's fifteen-year-old boyfriend coming out of the store a man. Sure made him feel different than the way he felt in the store. Changing from an embarrassment and extreme low instantaneously to a high, a high enough to walk with shoulders erect and even strut. But he didn't, he just smiled and hurried into the backseat.

Thanksgiving 1969, he had nowhere to stay. Nowhere to go. His brother asked if Joe would take him in. Something was up, and he didn't get it. Joe was really down. For some unknown reason and even though there was a huge difference in age, Joe and him liked one another. He looked up to Joe and his character. It was more than that, though. Maybe Joe saw some character in the young kid? It was more than that, though. Whatever was wrong with Joe that day, he was real slow to catch on. It took hours, then he knew.

Joe was cool. Tough too. Had to be. Had an older model Chevy with a column shifter. The car was mint. Dressed out with large back tires and chrome mag wheels. We call 'em muscle cars today. And for good reason. Joe's family situation was worse than his own family but very similar. Joe drank. His dad drank but was not anywhere to be found. His dad pretty much stayed at the worst bar one could imagine. Dirty smells like stale beer, puke and even pee outside the door. Yeah, no one would want to use the bathroom inside. It was really bad. Known as the Village Inn out in the middle of nowhere, but it would draw a big crowd very late at night. The county had a hard time keeping it closed after one or two in the morning. Back then, there seemed to be a lot more tolerance than today for gatherings and cutting loose on weekends. Most who were labeled as troublemakers weren't really troublemakers at all. It was just that they worked at the lowest paying jobs of the Lower Eastern Shore imaginable for the least amount of money possible, and most were just trying to have gatherings, getaways, and have fun on weekends. The elite call these girls' getaways. The rich men called it golf outings or hunting expeditions. Back then the gratuitous called it spring break from colleges before they reach elite status. Even the college student weekends wore a cloak of exception. He himself never saw the need for the piece of paper to reflect exceptional partying, favorable hazing, and professor-led indoctrination.

Joe's dad had died recently. Heart attack? Joe's mom was a heavy drinker too. It was Thanksgiving Day. Joe drove with just him in tow just a few miles to over State lines because booze (liquor) was cheaper in Delaware. Delaware assessed lower taxes on alcohol than Maryland did making liquor much cheaper. It was for that reason Brownies Liquor Store did well on the border. Joe was about seven years his senior. He himself was about fifteen years old. At the time, the legal age to drink alcohol in Maryland was twenty-one, and in Delaware, twenty. It was not long after the Vietnam War was nearly over that the legal age across the nation was lowered to eighteen. It was felt that if one was old enough to die in a jungle on foreign soil or kill an enemy, certainly they should be able to drink beer, wine, or even liquor. It was for similar reasons the voting age was lowered not long after WWII and the Korean War. Of course, all these age limits were lowered for the elite college students who were not normally drafted—just another reason he did not like college. It just didn't seem right. It may have been called class warfare back then, but he didn't know a classification existed. He just knew the difference between right and wrong. He would have to learn. The drinking age was one year lower in Delaware than Maryland too.

Didn't matter Brownies in Delmar, Delaware, just across the Maryland border would pretty much sell to anyone to make a buck. Joe bought a half gallon of Jack Daniel's, a case of Bud, and also a pint of schnapps. Joe broke bad with the car and we got stopped by the Maryland State Troopers at the border. Joe said hide the pint. He did down his pants. The cops asked how much booze Joe bought at Brownies. The cops didn't care about the burnout and banging of gears; they tried to get Joe for interstate transportation of hard liquor. Anything over a half gallon was against interstate transportation laws. The cops glared at the long-haired youngster in the passenger seat. They seemed perturbed at Joe for having him along, saying Joe was a bad influence. The Maryland State Police made Joe get out of the car, checking to see if he had been drinking. Hungover maybe, but Brownies opened at noon, and it was 12:15 p.m., and Joe knew not to drink until we were clear of the high visibility State line area. They gave him a hard time about the case of beer, combined with the fifth, being borderline over the interstate transportation liquor laws. Plus a fifteen-year-old being there. The amount was close but not illegal and neither had drank anything. Yet Joe knew the pint, combined with the fifth and case would've put Joe over the limit of law. If the cops had forced the youngster out of the car, the cop might not have been able to believe the bulge in his front pants was something which originated from birth. They never made the youngster get out of the car. Although the one-sided hassle was evident, it was clear there was no wrong to be found. The cops wrote Joe a warning for reckless driving or something and let the two go. Was it harassment? Was it racial? The whole thing had nothing to do with color. But definitely police were surveilling. Is police intimidation something new? This all occurred around 1969. It was clear Joe had what later became known as an Indigenous Heritage but he doesn't recall anyone ever mentioning. Besides no one ever knew his own heritage. His ancestry was always simply an assumed. They were all wrong.

As soon as they got on the back roads, they popped the tops. And hit the Jack too. He knew it was too much for him so he mentioned the schnapps. Joe told him the schnapps was for his mom and began explaining Joe's dad had died and how hard the holidays, Thanksgiving, Christmas, and New Year's celebrations, were going to be on Joe's mom this year. Joe didn't care about the joys of the season. It just meant sometimes paid holidays from building chicken houses. Somehow, someone thought it a better idea not to mention in schools the biblical reasoning of law, liberty, and morality to much of the middle class who were busy catching up on household chores during holidays and Sundays. But it was Joe's mom who always wanted for her boys, her sons, to experience the joy of the holidays and family time. Some mothers greatly looked forward to family gatherings. Some adults have fond memories of the smells of the different foods, the bonding, the family discussions, and sometimes the arguments in their early years of seasonal family gatherings. On the rare occasion of an argument, making up led to deeper understanding and bonding. Since they were poor and Joe's dad struggled with alcohol and depression, much of the household responsibilities seemed to rest on Joe.

He was pretty loaded when they arrived at Joe's mom's house. Honestly it had been tough sleeping in a makeshift "fort" in the woods, and he was just hoping to pass out. He could hardly stand. They came in through the back door of a very old house, which opened to a small kitchen. Joe's mom was in a heavy nightgown at the kitchen table. The ashtray was full. Joe's mom was crying out loud and in emotional pain. Joe gave her a really emotional hug. Then Joe gave her a couple of packs of smokes and the pint. She took them and thanked Joe. Joe introduced him. All he could do was hold up the counter. Joe's mom got up and gave him a big hug. Totally unaccustomed to this emotional exchange, at first he arched his back but then leaned in because it seemed like the right thing to do even though she was in a nightgown. But Joe's mom started bawling. He was very sad. It was very upsetting. She said that she didn't even have a turkey for Thanksgiving for the family and her boys. Joe hugged her again and consoled her, telling her Joe would go get a turkey. No problem. Then they all toasted a shot to a happy Thanksgiving. Her a schnapps. Joe and he a shot of Jack. *Whew*, he thought, fighting back puke.

Joe looked at him and said, "Let's go!"

He headed for the car. Joe said, "No, the truck."

"You got a truck?" he asked.

"No, it was Joe's dad's," came a soft reply. A two-door late fifties to very early sixties bench seat. Clutch column shifter.

"Where we going?" he asked.

Joe said, "To get Humphrey." He didn't understand what was up. So he asked. Joe said they were going to a farmer's house to take a turkey. He asked why was the other guy needed; he could do it. He definitely did not agree or want to steal, but he was torn that if he could help Joe's mom be a little happier, he definitely would.

They pulled up at Humphrey's house. He hopped out to let Humphrey sit in the middle. Humphrey was very large, about Joe's age, and wearing an army coat. Definitely not a veteran. Not the type. Humphrey kind of roughly said, "No, you're in the middle, punk." Now all doubts were erased; he did not like this guy. Something was off.

Joe shut off the lights and coasted a good stretch toward the farm. Joe said he would wait here for their return with a turkey. So then the little guy in the truck spoke up and tried to explain; if they simply knocked on the door and asked, the farmer might actually give them a turkey. But that was not going to happen. Joe seemed to pause and give thought. Humphrey saw the pause and angrily shot a look at the punk in the middle then pushed the negative results and impossibilities of asking. After momentarily staring at the farmer's front door, Joe looked into his eyes, reflecting an absorption of the thought and a desire, but said, "It wouldn't work." Whether it was pride or Humphrey and Joe knowing something about this farmer he didn't, we'll never know. It seemed Humphrey was familiar with the farm and somewhat familiar with the layout of the land. It was pitch black. He was young and of smaller stature and he had been drinking all day; he had to pee. Certainly, all three knew—wrong time, wrong place. After a slow, methodical surveillance of the situation. Even the pigs did not care they were there. Barely a snort or grunt. He especially looked toward the farmer's house with a very long, tense gaze. He did not want to get shot by an angry, scared farmer protecting his life and property. If he was shot, he knew it would've been rightfully so. His situation was such that he had extreme empathy and felt a strong connection with Joe's situation. He'd have much rather gone and knocked on the door, try explaining, and offer maybe the change he had in his pocket for a turkey. He felt maybe the farmer might understand. But that was not going to happen. It seemed the other two knew things he didn't.

There were bright outside lights to be avoided but no sounds, no movement. So quiet, what could be the harm? He told Joe it was all clear. Besides, he really had to pee! That seemed to make Humphrey more annoyed with him, even mad. But while he was getting ready to let loose, he noticed something odd. A small post with a little white glass thing. Glass insulator? Bare electrical fencing wire about four inches off the ground, post to post. He whispered, at risk of still getting on everybody's last nerve, "Hey, Joe, is this electrical fence wire hot?"

Joe whispered, "Uh, yeah. Probably, be careful." Mostly, the pig snout is carried pretty low; still, if the pig snout missed the wire, it would zap their short legs. While he was peeing, trying not to hit a bare wire in the dark, he warned Humphrey of the electric fence.

"Of course," came back, "yeah, yeah, I know. Where?"

"Right there," he said.

"Where?"

He moved closer to Humphrey and the wire, pointing and whispering, "Look, right there." "Watch," he said. He zipped up and stepped over. So did Humphrey. It was about 150 yards to come up around the back of the barn, right by a gigantic tree between the farmers house and the barn. The tree was full of turkeys. He'd never seen white turkeys in a tree. Looking and listening, there were none on the ground. *That's weird*, he thought.

All was quiet. He looked at the farmer's house. No noise. Silence from the farmer and the house. Luckily, the pigs never made a sound, and neither did the turkeys. *Quite odd,* he thought. And turkeys all up in a tree? Easy in, easy out. Then he saw. Oh no! A young German Shepherd. He grabbed Humphrey's arm, whispering animatedly, "A dog!" But the dog didn't bark. *Whew!* He thought. Then he saw the dog causally approaching directly up to them. It was coming right up to them. But the dog was wagging its tail. Whew, another relief. As he leaned to greet the dog and caress, rub, and pet it, Humphrey grabbed the dog. With one giant hand Humphrey muzzled its mouth closed. Lifting its head exposing its throat, simultaneously revealing now a bayonet. Humphrey, with all intent and purposes, was to kill the dog right then and there. He was shocked. His first thought was, *This guy is an animal.*

Almost coming unglued, he said, "Stop!" He actually reached his small hand, grabbing the giant's forearm.

"What are you doing?" Humphrey said. "The dog is going to bark."

He firmly replied, "No, it's not! If it was going to bark, it would have barked already. Let it go."

Humphrey said, "No, I'm killing it." As the young lad squeezed Humphrey's forearm as tight as could, he had to think quick.

Humphrey was hell bent on killing. He was unable to make eye contact.

So he began loosening his tiny, firm grip stating, "The dog is not going to bark. Let go of its mouth. If it starts to make a sound, then kill it." Then the young lad let go of Humphrey's arm, hoping he had struck a deal.

Still holding an army bayonet against the dog's throat, Humphrey slowly released the grip on the dog's mouth, slowly opening the hand wide. "See?" he half-asked, half-said. "Put the bayonet away." The dog actually seemed to realize its predicament but never struggled. The dog then moved its head to the left, more toward him, and he gave it a brush on the back with a good push to get it away from this guy. The dog slowly moved away but wanted to hang out. It was then he realized why the turkeys were in the tree. The dog probably wanted somebody to play with and probably messed with the turkeys. Turkeys might be more comfortable in trees. These were domesticated birds which just hung out behind the house.

Then the dog happily and playfully danced around their feet. While Humphrey was still too worried about the dog, he noticed a giant turkey right there only a couple of feet away. A low branch was located where he could easily grab both legs. He whispered, "He was getting that one."

Humphrey said, "No me!" By now, he clearly understood, and Humphrey was not going to get a chance to screw this up. It was too late. He leaped from the crouched position, grabbed both legs with both hands from behind. The bird flapped madly. He simultaneously switched from a two-hand hold to a one-hand hold of both legs. He was already running, rounding the back of the barn and towards the truck. Humphrey was pissed but followed. Humphrey was barking whispered commands. He ignored them. *So weird*, he thought, why the giant bird never really bit at him or made any noise other than widely flapping sounds, somewhat normal sounds that might not alarm a farmer. Because birds commonly jostle for position or domination by flapping wings, which might seem somewhat normal. But the bird made no squealing, panicked gobbles, or panicked bird calls.

Humphrey kept barking, "Wait, wait, let me carry it." He ignored him until they got closer to the truck then remembered the wire? He purposely let Humphrey catch up and grab one leg of the turkey. Humphrey began to argue again and now tug. Just then he noticed the small pole with the glass insulator. He let go of the turkey's leg he was holding and took a high step in stride over where he thought the wire was. Still holding one leg and running, Humphrey fell flat on his face. Quickly, he stepped over and grabbed the super-sized bird. It was bad, but he actually hoped Humphrey got the piss shocked out of him. He jumped in the back of the truck with the turkey.

Then came Humphrey demanding, "Give it to me."

He couldn't stand it anymore. Turning over the bird, he leapt over the side and climbed in front with Joe, so happy to be away from that guy. He said, "Got a big one, Joe." Joe was so happy, smiling and patting him on the shoulder. Joe almost laughed a little, probably didn't think the whole thing possible. Joe was now relieved.

While on the way to Joe's, his heart racing a little, he told Joe, "That Humphrey guy was really strange. That guy tried to kill a dog for no reason." He looked over his shoulder toward the back of the truck bed. Humphrey had his back to the rear window with his shoulders strangely straining downward towards his lap. He had no idea what that guy could've possibly be doing now. He took a double take. Very strange guy?

They got to the house. The turkey was dead. Humphrey quickly blamed it on him. He began to argue. You tried to kill a dog too! Humphrey then declared to Joe, "If the farmer had come out, the farmer would've died too." He then revealed a revolver from his army coat.

"Oh my god. You are absolutely crazy," he said.

Joe quickly stepped in as tensions began to flare, saying, "It doesn't matter. The blood has to be drained quickly before it goes bad." Joe gave him a convincing look, letting him know that he had seen the turkey alive and well before Humphrey killed it.

About seven years later, on August 19, 1976, David Humphrey was witnessed carrying a bag with Louis Conti and George Whayland from the Beer Market where they worked in Salisbury, Maryland. Mr. Conti and Mr. Whayland's bodies were found on August 20, 1976, on the Route 13 bypass in Wicomico County. Both died from gunshot wounds. David Humphrey received two consecutive life sentences for murder, two twenty-year terms for robbery to run concurrent with each other and consecutive to the two life imprisonment sentences and a three-year term for a handgun conviction (https://law.justia.com/cases/maryland/court-of-special-appeals/1978/1024-september-term-1977-0.html).

At fifteen, unbeknownst to him, he had stayed the hands of a killer. Even it was only to save a dog. All that had happened the night of the Thanksgiving Turkey, might've saved a farmer too. He would learn later that it was not his own hand that had quieted all the animals of a farm. The strange quietness of an entire farm so as not to alarm an innocent protective man (farmer). Pigs, turkeys, even a future guard dog. He was not alone. Although none would ever condone the actions of a sinner in the midst of sinning. There is but One. One who had ten years prior turned His face toward a young boy. His Face would never turn away. It must be horribly difficult for a Father to watch His child while in the midst of thievery and sinning. But forever seeing, He does. It's kind of difficult to have favor of a child in the midst of sinning. But the Father may have had another One present who said, "See, Father, your youngster, in the midst of great risk, torn between right and wrong and facing overwhelming brute force, turmoil, and difficulty stays the hand of a brutal, unjust killer." Only gone ten days, he went home on Sunday, the day before returning to school as if nothing had happened. Home wasn't like he thought. Things changed after that. He had continued to erode trust and favor of loving and caring parents. He would continue to bring them heartache and great difficulties. It was just the end of junior high school.

For this generation, man thinks he is like God and that man is capable of the highest level of technological surveillance while maintaining moral integrity—when to intervene, when to apply mercy and grace, and when to administer punishment, wrath, or vengeance. Man is not capable. The human brain is too susceptible to sin. Morality shifts just as the shapes of desert sands shift from winds. Correctness is determined by a minority of elites seeking followers, favor, or likability. Political majorities become monarchical decision makers with agendas either monetarily driven or for power and control over people, ultimately eliminating freedom. It seems free people are to be considered dangerously sly and cunning and must bear watching unto the most private recesses so that there is no place for privacy. Originally, in America, it was the people that were to have authority—that a government would never be able to become a corrupt monarchical force eliminating freedom, equality, and the right to pursue happiness. The cries of change and the ease of willingness to accept change brought the sacrifice of freedom and the right to pursue happiness. The people are not trusted, yet it is humans that comprise the government. What's the difference between those who watch and those who are watched? Authority. Authority was taken from the people. By who? Fallen angels. Fallen angels chipped at weaknesses and vanities, distracting with idols and dangled riches and offering power. Finally, they empowered a majority. Originally, the fallen angels rebelled against God. It had become easy to convince the rich and powerful to maintain their status that they must become like God—like the fallen angels. By giving a free people no place to hide, the fallen angels ultimately sought to prevent the return of Christ. Their purpose is that the fallen angels would ultimately rule. With the web cast, the false promise was set. With the snare of the fowler complete, man could have no secret.

The only problem is that the human mind is not capable of total voyeurism. It becomes an unwitting and unmanageable perversion the human brain is not capable of. It causes a corruption in humility. Voyeurism magnifies a judgmental feature in the brain. The controls of what is watched by high tech captures the youngest and the most vulnerable in compromising yet most innocent and guiltless behaviors without privacy. Most states have statutes, ordinances, and laws against Peeping Toms and voyeurism, but somehow, that has all been tossed away and entrusted to fallen angels, who number now in the millions and simply follow orders from those with agendas and secret collaborative agreements. This truly seats them above their neighbors. This breaks down the fabric of trust. It is no longer "love thy neighbor" but "spy on thy neighbor." Then who is left to be trusted? The people or the people in government? Watchers had no love for man, only usefulness.

When by watching there can be no secret and no place left to hide, a self-perpetuated power is created by the watchers of which a monopoly is born. Although with no secret possible and no place to hide, this is thought to define utopia; peace cannot be obtained within the containment without righteousness. Humans are not capable of being mistake-free and of pure righteousness on their own. A forced righteousness is not possible because the use of force to obtain righteousness in itself becomes a crime and immoral, so those in power become slave owners and immoral. A monopoly watching and selling the most personal and private of information equates to defrauding the people of their soul and selling souls for profit. Every monopoly eventually becomes so powerful that within itself, a toxic environment of power and invincibility results in a drunken stupor. Corruption is ultimately brewed into a poison that the monopoly gulps in large swallows unto its own demise.

It is this young sinner to whom all this is revealed, just as God's First Scribe was shown. His story follows. But before the earliest beginning of man walking with God and his angels, let us continue as this young sinner struggles in the world toward manhood.

THE DOPPELGÄNGER'S
BEGINNING

It was when he was around fourteen or fifteen that he began getting obscene phone calls from a guy? Disturbing, to say the least. And this was like, 1970? Scary and disturbing for girls to get calls like that. But a guy? Just plain disturbingly weird. Over time, the problem escalated. The phone rang in the den. He picked up and said, "Hello."

A young girl's voice said, "That's him, Mommy." Her mom took over the call and asked to confirm his name. "Sure, yeah, that's him." Then the mom progressed into a profanity-laced if he ever called her daughter again, she'd kill him.

Baffled and extremely angry, he said: "Listen, lady," if he were to call her daughter—which he didn't, and he had no clue who they were, but if he did call with an obscene call—would he give his right name? "Come on, think about it, lady."

The mother paused. He could tell she momentarily reasoned, but the girl's mom had to still prove to her daughter she would defend her, so the mother proceeded to unload on him with some disgusting expletives finishing with, "And bend over on his elbows, and walk down the street backward!" They hung up on him. He got so mad. He'll never forget those exact words. This would continue to horribly escalate. No one will ever understand how this would come to horribly disturb him. Even becoming gravely dangerous.

Weeks later, the phone rang. He answered. The guy with the obscene phone call. Oh, he was furious now. Called the caller out. Said he'd be more than happy to meet. Then named the place and time. The caller agreed. He watched the appointed place. The time came and went. His older brother overheard some of these calls and asked, "What's going on?"

He was so mad. His brother said he needed to kick that guy's back side! His mom called to him, "Keith's here for ya." He went out the back door. Keith about the same age, lived a couple of houses away.

"What's up?"

"Just visiting" came the reply. Then he kind of went off, explaining he wanted to kick some butt. Keith laughed, and they talked. He didn't get it. It didn't sink in. This combination of him receiving calls and a caller calling girls in school his age saying it was him and giving them obscene phone calls. This pattern continued to escalate.

One time, sitting on a bench, an older man came and sat near him, very angrily and oddly staring at him, examining him. He found out later from one his best friends that was his older sister's boyfriend and he was planning on beating him up. They all explained to her boyfriend that they knew him and was just not capable of such behavior and that it wasn't him. But the guy had to personally see. Never said a word, just oddly observed. Never before had he felt so uncomfortable with no idea why, who the guy was, or what was going on. This actually escalated over a couple of years, continuously worsening.

On one occasion, Keith asked him to go drinking, ride around on a weekend. Keith's mom and dad had money and helped him get a nice green Nova. It got dark. They rode through some back roads he was unfamiliar with. Turning down a dirt road, they came to a stop at a field. He got unusually worried for some odd reason. "Is this safe?"

"It's a farm field."

"Where's the farmer's house?"

Keith replied, "Miles away." He made him turn off the radio. He listened a long time, straining his eyes to see out of the car into the blackness. Something was off? Keith broke out some pot. He took a few hits. After a few minutes, something came over him. No idea what it was. He started to feel odd. It was not the beer and the high. Something else. It seemed like a dark pressure on him, as if something that couldn't be seen closed in on him. His vision narrowed and blurred. Total blackness was outside the car. Fog and total darkness left the windshield black. Then it seemed like he became claustrophobic or something. He had to get out. Out of the car. He jumped out.

Keith was freaking out. "What's wrong?"

There was no answer to give. No way to explain. Something was closing on him with pressure.

Getting out of the car, following the contour of the car toward its rear, he started to feel better. The fog that had previously hung so heavy in the air leaving everything soaking wet now began to lift. As he looked to the sky, it was still a very black night with no stars visible as yet. His eyes now continuing to adjust, his pupils widening, he was beginning to make out the white of sandy dirt at his feet then a nearby tree line. The unknown heavy pressure still seemed to weigh him down. For some reason, the further he got away from the car, the better he felt. It was then he realized he just had to get away from the car. Maybe he would let some beer out. He'd feel a little better.

The further he slowly moved from the car, the better he felt and even in complete darkness could see a little better. Noticing a slight clearing just in the woods, he decided to venture just inside the tree line into what seemed like a small clearing just beyond the tree line. *Good place to take a whiz*, he thought. The noise of the stream was actually pretty loud in the quiet of the night. He now noticed other than him peeing, the silence was deafening, and all was still. Not even insects? Why? It was like something was holding its breath while hiding. While finishing up, relieving himself, starlight began to fill the clearing. The clouds must've been lifting. He began to naively but observantly gaze around the clearing. There had been a fire. Logs were placed as seating around the fire. A bull's head? Kind of fresh? Still skin on it. Brownish blood on it and the ground. Yes, a bull or steer's head! With antlers just on the edge of the ashes of a fire pit. Then he saw a pentagram drawn into the ground. Suddenly, the hair stood up on the back of his neck! No, for real. His pores immediately opened throughout his entire body like static electricity covering his body. A very real sense of urgency swept over him. Then he performed a quick 360 surveillance of the area, while listening. Nothing, dead quiet. Not even insect noises? Then the sudden realization of his current situation—he was currently standing at the site of a recent occult sacrifice and ritual. He first thought, *Leave!* Second thought, *Leave—now!* A realization set in and it was then he knew that he should leave now. So, he would leave immediately either by foot or car.

He shouted for Keith more than a couple of times. He became perturbed and dumbfounded at what was seemingly Keith's ignorance and lack of response to urgent shouts for Keith to come. Like Keith was ignoring an upset shout for help? Keith slowly and nonchalantly came through the edge of the tree line. Was it that Keith's eyes were still adjusting? He stared at Keith's cretinous, nescient, and mindless behavior in disbelief. He animatedly began to explain what they were standing at. Strangely, Keith began to display, an awkward outward appearance like, No big deal? He was coming unglued. This was not time for complacency, ignorance, or disbelief. Keith's odd behavior solidified that he was leaving. And leaving now! But it was Keith's car; Keith was driving and said no. He made it perfectly clear. They either left together or he was taking Keith's keys and car from him and leaving. They left. He knew adults could be mean. Now he discovered people could be evil and that evil existed. At the time, he didn't realize he was being attacked. He knew since he was young that God was real. Now he knew evil was just as real. He was also being shown a physical reaction to pure evil. Now he knew people collaborated with evil. He just didn't know who. Still loving and caring but combined with being inexperienced to naive and trusting, he had no clue who the evil people were. Doppelgänger would return.

Beginning with first grade, it only took him thirteen years to become a high school graduate. He would like to explain that in his last year of high school, the school liked him so much they invited him back for another year. He always thought the invite came a little rough; at least the offer was genuine and sincere. He only needed half a credit in his last year to reach the required number of credits to graduate, and in his last semester, the vice principal demanded he leave. Oh, for sure, years of trouble in school. What would be the final straw?

He got an invite for a car load to head from Salisbury, Maryland, to Union Grove, North Carolina, for a blue grass festival. Never heard of it, never been. At a time when people had been interested in events like Woodstock, New York, and other rock concerts, he and some friends went off for the unknown. What was blue grass music? Long before GPS and electronic mapping, they checked a folding-type paper map and found themselves somewhere in North Carolina, near where they needed to be. Out of the car looking at a map, someone wandered by a pole and called everyone over. There was a very small poster stapled to a wooden telephone pole. They all gathered. Hey, the Allman Brothers Band were playing this weekend. They checked the map about seventy miles away. He injected his opinion that they had come this far for the festival and that they could see the Allman Brothers Band anytime. They all did not agree, but off to the festival they went. He had never been at a more welcoming and friendly event in his life and still didn't know of a time he has spent with that many kind people at one very large event sharing food and drink. Really sharing. Giving food and drink to those hungry and thirsty. Making sure tens of thousands of people were comfortable and happy seemed to be a common goal of all. The dancing and bonding was incredible. He would never forget.

Monday back in school. Then math class. A substitute teacher today. Sometimes a common unwitting "take advantage of the situation and substitute teacher" happens in school classes. This day was one of these days, he guessed. All were seated before the bell rang. All were conversing in pairs and threesomes, et cetera. The bell rang. Many students kept talking. He looked up at the slightly elderly teacher, and she was writing looking down at her desk. Kind of bursting with wanting to share with someone the very long, exciting weekend, he turned around and began telling Raymond. Raymond was sitting right behind him. Raymond was genuinely interested, saying, "When is the next one?" He didn't realize at first she was addressing specifically him until everyone got quiet and were facing forward.

The class had been talking very loudly. He didn't even hear the bell ring. He turned around slowly and looked at the sub.

She said, "Get up here."

He stood beside her until she finished writing half a page of discrepancy. *For what?* he thought. *Talking?* He got to the vice principal's office, and it was if he was expected. He handed the sub's note. He never even read it. So silly. For talking? After spending a few minutes reading the entire note, the vice declared, "You're out! You're finished for the year! You're expelled."

Shocked, he exclaimed, "For what, talking?"

The vice said sarcastically as if the accused assuredly knew, "For being a rebel and leading a rebellion against poor Ms. Substitute Teacher (never knew her name)." He quickly thought, *What?* She actually lied. He was getting expelled over a lie. He exclaimed, "But!" then stopped. He knew there was no turning back their combined momentum. Maybe she felt she was only exaggerating. To him, it was a lie. Since he was done, thrown out, he spun to leave. He got about twenty-five feet away from the vice principal and remembered he still had the wooden hall pass. Without need of the hall pass and no need to walk back, he gently tossed it. It spun through the air just enough to land on the asbestos-tiled floor and slowed to a perfect stop at the vice principal's feet without touching the vice principal's nice shoes. The VP angrily picked it up and glared. He turned and hit the crash bar hard. The door banged when it hit. He really did nothing that wrong to be permanently expelled in his last year. He figured it was just the final straw, maybe. But to be finished by a lie was a kick while down.

His dad was furious with him. They had another meeting in school. They went. The vice principal talked. His dad made good sense. He sat in forced silence, no self-defense. Then the vice principle added, "You threw the hall pass at me." It was a frontal assault! He was shocked. Even the vice principal lied, for surely the vice principal knew. He looked at his dad and was angry, but this time, for once, he kept his cool. He responded to the accusation, revealing humility, for this is what he knew they wanted to see: that he really never intended to hit the vice principal, that even the vice principal himself surely knew if he had tried to hit him, he could've, that it was just a simple toss but that tossing it like that was disrespectful, and that he was sorry. Actually, all three were shocked that those words were spoken. And they were the only three in the room.

The decision of expulsion was set but, Vice said, "He could return next year for half day of school. Civics and Problems of Democracy was mandatory." The vice principal let him pick an additional course required to fill a half day of school. He picked chemistry. Vice seemed a little surprised at the chemistry pick. He could've picked art or home economics. He figured since he had to be at school a half a day for another year might as well take something interesting. Oh, boy. He about came unglued at first. Didn't matter now what he was about to say. Never believed anyway. Now this? He was sorely angry but settled in for what must be; that he was to live a life of injustice when it comes to arrogant and lying people in positions of authority. Of course he didn't realize it immediately but a little later did come to agree his behavior all throughout school did deserve a type of ultimate disciplining. He got another wake up call but still couldn't hear it clearly.

So his last year of school, he got a job insulating houses with the other half of a day. He would come home from high school prior to lunch and then go to work. Their boss was a small business owner, and this side venue of insulating existing homes in the seventies was to save on energy cost. Many older homes were not insulated properly or not insulated at all. Heat would just escape through walls and roof. In the young man's home and in some places he lived, a candle's flame would lean with the flow of the draft and wind passing through houses. This was not something the owner of the small insulating business had to do, but it made a little money and paid some young guys out of high school a little money. But this was mainly beneficial to the community. Most customers were the elderly. Their boss was a very nice man—Mr. Barron. He cared. The cost to the homeowner was extremely fair, and advertisement was by word of mouth from satisfied customers. Changes in the home were felt immediately. It was cooler in summer and warmer in winter, and it was more cost-efficient. At the time, most homes were not air-conditioned. It was a nasty job crawling under houses and up in hot attics. The fiber glass insulation itched some crazy horrible. We called it an *itch*. But it was actually a burning from the sun, fiberglass, and minute particles of glass mixed with fire-retardant chemicals getting into our pores and flesh. We wore long-sleeved flannel shirts in the summer. There sure was some crazy heat in the attics. It was absolutely brutal. Showers were mandatory and provided some relief. Relief from the pain and itch required technique. Running cold water first to rinse off excess then run hot water to open pores to try and clean any remaining spun glass stuck in the skin pores. Then cold again to close the skin pores. Some insulation was made of a chemically treated paper-type dumped into a bin or hopper then blown into the attic. Manufacturers of the insulation claimed their product was noncombustible, which, to him and others, meant it would not ignite easily. Adding chemicals guaranteeing the insulation was fire retardant puzzled him and other young coworkers. So they would run their own test by throwing lit matches into insulation to see if it would burn. Sometimes the insulation would catch fire, and on other occasions, the match would smolder and the area wouldn't catch fire. Very often, they couldn't help inhaling the fibers and dust from the insulation. And at times, they would be covered from head to toe. Their fire-retardant chemical test did raise concerns about what they were inhaling and being covered by so, they told their boss. Their boss provided a little white cloth mask that covered their nose and mouth. While long sleeves, mask, safety glasses, gloves, and long pants did not eliminate discomfort and their health and safety concerns completely, having a paycheck on Fridays seemed to ease some pains. All the misery and worry generated a feeling of really earning and deserving the pay. A type of pride from sacrifice?

HE DID NOT KNOW IT
WAS HIS DENTIST

Once again, drinking would be his downfall. At a friend's house in the city, he become inebriated, and at that house, there were two girls and two guys. His friend fared well, and the other turned him down for many reasons, one of which was he was absolutely unsightly and unbecoming. He left. It was late at night, and there was nowhere to go. He went behind a city building, climbed some trash cans, and lifted a hinged window to enter the building. The opening was covered with drywall. He broke a hole and entered. It was a dentist office. He went to relax in the chair and thought he better go. He grabbed a trash bag and put some dental instruments inside. He started out the front door, but a police car pulled up. So he left the way he entered, walking along the street in a neighborhood not far from the dentist office. A police car pulled up beside him. He decided not to run. It was a neighbor of his. They knew each other. He wasn't even handcuffed till booked. Why did he do it? You're not going to like the answer. Here it is anyway: it was probably another reason to be loved all the more by all of heaven when he would finally figure out he needed to be saved and ask for forgiveness.

He was released on his own recognizance, and once home, his dad informed he had broken into his own dentist's office. His dad took him for a dental exam to face up to his guilt and apologize. His dad picked him up from school. The whole thing was horribly embarrassing. He sat in the dental chair, and his dentist came in, was angry, and asked why he would do that to him. This caught him off guard, and he tried to blurt out that he really didn't know it was his dentist. His dentist was still in disbelief. He said he was sorry, but that the apology wasn't welcoming. It was sour, and sincerity and pureness was there, but no sweetness. His dentist was too hurt and too personally affronted to fully forgive. He couldn't do dental work for him today but really liked his dad and went to talk to his dad. His dentist would not pursue additional effort at his trial for full prosecution. Didn't matter. The trial backfired like a loud old truck engine.

He was going to plead guilty, and the prosecutor and the public defender had worked out the first offense deal—probably probation. On the way to court, bad habits snuck in. He forgot to brush his teeth. In the car, his mom offered gum. Sometime before he was called, she offered him a napkin, and he took it but got interested in the cases beforehand or something. He just honestly forgot. It was his turn now. He sat, respectfully listening to the charges, and suddenly heard, "Boy! Are you chewing gum in my courtroom?" The judge took off his glasses as his voice climbed louder. The judge continued, "I could give you fifty years for these charges." As he was being chastised, he suddenly remembered the gum. He started to swallow it. His lawyer quickly said, "No." He looked this way and that for a trash can and readied the gulp. His lawyer repeated louder, more forcibly this time, "No, don't. Don't swallow it. Spit in here." He finally regained composure and looked at his lawyer holding a handkerchief. He took the handkerchief and put his head down to the side, releasing the gum, still not being sure, and of course, everyone in the room could read what was happening and leaned forward. Well, everyone probably, except his mom. The judge calmed a little and said, "What's a matter boy, ya nervous?" The only thing he could do was nod. Dressed okay but long hair back then? And gum? It was over quick. He stood with his lawyer. The judge said, "I sentence you to two twenty-five-year prison sentences, one for breaking and entering and the other for grand larceny, but suspend them to three years supervised probation to run concurrent." *Wham!* That maple mallet? Happened as a minor, tried as an adult. It didn't matter; he was a felon for life. But worse, he sinned. He was a thief. There would be more.

He lost his part-time job insulating homes. His boss invited him in his home for the first time. His boss felt bad. His boss liked him and offered him a beer but couldn't keep him now. Since it was a small town everyone would know he was thief. They finished their beer, and he wrote his last check for the hours worked. He left. He had mixed feelings about it. He made a horrible mistake, but it had nothing to do with work. Now it was getting harder for people to figure him out. It began to seem like he wasn't turning out to be the type a girl would take home to meet her dad. As he left, it was like the end of the world. He was fired for being a thief. One weekend, and his check was gone pretty quickly. Then Johnny called. Johnny was his age and lived on the next street over, and he started his own insulation business. Johnny did not care at all. Johnny needed help, and they knew each other. Johnny trusted him and had no reason not to. Half a day in school and half a day working was great for a while. But Johnny always needed more. It was just the two of them, and the business was booming because there were many houses around the Delmarva Peninsula that were older and not insulated. The savings of insulating the home paid for itself quickly. Johnny wore him out too fast. He wasn't ready to work every day yet. He did help get Johnny started, though.

The Return of Doppelgänger

Debbie asked him to go to the prom with her. He liked Debbie a lot. He was committed. They had dated over a year. Having no clue about formality. Absolutely not wanting anything to do with going to a prom. It was not his thing at all. Dressing up so people can show off and strut themselves. Nope. Something for him to avoid at all cost. The pressure was intense. His mom wanted him to go. Pressure from even his brothers? Got to be kidding. Then came his mom's yank at his heart. Debbie wanted to go, and it would break her heart. He actually said he could get someone else to go with her. Then came his mom's firm lecture. Birds, bees, being a man. Okay, he'll do anything just stop. His mom actually had him almost in tears. He was still stubborn though. So his mom went to the store and came home with the corsages and boutonnieres. What? He had to wear that?

Debbie drove. She came over. Made his mom beam. Took pictures and then went over to Debbie's mom. Debbie's house. Seemed like forever. So uncomfortable. Finally ready for a picture. The phone rang. Debbie and her mom both went to the phone. An oddness quickly settled in. They acted weird as they went to the phone. To him, he was so uncomfortable in that tux; it was hard to notice some awkwardness, but he did. The two were acting weird. Trying to remain courteous as he could and not be nosy, he couldn't help it. Curiosity got the best of him. He leaned forward, looking around small columns from the small living room of an older city house, into the small dining room looking at the mother and daughter acting strange, both holding the phone to their ear and staring at him in disbelief. Yet relief? A very strange feeling. Debbie stepped back, smiling.

The mom said, "It's for you."

Weird, he thought. No one knew he was there. Maybe his mom? He tried to act confident taking the phone. Although confidently, he quizzically said into a large yellow handset connected with a coiled stretchy yellow cord to its base, "Hello."

Then came: "What are you doing with my girlfriend?"

He demanded, "What? Who is this?"

Then came a strange reply: "You're not taking her anywhere."

He suddenly went blind. Although there were two others present at the time, now there was no one else in the room. Except for him and whoever that voice belonged to at the other end of a line. Those two. Then the most godawful words that had ever left his mouth spewed forth. "Anytime, anyplace. You pick it. As a matter of fact, you are the homosexual that has been calling me and now you're calling my girlfriend. No matter where you are. No matter who you are. I am going to find you." Those were his words but combined with a tirade of expletives laced with a great deal of profanity. He continued to declare until the person on the other end of the line lost nerve. That guy? Although his words had fiery authority, the other guy's voice had none. That guy hung up.

114

Shaken so bad, he stared into the phone until Debbie's mom gently took the phone from his hand. At first, he couldn't let go. Then the fire slowly cleared from his eyes. He could see again. The first thing he saw was Debbie's mom caringly and acknowledgingly look directly into his eyes. Water started to build in his eyes as he gazed into hers. He was so sorry and embarrassed at how he had handled himself in front of his girlfriend's mom, cussing and losing control. He began to hang his head, started apologizing and saying he was sorry. Dumbfounded and dumbstruck. Or was it something else? It was a humility he had never before experienced, overwhelming his entire being. All very slowly, although filled with rage, there came a certain peace accompanied with some clarity.

As he continued his gaze into the mom's eyes, she smiled. She put her hand on his shoulder, patting him proudly. Like "Good job, boy!" Her appearance was now clearly demonstrating some happiness and pride. For him? He wasn't getting it clearly.

Debbie rushed to his side, hugging him hard. Debbie exclaimed, "See, Mom! I told you it wasn't him. I told you that he's not like that." Quickly, Debbie said, "Come on, we gotta go." Again "We gotta go." Debbie grabbed his arm and pulled him. Seemed like she was pulling a big stuffed pillow that had legs which stumbled but moved. Debbie was halfway out the front door, him being pulled along. But then suddenly, her mom spun him around and gave him a giant hug. His body went limp into her hug but he realized she needed to be hugged too. They both needed it. He stiffened and returned the hug with strong but gentle love. They both needed badly to what just happened to happen. It didn't completely make sense. Not yet.

Now in the car and on their way, he looked back toward the front door. Her mom was smiling and waving adamantly. He gave a good smile and waved back. They were off. He still felt uncomfortable. That was extremely hard to shake off. He had to ask, "Has that guy called you before?"

"Ever since and even before we've been dating," she replied.

"What?"

And she never told him. He was obviously angry.

She said, "Don't worry, it's over now."

He asked, "Does he sound like me?"

"Exactly," she said. Debbie interjected quickly, "Although that guy's voice sounded like his, some of the things that guy said are not like you. But what was scary is, some of the things that the guy said were true, which left some weirdness."

He thought for a moment. "How did you know it wasn't me?"

Debbie said it had been really hard. All this time and she never told him. But she said it was very rewarding and reassuring that it finally happened while he was there. She said, "It's over now." For her and her mom to have to go through that was horrible. After over a year, for them, it was over. He became seriously sullen. He thought as he sat and actually felt something starting in him starting to break. That night after prom, he did not sleep. He watched the sunrise. The doppelgänger had to be stopped. There was nothing he could do. No one to turn to. Police couldn't help, and would be no help. There would be only one way to stop the doppelgänger. He and Debbie would have to break up. It may've seemed at times he was hard-hearted to her, but he knew a relationship would not be able to withstand what he was to face and endure. Before Debbie were a few others, and Donna was his first love. But it was the same. Although he cared deeply, deep inside there was much unseen that had to be dealt with before he could find marriage and everlasting love. Of course, he had regrets. He loved then but loves his wife more this day than girls yesterday. Did he sin in the eyes of God? Yes. Will he ever be forgiven by earthly men and women? No. But maybe there is something many do not know. A good father will always love his son. Are there times when a son must be punished? Yes. Does this mean the love of a good father stops? No.

It got worse. Now he lay in bed at night wondering whom. Whom could it be? He couldn't sleep. Then would come more doppelgänger attacks. Phone calls. Then another approach by a male stranger confronting him. The stranger said if he ever did it again, the stranger would kill him. He had no clue who the stranger was. But at least now he knew what it was about. It was coming from everywhere. He began to accuse people he had known for years of doing it. He lost friends. People he didn't even know were confronting him. This was getting extremely dangerous. He had been in life-and-death situations before. But this was different. One day someone would come to kill him. And justifiably so. It had been years. It was going to come to an end. It would have to. Now he lay in bed one night planning to kill. If he ever found out who it was, there would probably be no proof. To make it stop, he would have to kill the doppelgänger. But who was this perverted doppelgänger? How did he know some truths about him, and how did he know the same people? Now this was the second time he really wanted to hurt someone. The first was who shot at him. Now the second one? A perverted doppelgänger. This time, when he was weak from all the verbal assaults over the years, people avoiding him, and confrontations, darkness snuck in. His thoughts drifted to killing whoever this was if he ever found out. He thought he could actually kill. He never thought of it as vengeance. But it was. What else could he do? He would fight, maybe even dirtily like some kicking, a throat punch, or a choke hold, but this was becoming something different. He would be put to the test. He didn't know it then, but it was this day God would reveal to him exactly who it was.

Daniel 2:28 (KJV) "But there is a God in heaven that revealeth secrets and maketh known…"

At the time, he did not know. But it was on this day he knew that God had turned his face toward him long ago and never turned away. Today, he also knows (James 1:5, KJV), "If any of you lack wisdom, let him ask of God that giveth to all men liberally, and upbraideth not; and it shall be given him." Upbraideth not, in this verse implies that those who are seeking wisdom are with asking with good intentions. It is also true though that some secrets must remain till the end of the age.

He doesn't remember ever asking out loud. He wanted to know so bad he might have. But surely God knew his heart, his very being, was being destroyed from without but now also from within. It wouldn't be much longer before doppelgänger's identity would be revealed.

He finally told a friend, Billy, what had been happening. Billy said the guy had called Billy too and had told Billy it was him. Billy challenged the guy and told him he was full of manure. Billy called the guy's bluff. Billy said, "Yeah, the guy sounds exactly like you but says things that aren't like you." Things that Billy knew he'd never say. He confided in Billy, if he found out who it was, he'd kill the guy.

He was invited to a big party over Kevin's house. Kevin bought an old house and was having a housewarming party. He would rarely go around other people now. But Kevin was cool, and they had actually bowled in duck pin tournaments together and against one another. Duck pin is like ten-pin bowling except the bowler gets three throws, and the ball is about 3½ lbs fitting in one hand. No finger holes in the ball. No need. The rest is the same.

He left home early in the afternoon for an evening party. He walked. The walk was about eight miles through fields and small patches of wooded areas. Kevin said he could stay the night. He drank a pint on the walk. It was about 5:00 or 6:00 p.m., and the party didn't start till about 8:00 or 9:00 p.m. Kevin didn't mind.

The phone rang. Kevin answered and got all excited. It was Fred. Fred had moved from his neighborhood about three to four years earlier, moved to Arizona. Good for Fred. Fred got out. He was married and had kids now. It was a pretty nice phone call. Kevin asked, "Hey, did you want to talk to Fred?"

Still a little depressed, he jumped at the opportunity and said, "Sure, give me the phone."

He simply said, "Hello. Fred?"

Fred immediately said, "Uh, hey, Keith. How are you?"

He said, "No, Fred, it's me. It's not Keith."

Fred said, "Come on, Keith, this is a joke."

He calmly said, "No, Fred, it's not Keith, it's him."

But Fred insisted. Finally, it hit him, hit him like a ton of bricks. So he sounded like Keith. "Uh, yeah," Fred said. "Exactly."

He asked, "Fred are you absolutely sure that me and Keith sound exactly alike?"

Fred insisted again, "Exactly!"

Fred and he talked, but it was odd and uncomfortable. Very odd. Fred was excited, telling him of his wonderful home, children, and wife. His mind was filled with all these years. Situation after situation, confrontations, false accusations of perversions, and extremely disturbing emotional and dangerous positions he was left in and with for the rest of his life. That was it. He knew! After all these years. He knew who the doppelgänger was. Now the phone call was to end oddly, like something was left on the table unsaid.

Kevin seemed to notice. He couldn't say. He couldn't tell anyone what he now knew. This was going to get real. He could tell no one. So now what? He asked Kevin if Kevin minded that he started early. Kevin offered party food. He asked for a glass. He poured from a half gallon. Kevin said, "Hey, go easy." Shouldn't he eat something first?

He thought to himself, *Yeah, probably*, but answered, "Nah. Not hungry." Said he'd wait for everyone else. Next thing he remembered was waking up in a chair in the living room about 3:00 a.m.

He thought that must've been uncomfortable for others. A huge party with someone passed out almost dead center in a living room chair. Probably snoring. He felt awful. Still inebriated. He ran some kitchen faucet water into a glass. Chugged it. Twice. Grabbed some leftovers. Didn't feel like eating. At all. But thought he'd better force a little down. He was right.

He started walking for home. It was cold. Started to lightly snow. A wet snow. On this night he wore a denim jean coat and collared shirt. Not usually one to button the top buttons on a shirt, he did. Shirt and the coat. Turned the little collar up and "got small" inside the collar. A long walk, eight to ten miles. No gloves. He kept a good pace, noticing as he did the snow would hit his face; melt, roll down into his soft mustache and light beard, then freeze. He noticed if he tried to keep his hands in his pants pockets, the exposed part of his hands would burn. He found it best to walk with them out of his pockets. Swinging his arms to help keep a good stride would actually keep them warmer; the snow would hit his hands and melt. There was no one around to see him but if they did, they might've noticed the steam coming from his face and head. His head would only be partially covered with snow because the heat escaping though the hair on his head would partially evaporate the snow on his head, probably making an odd appearance. Stopping would not've been a good idea. His body temperature would've lowered once the soaked clothes lost the little bit of warmth attained by the brisk pace. Stopping could've caused hypothermia to completely overtake freezing him to death. As it was, he was experiencing only mild hypothermia. His brisk pace and small adjustments had helped a little.

It began to snow harder making it extremely difficult to see. He wondered about snow-blindness as he looked into the direction of the winds at times. He thought he gained some understanding of how the infinite number of patterns created by the wind blown snow might effect a persons mind and sight. Sure did burn though. The pain on his face and hands helped him keep his mind off what had to be done. As twilight approached with its soft purple glow, he was almost home. As the night sky changed to pink and yellow, the snow began to stop. As he walked up the driveway to the back door, he noticed the very colorful morning sky was reflecting everywhere off the snow. If it weren't for the trees and houses the sky and snow covered ground were almost as one. Eager to get in, he stepped up the few brick steps and grabbed the door handle to open the back door. The round handle turned, but as he pushed, the door was chain locked. He closed it and stood for a moment without any thought admiring the beautiful colors of twilight reflecting off the snow on the ground. The door opened. It was his dad. It was first thing in the morning, but he must've been a sight. His dad peered at him oddly. His dad, obviously disappointed, turned without a word and went back to cooking his scrapple. The warmth of the house sure did feel good. The smells of breakfast? Well, people would've had to under-stand what scrapple is before they might possibly admit, the morning smell of scrapple burning might smell good after about a nine-mile walk. He stiffly entered the back of the house slowly. Couldn't get his shoes off yet. His dad just thought he was drunk, disappointing his dad even more. He leaned against the radiator, trying to warm before he could bend. His jacket and jeans were partially iced over. He didn't notice at first, but then, the ice in his beard and mustache began to thaw. It burnt badly. He was at least slightly frostbitten. He would've looked very odd indeed if someone had seen him while he previously strutted head down into the snowstorm.

Finally he was warmed enough to take off his boots. He did and went into the bathroom. He looked in the mirror. He had never seen anything like that before. A little snow in his hair still. Water coming down and burning his raw red cheeks. Little balls of ice in his bear and 'stache. He had to reach up and feel that. Felt odd to say the least. What used to be a beard of the thin baby hair a young man such as he had now had ice balls. Still burned. His hands were red prunes on the palms. But it was raw red on the back of the hands. He tried to run water, filling his hands to somehow wash his face. It hurt. Maybe could've made some adjustments but said to himself, *Forget it. Just go to bed and get under the covers.* Upstairs he went.

All the boys except the youngest slept upstairs. It was like an open bay attic, slightly modified with some very cheap 4 × 8 foot sheets of ½ inch thick ugly blue insulation for wall covering. Like paneling? Ha, paneling came later. No air-conditioning in the summer. Only a window fan. No heat in the winter unless the entryway door to the stairs was left open. As he went up, of course he shut the door. Got the wet clothes off and under the blankets he went. Eventually warming, he thought, *How?* He needed a plan. Although he could tell no one, he confided in Billy.

He could say during his younger years, he had only three good friends. But these three were special. None of these three were really liked by anyone else. The four did get together a couple of times. Only because he wanted them to. But it didn't work out. So these three were his best friends, although these three only tolerated each other because of their mutual friendship with him. Anyway, he confided in Billy. Billy understood. He trusted Billy. They confided with each other some things which no one else at all knew about them both. Besides what Billy told him, he believed. Quite shockingly, sometimes he was able to give advice. What he told Billy, Billy believed. Billy not only would give advice, but Billy had a bad habit of being overly critical. He dealt with it. But Billy's criticisms and actual jealousy of his other friends was at times obvious and annoying. But to be clear, he told Billy on many occasions, the criticism was sometimes welcome but in the majority of cases unwarranted and unwelcome. He told Billy he was going to kill Keith.

FATE OF DOPPELGÄNGER

Now he knew who the doppelgänger was. No one knew what he was about to do. He acquired a big ole fat ounce of pot. Doppelgänger liked to get high. It was a Saturday evening. He called Keith and told him about the hefty ounce and asked if he would swing by and if they could get a six-pack of beer. They met up. Keith was driving his Nova. On the way out, they saw Billy, and he told Keith to stop. He wound down the window, told Billy of the plan to cruise and smoke, and invited Billy. Billy turned to him and said that he lost all respect for him. He just had to be quiet. He couldn't let on. So he said, "See ya later," and they drove off. He was a little disappointed, but his spirits lifted because Billy didn't know what was going to happen. He didn't either, really.

As he came out of the store with the beer, he asked to drive Keith's green Nova. Keith was reluctant, but he was convincing and told Keith he could twist up as many doobs as Keith liked. This time he would drive to a place of his choosing. He didn't know where; he just followed internal feelings. He drove into town. This surprised Keith. He drove to the end of a dead-end street not too far from railroad tracks. There was a dirt road, so he went just deep enough into the wooded area so as not to be seen. He had to be quick; this road would eventually be patrolled. He shut off the car and lights. Keith lit up. He cracked a beer and chugged then set what was left on the dashboard. He turned to Keith and said, "I know."

Keith was either clueless or acting as he must've always acted, saying, "Know what?"

Then it came quickly: "That you're the pervert that's been calling everybody all these years and saying its me."

Keith acted like nothing was just said and tried to pass him the joint. He didn't take the joint but turned toward Keith and said, "Keith, if you ever do it again, I will kill you."

Keith kind of laughed, stuck holding the joint, and was now looking at it.

He noticed Keith did not take him seriously. Then things went kind of dark. He waited for eye contact. Once eye contact was made, he scooted a little to make the reach much easier and followed with deadly seriousness. "Keith, if I ever hear anyone say I called them with a perverted call, and even if you didn't do it, Keith, I am going to kill you." This time he could tell it sank in a little. He scooted back under the steering wheel, started the car, dropped it in gear, and punched it. No lights on. Keith hollered, "Stop." He got up to about 55–60 mph, and suddenly the car was airborne. It seemed like a long time. The appearance was a blackness, a sky without lights. He couldn't tell what was ahead; he had never been here before. As the Chevy Nova began its nose-up attitude yet downward descent, he could see a light shade of white closing in fast. Dirt or sand pit? He couldn't tell. The car finally landed, but it was a dead stop. The car didn't roll. He stuck it. Still into and unto an unknown. He heard a train coming. He dropped it in low and punched it. It didn't move, but the tires spun. Now he knew it was stuck. He opened the door of the driver's side and looked down. Some kind of sand pit? He quickly made the assumption it was a deep sand pit, not totally uncommon for the Lower Eastern Shore. About thirty miles inland from the ocean, the sandy area was almost entirely surrounded by pine trees except for up ahead and slightly to the left where an opening with railroad tracks were visible. Keith was in deep shock, mumbling something like, "Stop." He already had. Seemed as his point was well made and most likely sank in. Then came the sound of a train accompanied by a train whistle.

He grabbed the bag of pot off the seat, shoved it in his pocket, and ran for the train. It looked like it was headed south toward Little Jimmy's Bar. He could jump off there. Satisfied he made his point with doppelgänger, now he needed transportation. Hopping a train at night in boots was harder than it seemed. He was running in boots on the big rocks and barely made it. He decided to get to a better car and stepped for the connection, but it moved about a foot with the train rocking and swaying. His foot went down into the darkness. His heart went empty. He grabbed up and forward for anything as he headed downward under the train. To this day, he does not know how his hand landed on a hand railing. It was a very difficult stop from falling, pulling himself back onto the train platform between cars. He leaned against the steel of the car, caught his breath, and decided to become part of the train right there. He looked back at the Nova. That car was not going to be easy to get out at all. He thought, *Good enough.* He jumped off at Little Jimmy's and had a few drinks. He assured himself the mission was complete because if it happened again, things might not be so friendly.

His First Concert

Neil Young and Cat Stevens were to perform at the Baltimore Civic Center. In eleventh-grade art class, Jack had an extra ticket and asked him if wanted to go. Jack was a little taller than him. Same build and soft-spoken—a very nice guy. Jack seemed more reserved than he and was quiet; he didn't get into much trouble, which was good. Jack was a good guy. Jack had kinky brown hair combed to one side like Sammy's, but Sammy's was blonde. He thought Jack and he were an unusual pair to go to a concert. At first he responded no—wasn't interested in the bands or location. But free ticket and ride there and back? It was his first, so he agreed.

January 19, 1973. Baltimore was over ninety miles from where they lived, and it was from farming and rural area to a big city. There were no GPS or iPhones back then; finding your way to a concert in a large older city was quite a major road trip. They found the Baltimore Civic Center okay. Parking was tough. That part of town had always been a tough part of the city. Neil Young opened with a band. Like he said, it was his first major concert, so seeing what happened next was very memorable. It was a good sound, and he looked out over the crowd from where he sat. Since it was a sellout, the center was packed. He had never seen so many people in one place. Someone handed him a joint and then a small pipe. He whispered, "What's this?" An answer came back: "Hashish." Then another little pipe came; this time, someone next to him, sympathetic to his simple curiosity, whispered, "Hash oil," as he handed it to him. *Wow,* he thought. These were kind people in his row, trusting their pipe down a long row of strangers. Then he looked down at the rows in front of him and Jack; it was the same thing—lighters lighting up, people whispering and such. *Quite curious,* he thought. He looked up and saw the band left Neil Young alone onstage. Neil Young was seated at a piano and said to the audience he was going to play a special song, a "soliloquy"? Guessing in the music industry, it's called a solo performance. But in this circumstance, it ended up being more like a "solo soliloquy," for the unusual took place. Neil Young was actually playing the piano, acoustic guitar, and harmonica at the same time and singing. Of course, there were times in the song where that was not possible, like harmonica and singing or guitar and piano. Hopefully, you get the picture. Musicians have done this in the past. He had seen others do this for this generation. Mike Truitt, Plain Slice Mike, does something similar for donations on the boardwalk in Ocean City, Maryland. Anyway, so as Neil Young played this soft song, he noticed something was not right. He could hear everyone in the whole center talking. He looked out into the darkness. But it wasn't dark. There were lighters everywhere flicking off and on or burning to get a good stoke. This was long before the tradition of people just holding lighters in the air. Guess for this generation, lighting one up has morphed into holding an iPhone in the air. It was January 1973 at this concert, and there happened a very strange occurrence.

When he heard everyone talking kind of as loud as Neil Young sang and played music, he sensed trouble. *Uh-oh,* he thought, *this is disrespectful. Not good.* And sure enough, Neil Young stopped playing right in the middle of a song, grabbed his guitar, and left. He walked off the stage! He turned to Jack and said, "This ain't good." Jack was too high to even realize what happened. Everybody was.

Jack said, "They'll be back. It's just a break."

When people all around didn't get it, he prepared himself for what was to happen next. Someone handed him a joint. He said, "No thanks." They tried to skip him and hand it to Jack. He said, "No, Jack. Stop." The guy was a little gruff but withdrew the offer. Jack was okay; they were friends and partners in this. Jack settled back. He was really too high anyway. Then an announcer walked up to the mic and said, "Neil Young has walked off the stage, left, and is not coming back. And Cat Stevens has refused to come out and play."

He immediately stood up, helped Jack up by his right arm, and said, "Come on, we gotta go. Jack was closest to isle so Jack would have to exit first."

Jack was like, "Nah, it's okay."

This time he got way more animated. "No, Jack, this is not good. We gotta go. We got to go now!"

Jack pridefully got up and straightened up. Jack began stepping clumsily by legs as they moved, asking politely and saying, "Excuse me." Some moved politely. Some were annoyed at someone trying to get by. It was the same for him, except with a little more sense of urgency and purposeful manner. Some were getting angry, asking, "Where do you think you're going?" He just said, "Out of here!" and sped up.

The place erupted. There was screaming and hollering. There were people standing and shaking fists. The last ones in the row they exited from were shaking their fists and screaming. They ducked under the fists that were raised in the air. Jack stopped to turn back and see. He understood. He sadly, in an urging manner but forcibly, said, "Come on, Jack. We've got go. We have to go now!" Once in the hallway, they paused, eyes squinting from bright light. Which way? For obvious reasons, they forgot. He said, "Let's just get out! Come on, let's go this way."

Jack said, "I think the car is this way."

It didn't matter anymore. Trash cans were being thrown and set on fire. There were other fires being lit.

Jack said, "I've got to use the bathroom."

"You've got to be kidding me," he replied in astonishment.

Jack said, "No, it's a long ride home, and I had some beers."

He snapped back, "Go outside."

Jack said, "Where outside?"

He was getting out of there but would not leave Jack. He looked back at Jack and said, "I don't know. Pee anywhere outside, anywhere outside. It's safer."

Once outside, it was easy to see it was a good thing they left when they did. Windows to the civic center were getting smashed, and some cars near the front of the parking lot were set on fire. At least their car was parked near the back of the parking lot.

Jack said, "I really gotta go."

He saw the car. He said, "I got eyes on the car. Go ahead and pee."

Jack said, "Where?"

He thought, *Now that's a stupid question.* He shouted with arms wide open, "Anywhere!" He stood in the middle of a row with a view where he could have eyes on Jack and eyes on the car. Looking at the car, he saw some meatballs thinking about breaking into it or something. He shouted, "Hey, not that one! Better pick another one."

Jack and he were a little distance apart, and Jack couldn't see the car. Jack said, "What's wrong?"

"Nothing. Just finish."

It was the disruptive taking advantage of chaos. They decided on easier pickings and scurried on. Jack and he got out of there. It was shaky. Riot police were showing up and blocking roads. They got out just in time. It was late and a long ride home. To help Jack stay awake and alert, they talked about some of the events that had happened earlier, and he certainly mentioned that he thought his first concert was one for the record books.

That night Neil Young may have been trying to kick off a breakout moment for his song "Light a Candle," written as a song that had deep meaning for a movement of soulful expression; the song was having no effect on this large audience. The audience was numb to any deep soulful meanings, and the people were only at concert for the event itself and self-absorbed with getting high while having live entertainment as a backdrop. It might have been too much for Neil Young to take, playing a song written as meaningful as "Light a Candle" and looking up to see about thirty thousand lighters lighting pot to get high when the song was written to move a soul toward the light. They didn't have another live concert at the Baltimore Civic Center for about thirteen years or so after the Neil Young walkout of 1973. It's at events like these that cause shifts in hearts and minds.

BROKEN NOSE

This time he was unsightly in the eyes of God and broke man's law for which he remains an unforgiven by man's law to this day, some forty-four years later. As he recalled while bent over, throwing up, a man asked what he was doing. He thought it was kind of obvious, but he stood to face a man in a flannel shirt, a pair of jeans, and pointed-toe cowboy boots and said, "Walking home." The man reached into his back pocket and revealed a badge. All he saw was a shiny object going in circles. The man demanded a driver's license. He responded that he didn't have one and told him exactly where he lived, about three miles away. He was drunk, no doubt, but it was obvious he was sick. He turned to continue walking home. The officer grabbed him by the arm and spun him around, again demanding a driver's license. To him, he hadn't really done that much wrong. He wasn't but a step or two off the sidewalk. He realized he had made an awful mess, but there wasn't much he could do about it. He did not want to be puking on the sidewalk or on the road. Most people don't want to be out in the open vomiting. Again he said he didn't have identification and only had a short walk home and pulled his arm away to continue walking home. This time the officer spun him and grabbed him by the collar, shaking him like rag doll and still demanding a driver's license. He thought if this guy was crazy, shaking him like that, the man was going to get vomited on. He reared his arm way back, not even being able to see from being shaken so hard, and took a wild-ass swing. He missed horribly, falling on his face. Next thing he remembered was coming too in an ambulance.

Then he noticed he was handcuffed, hands in front. Lifting his hands and looking at the handcuffs, he became furious and emotionally upset. He asked the paramedics what had happened. What did he do wrong? No answer. They just stared at him. They took him on a stretcher into the emergency room at PGH Salisbury. There came an attending doctor. He told the doctor to stay away from him. Now he trusted no one. The doctor said he needed attention. He refused treatment. After a brief discussion between the arresting officer and the doctor, the officer took him in a police car to jail.

He was awakened the next morning and told to exit the cell to eat breakfast. He felt awful. The room was spinning. He sat at the eating area but could not eat. He almost threw up. He immediately offered the food to a cellmate he did not know that was sitting next to him. The guy took it immediately. Another man demanded, "Next time, you give it to me." Then guys that knew him came over and said, "Come with us." The brute said, "You heard me," and walked back to where he was sitting. The brute chilled but stared at him. He was not afraid. He would give his food to whomever he chose. But he surly was glad to sit with people he knew. He was more comfortable.

He was seriously dizzy. His friends said, "Sit with us and move your stuff into our cell when we go back." He noticed his high school class president hollering out the window. His class president was in for murder, awaiting trial. He looked out another window and saw that David was hollering at a beautiful girlfriend five floors below and across the street. She was visiting as best she could. She seemed horribly saddened. After breakfast, he did exactly what his friends had said and moved his stuff to their cell. He was later released on bond and charged with simple assault on a police officer. His dad posted bond.

Four days later, the dizzy spells continued. His dad took him to a doctor. His nose was badly broken and had to be broken again and set. A couple of weeks later while over a friend's house, his nose felt strange. He ran his finger up to touch it and felt something hard and odd. He pointed to it and asked his friend, "What's this?" His friend didn't know but found it very interesting. His friend followed as he went to the bathroom to look in the mirror and see what it was.

While two faces were in the mirror, he got a hold of whatever it was and began to pull. He pulled slowly. A bone chip about 1/2–3/4" came out the side of his nose bridge. *Humph,* he thought, *guess it was trying to work its way out?*

At the trial, he humbly told his side of the story. Then the officer took the stand, telling his version. The officer said he was in uniform that night. He thought, *That's not the way he remembered it.* Then the officer said he could not let him go without identification and that the defendant took a wild swing, falling on his face. But as the defendant tried to get up, while on his hands and knees, "I punted him right dead between the eyes." The whole courtroom gasped loudly. He could hear people he did not even know saying, "Oh my god." The judge exclaimed, "Stop, I'll be right back!" The judge exited the courtroom, retreating to the judge's chamber. He returned almost immediately, opened a thick lawbook, and read, "A police officer can subdue or restrain a person for their own safety." The judge continued, "Although I believe excessive force was used, I find the defendant guilty of simple assault of a police officer, which is a felony. And although the defendant can be sentenced up to twenty-five years in prison, I sentence the defendant to one-year unsupervised probation. *Wham,* came the gavel. Dismissed.

So to this day, he is an unforgiven by man's law, losing rights other citizens enjoy. His public defender followed him out of the courtroom and down the main stairwell. His lawyer was now saying he could sue. "No," came his reply. As his public defender, the lawyer had never given him the time of day and was now saying that this lawsuit could be the biggest suit of the lawyer's career. His mom and dad stopped in the stairwell. His dad turned to him and said if he didn't let the lawyer take his case, this would affect him the rest of his life. Having no real clue, he asked, "Like how?" Probably not knowing how to answer on the spot, his dad said he'd never be a government politician. He said, "That's okay, I never would want to be one anyway." So he turned to the lawyer and said, "I would prefer to handle this with that officer someday on the street, man to man. If he and that officer would ever meet on equal terms, he would prefer to discuss what happened between them as two men. Did what he imply mean fight? Not necessarily. People might be surprised at how he handled himself, forgiving another man for taking advantage of a situation; he did not necessarily blame him. But if during a sensible discussion with the officer he could not convince the officer man-to-man not to always treat people who are defenseless in a brutal manner, well, then he would have to ask the officer if he would like to try his abilities with him when he was little more sober. But his mom, his dad, and the lawyer were extremely upset that he did not pursue compensation and atonement through the court system and possibly sue for lots of money. It was just not his style and certainly was not what God had chosen for his path. And just as well, he did not pursue it through the courts because it could've ruined the officer's good record and possibly hurt the officer's career. As it turned out, the officer ended up being very successful and helpful to a city.

As he got older, he really never held a grudge against the officer. He forgave and, quite honestly, forgot about it. No, really. He really forgot. A lot would happen, and none could ever believe he'd forgotten, but he did. Until he was forced to recall. The officer was Coulbourn M. Dykes, a Vietnam War veteran who served a year with the 501st Infantry and the 101st Airborne Division. He was awarded the Vietnam Campaign Medal for three major campaigns, the Vietnam Service Medal, the National Defense Service Medal, the Good Conduct Medal, the Purple Heart, the Army Commendation Medal, the Air Medal, the Bronze Star Medal, the Vietnam Cross of Gallantry, the Silver Star Medal, and the Combat Infantryman Badge. The officer went on to become the Chief of Police for the city of Salisbury, Maryland, serving with distinction from 1982–1998 (https://www.findagrave.com/memorial/112965549/coulbourn-m_-dykes). But he himself went on to be *unforgiven by man's law.*

In and out of work and needing the money, he took a job at a fast-food restaurant and was hired prior to the opening. He was told to say "Howdy, partner" when customers came in and as they left, to say "Happy trails." That was going to be tough to do, especially, if the customer knew him or it was a potential date? Didn't know how yet but he'd make it work. Instead, he got lucky. After four or five days of preparing for the grand opening he showed for work with a broken nose. A girl he was hoping to date was working there too. She saw his broken nose and asked, "What happened?" He simply told a short version of the truth. "He got sick while walking home drunk and a police officer kicked him in the face." The manger overheard him and fired him on the spot. He guessed the boss didn't want this type of person working in a new fast-food restaurant. *Whew*, he thought, *that was a close one. It was going to be hard saying "howdy partner and happy trails" to everyone anyway.* But finding a different job would be difficult without a car or way to work.

CHICKEN HOUSES

Building and remodeling chicken houses was about a two-year tour. A lot can happen in two years. Other than when he was a baby, his worst asthma attack happened about two or three o'clock in the morning. It was because of where he had worked for days. At around the age eighteen or nineteen, he labored as a "rough carpenter," building chicken houses on the Lower Eastern Shore. Many farmers subsidized their crop rotation with income from chicken farming. Since a farmer had the property of about an acre, a farmer could contract with companies like Purdue Farms Inc. for an approximately 420-foot-long chicken house. The company would help with the loan for the chicken house to be built and the logistics of feed, the arrival of chicks, and the removal of chickens. The chicken farmer cared for, maintained, and fed the chicken brood for six to eight weeks and up to maturity. There were not always new chicken houses to build for work, so his job also required updating, remodeling, and retrofitting older chicken houses with more modern energy-saving techniques like partitioning the four-hundred-foot building into three sections. Partitioning the chicken house into three large sections allowed the farmer to save money by heating less of the building. As several weeks pass and the chickens grow in size, requiring more space, opening the partition to another third of the chicken house would allow for more room for the chickens to roam, only then requiring more heat for the additional space. Chicken manure creates its own unique logistical effort, usually not attended to until necessary. Frankly, at times, he worked and walked on chicken manure eighteen inches to two feet deep. Chicken feces hardened to a surface like dirt except, depending on heat and humidity, the smell, moisture, and gases were not like dirt at all. The ammonia and nitrogen could be overwhelming, enough to make normal human breathing very difficult and vision blurry from watery eyes, to say the least.

Living a life of hardship from breathing with bronchial tube constriction and fluid buildup in the lungs with no solution from doctors quite often would leave him alone, not knowing what to do. That summer night with no air-conditioning upstairs and with the window open, every breath he took felt like a red-hot spear or rod through his lung. No, not just a spear, it was more like scalding red-hot rebar used in concrete construction or garden stakes. Rebar has a rough, knobby shape. That hot night was a long one. After 1:00 a.m., he stared at the ceiling, listening occasionally to the radio and looking out the window at the beauty of a clear night sky loaded with stars. The radio station went off the air as he struggled in pain for each breath until sunrise. Each minute that passed seemed very long as he labored to breathe. It was a very long night. He truly thought he would die, but he didn't. He heard his dad downstairs and figured since he lived, he might as well go to work. As his dad slurped coffee, downing a muffin with grapefruit, he stated he barely made it through the night and wasn't feeling well. There wasn't much his dad could do or say anyway, so silently they both headed their separate ways. It was off to work they went. No one seemed to understand or believe how bad the pain was or how scary the inability to breathe from asthma attacks was anyway. To him, no one could relate. It seemed no one believed or cared. He later would come to grips with knowing others really can't comprehend unless they go through something like asthma themselves.

He was fired by his first boss for theft when he was working on chicken houses. One morning they stopped at the corner store for gas and all prior to work. He was in line behind some guy he worked with. The guy in front said, "Put this on Cliff's tab."

Wow, he thought. He worked for Cliff too. He had a soda and bag of chips, so he said, "Hey, put it on Cliff's tab."

Everybody looked at him strangely as he got in the truck.

His older brother said, "What did you just do?"

"Nothing," he replied.

His brother said, "You can't do that!"

He replied, "That guy did."

Some in the truck laughed, looking out the window.

His brother said, "He's Cliff's nephew, and Cliff hired you. Cliff owns the company. That's stealing."

He replied, "Not really," and said that he'd pay Cliff back.

The next morning, Cliff called him into the garage and asked, "Did you charge to my account?"

He said, "Yea."

Cliff demanded, "Who do you think you are?"

He started to reach into his pocket and said, "It came to $1.50. Here, you want your dollar fifty?"

Cliff blew up. His face went totally red. He stormed out of the garage, saying, "You're fired. Get off my property," and walked away, heading for the house.

Strange, he thought, *this over $1.50?* He then hollered out, "Wait! Pay me."

Cliff turned, fist clinched. A big red head, a little overweight (okay, a lot), came for him.

He stood firm and said, "I worked four days this week. You owe me money. I ain't leaving until you pay, plus I need a ride home. Your crew picked me up. By law, if you fire me, then you have to pay me and close out on the spot, minus the dollar fifty."

Cliff said, "Joe, get this guy out of here before I kill him."

His friend Joe came over, put an arm around him, and convinced him he had to leave and that Joe himself would give him a ride.

Still reluctant, he said, "But…"

Joe said, "He'll pay. We just have to leave."

It was fifteen miles. He was embarrassed about his mistakes but kind of laughed, saying: "At least you get paid for driving me home."

Joe laughed a little, deep in thought. Joe came by later with his check.

His older brother came over to the house on the weekend and after some conversation said, "Go to Preston's house on Monday and ask for work."

"Who's Preston?" he asked.

"A building contractor. Does the same work as Cliff, chicken houses, and lives right down the street from Cliff. Just do it," his brother said.

Oh well, he thought. *Here I go. How embarrassing is this going to be?*

There he was on Monday morning. Joe was there and so was his brother and some others that worked for Cliff.

Uh-oh, he thought, *this is a set up.* He was going to get beat up. *Where's Cliff and his cousins?* he thought. He looked around. Everyone kept their distance like he had the plague. The owner, Preston, came out—a taller and thinner man than Cliff. He had brown hair and a ball cap. He was more like a farmer and contractor than Cliff, he thought, that's for sure.

He came right up to him and said, "What happened between you and Cliff?"

He looked down at the ground.

His older brother angrily said, "Tell him!" So he did.

"I charged a soda and chips to his account for breakfast."

"Then what happened?" Preston asked.

Right away he said, "He fired me."

"But what did you say?"

He said, "I said, 'Here, you want your dollar fifty?'"

Preston started laughing so hard he bent over. He even slapped a knee and spun around. Everyone started laughing. He looked over at Joe. Joe approvingly nodded his head, smiling. Now he got it. They all left Cliff over it. His brother said that Preston never liked Cliff.

Wow, he thought. Something major went down, and he had no clue. There would be much more that happened when building and remodeling chicken houses, but suffice it to say, if he tells someone he remodeled chicken houses when he was young, most laugh and come back with, "What do you mean by 'remodeling chicken houses'? Putting recliners in so the chickens can watch TV?"

So two to three years came and went. Although it meant nothing to anyone else, he gained a lot, including love from men. Right away, everyone thinks, *Sex?* It was absolutely the farthest thing from it, but was it intimate? Yes. For this generation, millions will never get that one. They'll never understand. It becomes disheartening to know that for this generation many men might not get the opportunity to know that type of love.

"VENGEANCE IS MINE," SAITH THE LORD

He did not know God was with him. God had turned His face toward him when he was around four to five years old. He did not learn until many years later that once God turns His face toward one, He does not turn His back on them unto perpetuity. The look may not have been a beautiful smile. He just can't help but think that God knew all the awful things he would do in life and that the look He gave was one of wrought. The look was not terribly bad or mean. The look was beautiful yet terrible and fearsome.

LEARNING POKER
THE HARD WAY

Robert Atkins and he were friends. Robert was closer to Joe's age—about five years his senior. He had curly red hair and was about six foot two inches, was light complected and freckled, loved fishing, and had a Ford Bronco. Robert and he would occasionally get a case of beer and enjoy driving through the dunes along the beaches in the borders of Assateague Island, Maryland and Chincoteague Island, Virginia. The two rode to work together. He would give Robert money for gas each week. They got along really well.

It was a Friday night with coworkers drinking and playing poker. He mainly thought the card game was just for fun. He didn't notice a heavier sense of seriousness in the air from others as Joe, Mike (his younger brother), Robert, and he readied to play. He was mainly interested in bonding and fun and had overindulged in liquor and beer. Mike had too much to drink and started losing. Out of money, Mike quit. Joe got low on money. He really hadn't noticed, but he was winning. There came a point he had a good hand at the five-card draw, nothing wild. Others folded. He found out he wasn't as good at poker as his dad had become. The game was harder than he had understood. Joe folded. Robert stayed in, but there came a point that if he raised enough, Robert would have to borrow a few dollars or fold. Robert wanted to go all in and check. Robert tried convince him to allow the play. There was no limit, and he was confident if he raised, Robert could get the money from Joe or Mike. No one loaned Robert the small raise. Robert angrily folded.

Robert was mad that he didn't just check; it would've been the honorable thing to do. He had too much to drink and, not thinking clearly, had just busted Robert.

After winning, he jokingly asked, "What's the big deal? What did ya have, Robert?"

Robert said, "Never mind now."

So he reached across to look at Robert's hand, his cards. That was it. Robert and he got into a brawl. It started in the living room and ended on the kitchen floor. The kitchen table and chairs got knocked clear. There was broken glass everywhere. He had too much to drink, and Robert finally gained the advantage. Once pinned and head turned against the wooden floor, he kept getting hit in the ear by Robert. In this case, it was unfortunate that he could take a punch and wasn't getting knocked out. Most fights wouldn't end until someone was knocked out or unable to move. He could tell the blows were either going to break his eardrum or worse—probably fracture his jaw or skull—so he called for Joe to pull Robert off. Everybody was hollering, "Stop," but Joe heard the submission and cared about him. Joe had to make Robert stop. Robert was actually scared to stop. Embarrassed and beaten badly, he walked about five miles home. He had way too much to drink. Drinking became a bad sin for him and would cause him many troubles.

He awoke the next morning for work very angry and planning to kill Robert when he showed to give to give him a ride to work. Basically, he was still not sober, not an excuse, just truth. Robert never showed, so he found another way to work. They all were on the rafters, laying the metal roof. A coworker working by his side saw how bad he looked and said, "I heard what happened. What Robert did was just wrong. Are you going to get him?"

He looked over at Robert. He thought, *No.* He had gotten what he deserved. It was over.

Robert heard the question and looked their way.

As humbly as he could, he answered, "No. It's over."

He and Robert were making eye contact. Suddenly it was as if Robert was pushed off the roof. On the way to the ground, Robert's elbow and ribs went through a two-by-four support beam as he landed on the dirt. It was about a twelve-foot fall. He and his coworker had no way to get to Robert quickly. There was no ladder, and it was too high to jump.

Someone on the ground rushed to his aid. While on the ground, wincing and thrashing in pain mainly to regain that first breath once it's knocked out of a person, Robert and he made eye contact. The quizzical look and fear in Robert's eyes was actually more intense than the look of pain. As all three took turns swapping looks with each other, Robert's eyes squeezed shut to focus on fighting pain. The coworker slowly backed away from him, leaving him alone, while all the others rushed to Robert's aid. Robert was rushed to the hospital. He had a broken elbow and cracked ribs. All three wondered, "How?" So he learned the hard way. He thought it was a friendly game, just having fun. But don't look at a man's hand after he folds. And if a man is all in, it's not a good form at all to raise even if there's no limit and you can. So he learned poker the hard way.

He saw Robert not long after. They talked. He told Robert he didn't realize that the fall was that bad. Robert replied it was kind of rough having a two-by-four stud break his fall. They laughed a little. He always liked Robert and always will. But Robert stayed clear of him and, after healing, got a job elsewhere.

Tornadoes on the Lower Eastern Shore of the Delmarva Peninsula were very rare. One day while building a new four-hundred-foot chicken house, a purplish-black cloud swirled in the backcountry. It was summer, and the large doors on each end were open. All side doors and about sixty windows were open too. The dirt picked up off the floor rather slowly at first, but then all was instantaneous. It went from a very bright summer day to complete black. The radio had broadcasted warnings of storms in their area. He lifted his hand to check if he could see his hand. He could not see his hand in front of his face. Someone hollered, "Close the doors." He thought that was about the stupidest thing he had ever heard. Oh well, the young helper has not much for rebuttal unless he was on break or at lunch. Even then, not much from him could be heard. He mainly listened. Even though he thought it was a bad idea, he went to close the side door nearest him. Unable to see in winds exceeding 75 mph, he found a door and attempted to shut it. The wind blew the door so hard that the door closed the rest of the way by itself, slamming his shin between the cinder block foundation and the *L*-shaped angle of the door. Both door and block made for a tight fit. Oh boy, that left a mark. Looking back, God must've come by, checking in on him.

This one coworker was about six feet and ten inches tall and maybe 265–270 lbs. in weight. He was like a mountain man but of the Lower Eastern Shore or from West Virginia. That's what he had heard. He really didn't know or care. To him, the guy was too playful, especially because he could get away with things because of his size. All day long, he was grabbing men's behinds when they were in awkward positions. After grab-assing, mountain man would laugh really hard. In the afternoon, mountain man got his older brother. His brother smirked it away and got busy. The big mountain man had a long black beard, long black hair, and a flannel shirt left unbuttoned enough to show his white T-shirt tank top. The four-hundred-foot chicken house was filled with his loud laughter when he grabbed someone's butt. He thought, *Not my brother,* and got angry.

He caught a moment with his older brother alone and quietly asked, "Why did you let him get away with that? I've seen you knock some really bad asses out before."

His brother said, "It wasn't worth it. Don't worry about it. The guy really means no harm."

He said, "I don't like it. He better not do it to me. I think it's queer."

His brother shot a look and made a statement. "What do you think you're going to do?"

He said, "Don't know. But that guy won't ever do it to me again."

After work they were all putting away tools to split up and go home. He noticed mountain man's wife drove up, and the giant waved for her to come over. There were lots of tools, and everybody always chipped in. Not mountain man.

As he reached way in the back of the Ford Bronco work truck awkwardly, he felt someone slide a hand up his inside leg to his crotch, then his butt. He lost it. Without thought, he belted out, "You must be queer!" It was then he realized what he said. There could be no going back. He righted himself to stand outside the back hatch of the bronco, clearing way of the vehicle gaining room and preparing himself. He had fire in his eyes.

Mountain man was standing beside the vehicle with his wife at his side, laughing, and asked, "What did you say?"

Filled with fire, he repeated, but this time very clear and loud, "I said, you must be queer!"

Mountain man's eyes fixed on the much smaller target and began to close the distance. Immediately Joe closed in on mountain man's right side, still wearing his tool belt and getting a good grip on his claw hammer. Baby Huey closed in on mountain man's left side. One would have to know Baby Huey to know what it would mean to have Robert (Baby Huey) close in at the ready. Both Joe and Robert were within inches, looking up. Mountain man must've gathered from his peripherals better to stand down and laugh it off, so he did, saying, "You're one crazy kid," and laughed. He grabbed his wife and left. Robert and Joe went back to business without saying a word. He thought, *Whew, almost died there.*

After that episode, he desired get to know Robert more personally. It was after work, and it had been another brutally hot summer day. The three were on the way home from working on the construction of a new chicken house in the back roads of Delaware. Robert was the one Preston trusted to drive the work truck. Besides, it was Robert, Baby Huey. If Robert wanted to drive, he drove. Robert was driving, and of course, he was in the middle on the bench seat of the work truck. Dave was older and had the window seat. They stopped at a half country store, half house in the middle of nowhere. Again some of those creative people filling the need would turn their home into a store. It was a great setup, actually. You can basically step from the house into work without driving. Some of these old family stores had everything imaginable that one might need—giant pickles, hot sausage in a jar, or mountain oysters. Some even made sandwiches to order. He got a quart of beer and sausage. Dave got a pint of bourbon and a twelve-pack. Robert got a Coca-Cola in the bottle.

They all called Robert Baby Huey from the cartoon character that was abnormally strong. Baby Huey was a cartoon character that was a giant childlike duck that didn't realize its own strength. Baby Huey was unusually strong with a childlike disposition. The similarity between the two was the unusual strength. But Robert was with a very kind disposition, genuine and sincere. Robert was all right with the nickname Baby Huey because it was developed from good qualities. Besides, if Robert wasn't okay with the nickname, no one would ever make the mistake of calling him by it twice. Let there be no doubt Robert was unusually strong, was very kind, and was thoughtful but also had some other physical attributes no other was capable of. Robert was a sergeant who served nine years in the Army and seven years in Vietnam during the war. Not many could say they spent that many years in theater.

He once asked Robert why he got out of the Army. Robert told him he was discharged for shoving a wine bottle up a "Puerto Rican's ass" (Robert's words).

"What?" He asked Robert, "What in the world? How?"

Robert told him that while working in the motor pool one day, this Puerto Rican didn't like what he said or something, came up from behind, and dropped his jaw with a lug wrench. Nobody that knew Robert would ever confront Robert head-on. Not anybody he knew anyway. But anyway, the lug wrench broke Robert's jaw. Robert was hospitalized and had to eat through a tube for a couple weeks. Robert told him as soon as he got out of the hospital, he went to the canteen and found the guy. And that's when he shoved the bottle up the Puerto Rican's ass.

"And they discharged ya for that?" he asked.

"Yea. But no," came the answer. "It was the wrong guy. It was the guy's twin brother," Robert said. So they kept Robert in the commanding officer's office for forty-eight hours, trying to figure out what to do. Finally, the commanding officer worked an dishonorable discharge just as a plane was leaving stateside back to the U.S. Robert said, "His CO liked him and told him to disappear and lay low, and he thought his CO might've gotten into hot water. But he never knew. Did exactly what was recommended."

That's when he understood and came to know Robert. Even with Robert's innate unique qualities, skills, and abilities, he lived in a very small home with his wife on the Lower Eastern Shore of the Delmarva Peninsula, building chicken houses.

On this day, in the truck, Robert turned to him and said, "I'll drink one gallon of water, milk, or beer straight down without stopping and without puking." Robert continued, "Bet me $5.00, and you choose. I'll drink one gallon down, your choice."

Dave said, "Do it. Bet him."

He was like, "Nah, if you're betting me, then I know you can do it. That's a fool's bet, Robert." He looked at Dave and said, "No because I believe he can do it."

Dave said, "Nobody can."

He said, "Baby Huey could."

Robert smiled. So then the discussion shifted quickly. Robert asked, "If you were drafted, would you have served?"

He thought a moment.

Robert added quickly, "Dave over there's a hippie-loving draft dodger."

Dave followed with, "I ain't dumb enough to go die in some faraway jungle over nothing."

Seeing this was going to escalate, he thought he should chime in and answer, "Yes, if was drafted, I would've served. But I would've probably enlisted."

Robert beamed.

Dave became obnoxious, saying, "I sing in a band on weekends and got a wife and a girlfriend."

It became obvious Dave was in competition over ideology, intelligence, patriotism, and manliness over the war with Robert. It was also obvious the two had gone at it before.

He nipped that in the bud really quick. "Well, let's hear ya sing then," he said.

Robert smiled.

Dave said, "Let me finish some more of this pint first."

"Why?" he asked.

Dave replied, "Because the singing hurts my throat, and the alcohol numbs it."

Weird, he thought.

Then Dave chugged, got ready, and belted out.

After about a minute or so, he cringed a little and looked at Robert then said, "Sounds kind of fake or something. Now I see why you needed to chug."

Dave said he needed the music, the mood, and his band.

Dave invited him to stop by the bar where he was playing and said that there would be chicks, and because he knew Dave, he would be in with the chicks. He was interested, curious, and agreed to it. He could sense Robert didn't like what he could be getting himself into. It was unfamiliar territory. Of course, Robert understood it was hard to turn down possibly meeting some young women.

Robert dropped them off. It seemed to him like they were in the middle of nowhere-ville. Robert was concerned that, for one thing, he was Dave, and another, they were so far from home without a ride. He assured Robert he'd be fine. He would get used to being in unfamiliar territory. He thought the band was awful. But he did meet a girl and got a ride home. They dated, but nothing meaningful lasted between the two. To this day, it was Robert and men like him he respected. He liked Dave. They were friends, but not close. It was Robert that was more genuine and trustworthy.

He and four friends rented an old farmhouse in Pittsville, Maryland, for $50 per month. They split the rent five ways plus the utilities, which was about $18 a month. They ran pipes from a well for house water. At first the brand-new water pump they got seemed to pull some air. He crawled underneath and soldered the old copper pipes to repair some leaks from expansion and contraction during winter and summer months without regular use, then the water pump worked. Then someone stole the water pump.

He spent three nights and days in the attic of the old farmhouse to protect the new pump. Lights were off, and there was no water. Basically, he lay in wait. It was a large attic and was clean. It had a wooden floor and an open wood ceiling. He made a room out of it with a sofa, a bed, a chair, etc. If he was in the attic, no passersby would notice any activity in the house. There was a brand-new pump that was installed this time, although the house was not ready to live in. There were different reasons that delayed each from moving in right away. This time he built a little pump house and ran a light to it so it wouldn't freeze up in the winter. One day while in the attic, he heard a car pull up. From the small window, he could see a guy he knew named Pat get out of the car and knock on the back door. A carload of guys stayed in the car. As Pat knocked, he thought, *Well, since I know Pat, it might be all right to go talk.* He had been alone for a while, and kinship might be good. He thought Pat turned to leave once there was no answer. So he ran downstairs to the back door—all good. They weren't breaking in. Or so he thought.

By the time he got to the door, all five were out of the car. Immediately something didn't seem right, so he asked what was going on. They acted surprised, but some still looked at the new $180 water pump locked inside a small pump house. One had a tire iron. He was probably set to break the lock, but now it could be useful for something else. He got it. He asked: "Pat, did you take our water pump?"

A little shocked at first but quickly assumed his leader-of-the-pack role, Pat answered, "Yes. Tron owes me money." He stood erect now, saying, "Five of us live here now. We all put out money for that pump. I helped install that other pump and now have put out money for this one."

"It's not just Tron's. Leave this pump and this house alone. Now you're even with Tron."

Pat said, "No, I'm not. Tron still owes me money."

From his peripherals, he noticed the four closing in. He got really close to Pat. Pat would be first. He said, "Pat, the pump was mine too." He was sure Pat could smell his shower-less body and breath. Then he said, "Next time you come, think of this. You did not know anyone was here. I watched you the whole time, and you did not know what kind of weaponry was fixed on you, shotgun or .270 mag rifle. Think about that next time you come. Pat, I still don't have a problem with you yet. But for now, it's time to leave."

The four closed in more. He locked eyes with Pat. Pat commanded, "Stop." He laughed and said, "Let's go." Pat then turned back as he was getting in the large four-door Impala and said, "Tron still owes me money."

He replied, "That is between you and Tron. But now know this. Anything in this house is partly mine. You mess with it, you mess with me. And know this now too. Tron has a friend."

They left. He watched. *Whew, that was close,* he thought. His investment paid off. The three days and nights roughing it worked well. Word got out, and the thievery stopped. Word spread that there was someone willing to do whatever it took to care for whoever lived in and what ever was in that house.

He had a wild dog for a pet, a small female shepherd mix. While working on constructing a new chicken house, this little shepherd kept coming by him and rolling in the insulation he was trying to install. *Cute,* he thought, but he tried to shoo her because rolling in spun fiberglass was probably not good for the dog.

His brother Stephen, with dark curly hair and glasses, saw a slight bond between the two and said, "You should take her home with you. The farmer is going to kill her."

After lunch she came back and was playing in the insulation again, being a little annoying and slowing him down but being amusing and cute. The owner (the farmer) came from behind, saw the annoyance to work completion, and was fed up. He said, "I got a pumpkin ball in the house for you. And I'm going to get it right now." Meaning, he was going to blow it apart with a shotgun right now. The dog stopped and looked, having no idea.

Maybe? He enthusiastically said, "No. Don't. I'll take her with me when I leave today."

The farmer walked away saying, "If she's not gone today, she's dead." The farmer could not have a wild dog running around his farm, chasing and killing animals.

At the end of the workday, there she was, hanging near him next to the Suburban work truck that they were all getting ready to leave in.

Stephen asked, "How are you going to get her in the truck?"

He said, "I'll pick her up and put her in." She seemed to like him, so he thought he'd just scoop her up in his arms in a bucket carry. She locked on his arm with teeth bared. He paused. It seemed like a warning. She didn't break skin, so he quickly continued and gently tossed her in the back of the vehicle. He named her Munchkin Lady.

It took a concerted three-day effort for he and his friends to pick off and burn away the ticks with cigarettes. The blood-filled ticks must've been annoying and certainly weakened her. He chained her to a cinder block ladened with extra concrete. When he called her, she would drag the block as far as she could to get to him. He got her to drag it farther and farther. He trained her to. Munchkin Lady's front legs and shoulder muscles became so pronounced that everyone could see the veins bulging. Her back legs became powerful too, just not as visible to most as the front.

One day he rode his bicycle to the country store for stock goods and essentials (food). On the way back, he saw the cinder block and chain broken about three quarters of a mile from the house, and there she was, playing with some dogs behind someone's house. He called her, and she came. Next time he rode to the store, he chained her to the front porch's white corner post, but upon return, she had broken the post and was playing with her friends up the street. He could only chain her to live trees after that. One day he walked with her into the woods. She nudged his leg to get him to stop walking. He stopped and looked down at her. She began stalking like a cat. *Weirdest thing,* he thought. He then heard something moving in the thicket. Then he got it. It was quail starting to move in the thick brush. She was hunting. As she got close, they flew. She leaped, snapping her jaws at their tail feathers, and almost got a few midair. She turned to look back at him as if to say, "You didn't see or hear them? We almost had some good food there, friend." He stood amazed then got down on a knee and comforted her with praises.

He traded for a .22 caliber rifle. There was a trash pit about seventy-five feet behind the house. He grabbed a stuffed teddy bear and set it against a post in the pile. *No challenge,* he thought. He wedged a dime ($0.10) slightly behind the black button nose, returned, then tried to sight the dime. He couldn't see the dime. It was too far, about one hundred feet. But he saw the black nose, so he aimed at the top corner of the nose where the dime was wedged. He shot. He went to check. He couldn't find the dime. He looked all over then went into the house. He sat for a while, then it dawned on him. He ran out to the teddy bear and stuck his finger in what seemed like a small hole at the upper left corner of the black nose where the dime used to be. He dug and felt it. He pulled the dime out. It was not dead center, but he had shot a dime that he couldn't see from a good distance. It took two shots. It was the first time he had ever fired that particular rifle, and he missed by a foot. The second shot hit the dime.

An out-of-work friend in hopes of improving odds of transportation called and told him of a government-paid training program for Vietnam vets. Neither were vets, but there were some open slots and a test was being given to weed out applicants for the few openings left for the program. They both tested, and he got the call. His friend was upset and embarrassed, but there were some no shows, and after talking with the instructor, he got his friend into the program. The training was the same training for union-certified journeyman carpenters but for vets. Upon completion of the training he became a journeyman carpenter, and if hired, the employer would be reimbursed up to $4.50 per hour of the employee's wages. After completing the training, he heard the city of Salisbury was building a larger civic center, and a large job like that certainly there would be opportunity for work.

Working some short stints building homes including some finish work, had worked flat-roofing with hot tar, built chicken houses four hundred feet long, plus he came with a program the boss would get paid to take him. Surely, he had a chance getting hired at a large project in a little town like Salisbury, Maryland? He walked up early on to the job site and asked someone. They said, "Ask him." They pointed over to a feisty, tough little man, who seemed to be somewhere in the late forties to early fifties of age. He found out later he had done a couple of tours of duty in Vietnam. He walked over and presented himself, and that's how he began climbing steel. An iron worker. After working as an iron worker for some reason, pressure came to change iron worker's title to "steel worker?" The explanations came and went. It wasn't iron and rivets, and more buildings were made with steel, nuts and bolts. The ideology seemed to be a way of union strengthening to combine or keep in combination the steel manufacturing industry labor force and steel construction labor force. He didn't care. He was not in a union. He was an "iron worker." Even so young he had great difficulties with groups whose leaders might profit from his efforts and sacrifices in the workplace. One boss was enough. Even being young, he witnessed intimidation of fellow workers and friends. He didn't like it and wanted no part of it. He knew unions had their purpose in our country, ensuring safety and improving conditions in the workplace throughout the years, but unions were not for him. Organized crime or unionized strength funding organized crime on to funding political parties was not for him. If political parties are funded by organized crime, doesn't that mean the political party is criminal? Public unions never made any sense to him. Unions were formed for safety reasons and labor force monetary protection. Unions put pressure on or forced companies or corporations into capitulation to treat their employees better. Why public unions force the people, the citizens, into doing anything toward their own betterment was beyond rationalization. There is always the option to not work for the government. Aren't government jobs usually the best, best benefits and best wages? It's like a company of army soldiers forming a union, taking money from banks, and kicking in the doors of the people or the citizens for better pay. This mentality he could not bear.

THE SILVER GHOST
ATE A POLE

He made enough money as an iron worker to buy his first car, a 1964 four-door Chevy Bel Air, for $275. He loved his car. A gray car with a rusted roof. He bought a can of silver spray paint. It looked gray when he bought it. He sanded the roof then painted the roof silver. Who cared? He didn't. It did seem people would accidentally pull out in front of him more often, he thought, than other vehicles he had ridden in. He learned he had to be on his toes driving. Others that rode with him noticed what must be a camouflage phoneme from the paint job on his car, causing other drivers difficulty seeing his car. They named his car the "Silver Ghost." It seemed to fit. His 1964 four-door Chevy Bel Air, the Silver Ghost, ate a telephone pole. It would be the first time he died. It was a rainy day, and they could not work the steel. They cashed their checks and headed to the bars. Bars weren't open, so they drank first then pretty much closed the bars. He awoke on the sofa at his mom and dad's house without any money at all. It was hard to believe he had spent his work check when had plenty of money. He couldn't believe he cashed his check. So he took off to head to the last bar they were at to see if he had dropped his check. It was about 2:00 a.m. in the morning. The speed limit was 55 mph on a two-lane road. It was extremely foggy, and a slow car was in front. There was a double yellow line, so he couldn't pass. Finally, dotted lines appeared. He pulled out to pass and accelerated. There was a car headed right at him. He turned the steering wheel left as hard as he could, heading off the road into a field, but there was, of course, the one telephone pole. Skidding sideways, he hit the pole at the passenger side door just behind the right front tire—immediate stop. The pole stood stronger than his grip was from climbing steel; the steering wheel pulled from his hands. There was a very large hard plastic speaker hooked to his radio beside him on the front bench seat. His head hit the speaker as inertia took over from the sudden stop.

The next thing he remembered was being lifted to the sitting upright position, and the telephone pole was hanging from the wires, just swinging in front of the windshield. The bottom five feet of the pole were gone, the top half silently swinging back and forth. It was eerily silent, foggy, and dark, and some smoke was rising from fluids on the hot engine. A cop came. They both went to sit in the police car. The policeman was acting like he was writing a report and kept asking if he wanted to go to the hospital. Blood was pouring out the right side of his head, but as long as looked straight ahead or to his right, the policeman couldn't see it, he thought. The cop gave him a ride home. It wasn't far. His car was towed and the title traded for scrap. The next day at work, his back went out. He went to the hospital and was diagnosed as a backbone contusion. He was out of work for ten days. But he never told anyone about the possible skull fracture (more like probable or more like "a skull fracture"). To this day, the area hidden by his hair is a discombobulated mess of a scar. Crew cuts are out of the question.

He started off iron working at the bottom of the rung as "bolt up." Surely couldn't be hard shoving bolts in holes? Shouldn't require a large amount of technical skill, right? Everything about climbing steel and bolting connections is hard. On one job, an eighteen-year-old was walking with an impact wrench on a steel I-beam to work on another connection. The air hose connected to the impact tool slipped off the steel. The falling weight of the hose once reaching the impact tool, caught the young iron worker off guard, snatching him off the steel then falling five floors onto a pile of steel beams. The young iron worker had hit so hard the doctors at the hospital found four of his teeth in his lungs. The young iron worker came too that night and talked with his brother giving everyone hope, only to die the next day.

A building inspector came behind him and checked his bolts, telling him them weren't at the right torque value. The foreman told him from then on to use a torque wrench. Tightening a bolt and nut to its correct preload requires a torque wrench. Carrying a three-foot torque wrench many floors up on a steel frame that sways in the wind for twelve-hour shifts on summer days, to say the least, was not preferable. No one taught him how to torque bolts with an air-operated impact wrench (air gun, air wrench, impact wrench, impact tool). As long, hot summer days passed, tightening bolts with the long cumbersome torque wrench continued. One day, he observed two others tightening bolts with the impact wrench. He noticed as the bolt tightened, the steel flange attached to the corner of the I-beam started to flatten or compress; the sound of the air gun changed. As the bolt began to tighten, the sound of air-operated impact tool, the bolt and the steel, connection would change from a mix of all the components making rattling sounds to a slower rhythmic, ratcheting sound. As the nut and bolt tightened, the mixed sounds of vibration from component rattling would change in pitch then transmit uniformly through the steel, causing the steel to "ring." He got it! As the bolt reached torque value, the clanging sound of the air gun would change, transmitting a "tinging" or "ringing" of sound through the steel. So he took it on his own, grabbed the impact gun the next day, and went to work tightening bolts with a newfound confidence.

A while later, the building inspector came checking bolts and challenged him, telling him he wasn't allowed to use the air gun. He told the inspector to check the bolts and if they were the right torque to leave him alone. After checking the bolts, they both made eye contact. Without a word, only a sly grin, the building inspector turned and left. Although this older method is acknowledged and accepted, the technique is considered less reliable than today's precision torquing tools and not preferred. The technique is known as a type of "sounding."

For safety reasons, the learning curve to climb steel productively may've needed to be slow; for him it wasn't. With no safety net, belts, or lines, many would "coon" the steel. Yup, looking like the animal walking along a smaller branch in a tree. "Cooning" was traversing the steel I-beam with feet on the bottom flange and the knees sliding yet holding tight on the top flange of the "I." In this way, a worker could hold the steel with hands too, slowly scooting along more safely. Sacrificing speed and agility for safety five to six floors up. Some would walk. He would run. One day, making a connection at the end of a 240-foot long 60-ton truss with four other iron workers, he noticed them all leaving. He looked at the workers at the other end; confident in them making one bolt, they were leaving too. Bailing out? The bolts for this truss were about two inches in diameter and over ten inches long. Having one in the other end 240 feet away was a little comforting, but with both hands holding on to the bottom of the truss, his end was very slowly swinging into the building. Strangely enough, he could feel he was slowing it down, but no matter how he leaned or pushed, he couldn't stop it from moving. He heard everyone screaming, "Let go!" He looked down on the ground and thought they couldn't be talking to him. He looked back in the building where this truss was moving slowly towards and saw people pouring concrete and working, not having a clue this truss and catastrophe was silently heading toward them. Hearing more screams of "Let go," he thought, *Are they crazy?* If he let go, all those people would die. Hearing the screams of "Let go" again, he focused more intently down at them because they had to be out of their mind. Now looking intently, he saw the sixty-ton crawler crane was lifting off the ground and tilting forward. The bottom flanges of the truss he was holding were now past him and he thought, *I'm slowing it down, but I can't stop a crane from falling,* so letting both hands go he was the last to gather near the back of the crane as it very slowly continued falling forward with its half of a 60-ton, 240-foot-long load. The end of the truss started to build a little speed, now seeming like nothing was going to stop the crane from falling. He started to picture what the crumpling steel would look and sound like. The swinging truss caught a plumb cable and started to slow. The crane started to slow. The immense size and weight of the truss and crane now beginning to precariously balance on a wire rope about ½ inch in diameter. The rope seemed to stretch. The behemoth and load slowed till there was no more movement. Slower and slower as the wire rope stretched to its breaking point. It stopped. The crane and truss stayed. The foreman had his head on the tool box of his red and black truck, shoulders bouncing as he cried. The iron workers frantically barked to each other ideas like get on the back of the crane for weight. Some threw 4 × 4 pieces of wood under the front tracks.

None of this is going to do any good, he thought. *That wire rope is not going to hold the crane and truss balancing on this precarious fulcrum.* He said to the lead connector, "Tell the boss, 'Get the third crane, rope and clamp it to this crane, and pull it back.'"

The lead connector said, "That won't work."

He shot back, "This ain't going to work either! Tell the boss."

The connector told the boss. They pulled the crane back, and the truss amazingly came back upright. Undoing the bolt on the other end, they lowered the load to the ground, rerigged the truss, and got it in place before the end of the day. He thought for sure for a moment that day they were all going to be on the news that night.

Was it possible that he had slowed a sixty-ton, 240-feet-long truss enough that it would hang up in a one-half-inch steel plumb cable without simply snapping it? Good thing Carl (the crane operator) did not jump out of the crane to save himself and kept his foot on the brakes. As it came to a stop, everyone on the entire job site heard Carl's booming voice, *"Whoooaaaa!"* God was with him that day. He did not know it then. He knows it now.

People would stop their cars and watch, amused but busy; they never had much time to notice what was happening at ground level anyway. Someone had stolen his 4 lb. maul. This really frustrated him, and he wondered why and who. Looking for a replacement at Sears, he thought the 4 lb. never really gave much advantage. He brought an 8 lb. sledge home; his brother said he wouldn't be able to get around on the steel with that size of a sledge in his belt pouch. So he shortened the handle, and to prevent future theft, he spray-painted the handle a "slime lime" green. One day someone smacking with a 4 lb. maul on a difficult make said, "Make it for me." Smartly handling and landing a perfect blow five floors up, he made one hit and made the connection. That was it. From then on, other iron workers nicknamed him Hulk and his green sledge the Hulk. Up on the steel would sometimes come some light repeated banging, the sounds which to an iron worker's ear lasted too long. A difficult make? The job sites where he was present, the light banging on many floors up would not last very long for invariably came the holler, "Hey, Hulk, bring me the Hulk." Unfortunately for him, since he wasn't a willing partner yet when God moved him, it was always hard. Living in Reston, Virginia, required driving to jobs all around the Capital Beltway between Maryland and Virginia. He got arrested for drinking and driving and was ruffed up by police in the Fairfax County courthouse. He got charged with a DUI; the judge took his license for a year. This kind of twisted his attitude about where he lived and what he was doing, so he did another hard thing at twenty-three years old: he called his dad and asked if he could come home.

His dad started work picking cucumbers on a pickling farm at about thirteen or fourteen years old. His dad worked alongside German prisoners of war (POWs) during WWII. He asked, "Was there barbed wire and fencing?"

"Oh no," his dad said. "They didn't want to escape. No way for them to get back home. Besides returning to fight in a war and die in battle was not something any of those prisoners wanted a part of."

His dad had two jobs before the age of fifteen. His dad was a kind, very hardworking man, well-respected and committed to his work. Was his dad's work a lifelong dream? Absolutely not. His dad quit the last year of college because his mom was pregnant. His dad's family never got over it because his dad had a full scholarship and gave it up for his love and family. Had to get a job. His dad was born near Dagsboro, Delaware. Driven more than most kids his age, his dad modified a bike with a smaller front tire than the back in the 1930s to affix a large basket in the front to load and deliver newspapers. Remembering his dad worked on a pickle farm with German Prisoners he asked, his dad, "Did they ever try to escape? Wasn't it weird working with prisoners, fence, barbed wire, and guard dogs and such?"

"No," his dad said. "That was movies. Only a few guards and really weren't needed. The German prisoners didn't want to escape."

What? That didn't make sense! Weren't they patriotic?

His father explained, "There really wouldn't be any way to get back to their home in Germany. Life in Germany would be horrible. Germany was being bombed night and day. As German prisoners in America, they were fed and clothed." His dad described how on the farm was much better than being at war.

These explanations caused much reflection, curiosity about patriotism and of war. His dad's older brother had served in WWII. He questioned his dad, "You must've been old enough to serve in the Korean War."

His dad told him, "No, in the Reserves." His questions for some reason drew responses that seemed to cause the subject to end rather abruptly. Being young, he thought his dad was not patriotic. Not until he was much older did he find out his dad had gotten only one B in all his years of schooling. The whole family pressured his dad to continue in school. His dad's family tree had always been poor. Hard workers but never highly successful. His dad's family felt he would be the one to break the mold to have a chance for a successful life. His dad always got straight A's. No exceptions. Well, except for that one B. So all his family funneled him toward school and away from the military. They convinced his dad they relied on him to be the one. It seemed his dad let the entire family down.

As high school salutatorian, his dad's speech consisted of Russia's Joseph Stalin's cruelty, false promises, and the threats of communism. His dad's graduation speech exceeded expectations for a high school graduate, earning a standing ovation of over ten minutes. His dad earned a full scholarship to any school in the country of his choosing. His dad chose Northwestern University, Chicago, Illinois, majoring in journalism. Everyone in the family expected his dad to be another Walter Cronkite, his dad's sister once told him. But his dad didn't seem to enjoy fraternities and felt he was only becoming good at poker. He asked what his dad learned at Northwestern. His dad said he had learned to play bridge and poker. After about three years at Northwestern, his dad came home for a visit. Met his mom and fell in love. This greatly disappointed his dad's entire family especially after Dad met his mom. She was very young and, everyone said, really beautiful. They fell deeply and madly in love, marrying almost immediately. Their marriage caused an everlasting rift in his family. He left college straight away after marrying his mom. They needed a home and money for a baby that was now on the way. Dad got a job as the terminal dispatcher of a lower eastern shore trucking company. As the company changed ownership throughout the years, his dad stayed loyal until retirement. His dad became highly respected within the trucking industry on the Delmarva Peninsula, never attempting the dreams the entire family had hoped for, becoming the famous writer and journalist they all knew his dad could be.

His dad did write a book. Finished it. The family knew because his aunt typed the entire book on an old-style key-and-swing arm type-writer. The only manuscript disappeared. To this day, no one knows what happened. Sadly, the book disappeared, never to be seen again.

He played bridge for a wee bit of social life at the Elk's Club. His mom would get the chance to get out and dress up. His dad was extremely competitive at bridge, which caused a great deal of stress, also some notoriety within the Salisbury, Maryland, community. The card game of bridge is a tournament-type play with partners and bid-ing. Ranking is national, therefore many groups are very competitive, and for obvious reasons, husband and wife partners just wouldn't always work. His mom and dad were a very loving pair and as bridge partners were a force to be reckoned with. The stress was high, though. His mom was beautiful and drank. His dad drank a little but was extremely competitive and would become angry if the pair lost for any of the imaginable reasons. The pair won many tournaments, leading to travel tournament invites. Their travel was limited, leaving five extremely difficult boys home alone. Their success became lim-ited because of their family responsibility and income. About thirty years of major surgeries stopping the heart, to "roto-rootering" (drill-ing) clogged arteries blocked by cholesterol, bypass surgeries, and replacing heart valves to include repairing the mitral valve. His dad's only complaint was not being able to eat a real egg again instead of liquid eggs from containers. He had great respect for his dad more than anyone could imagine for his dad lived life as a good man.

His brother, Stephen's son, seemed blessed with the better qualities of the family linage like their dad. The same maladies of heart and compassion of the grandfather. Quiet and shy. All straight A's. Never lower. Not even one B. Earning a full scholarship anywhere in the United States, his nephew chose Lower Eastern Shore Community College. As he died of heart disease in his early fifties, his brother would never come to know and feel the pride of his son's accomplishments. Among the many challenges his older brother Stephen faced, his third son was born with severe water in the brain. No natural physical way to drain the fluid from the brain. Doctors at John Hopkins asked his oldest brother if he wanted to save his son or let him die. His brother would become very emotional and disbelief of given the choice. For his brother, he had no choice. The doctors made a tube that the fluid would drain into the stomach. There were times during the younger years it had to be replaced. For growth and one time bouncing or jumping on the bed, the tube must have kinked or dislodged from the brain or stomach requiring emergency major surgery to save the lad. Today, his nephew stays busy working full time and loves following Oriole baseball.

He found work, but it was only part-time as a bouncer in a small local bar in Salisbury. It was hardly a job that earned what he was used to, but he hoped it would lead to a better job. It didn't. One of the bartenders was pretty and was a few years his senior. That didn't stop him. He always asked. Early one afternoon, just her, he, and van full of ruffians came in. They were mostly playing pool, so he walked around the outer perimeter of the building, which was part of his assigned responsibilities. As soon as he walked back in, the bartender was a little panicked and said, "They got to go."

He looked over, saw he was greatly outnumbered (seven or eight to one), then looked back at her and said, "Why?" He was hoping there was something that could be worked out.

She said they were groping her and roughed her up a little.

Well, okay, he thought, *but how?* So he walked over to the biggest one and said, "Hey, you all can't do that to her. You all have to leave."

The big guy laughed, finished his beer, and said, "Hey, let's go."

They left. He was shocked. He went over and said to the bartender, "That was close. How about a shot?" They took a shot together. He tried again. Of course, not happening. Nobody was inside, so he went outside to walk the perimeter. He walked out the door and turned left, and there they were in the van. The one in the passenger seat was twirling a revolver. They all looked at him and laughed. He spun around and went back inside, saying, "Call the cops. They're still here, and they have a gun." The police came and acted like he was an idiot because nobody was there.

One night Ian Anderson and the Jethro Tull band played at the Salisbury Civic Center. The bar's manager he worked with ran into some of the band backstage and invited them to the bar he worked at. He thought, *Fat chance of that. It's a little hole-in-the-wall.* Sure enough, a bus and limo pulled up out front and unloaded. They all had center tables at the bar in front of the dance floor. Salisbury was a small town, and word spread fast. It got crowed. He saw Ian Anderson. There was a huge crowd gathered around the band's table. He almost introduced himself or said hi but thought it really wasn't all that. Plus, he was working, and besides, he'd met band members before. Band members were just other people to him. He surely did not idolize them or think of them as "stars." It was all about the same to him, especially after his experience at the Bayou in Georgetown, Washington, DC.

He was with his girlfriend, Nita, listening to the band 38 Special. He got tickets from the radio station DC101 for $1.01 each, so he thought the adventure might be worth it. He could also show Nita that an iron worker from the Lower Eastern Shore of the Delmarva Peninsula could take a young woman from the city to downtown Georgetown for a good time. On this night, the Bayou was packed. The band took a break. They were at a booth near the front, and the waitresses seemed really busy. So he told Nita he was going to get them a drink and that he'd be right back. He left Nita alone. The bar was awash with people smashed together, pushing and shoving for position. He paused for the right moment and strode in. He got two drinks and a shot. He headed back to the table with two drinks, one in each hand, watching out for passing people and being careful with the drinks. When he got back, for a moment he thought he was at the wrong table. Then Nita looked up at him, beaming and ecstatically saying, "This is Donnie Van Zant, the singer, and he said that I could try out singing for his band." Without a word, he set a drink in front of Nita and on the table where he stood. He waited. He knew Donnie was familiar with this scenario. He still waited. Once Donnie finally looked up, the eye contact made it perfectly clear: where he stood and where Donnie sat was at that moment all wrong. But he said it anyway: "Get out of my chair."

Donnie laughed while Nita struggled in shock for words. Donnie leaned forward as to kiss his girlfriend, and starstruck, she returned the kiss. Donnie slid out of the booth. He didn't move a hair as Donnie passed. You probably could not have fit a king of hearts from a deck of cards between them.

He slid his drink over, sat down, began to sip, and said, "You kissed him."

Nita came back with stuff like, "If a star was to kiss you, you would—"

He cut her off. "No, I would not. That's not right, and that's not who I am."

Maybe now might be a good time to explain. Could he have knocked Donnie out for disrespect? Maybe? Certainly, Donnie's black Silver Dollar hat would've gone flying into the crowd. Could he have beaten Donnie up right at that moment? Maybe? But you see, the choice was his girlfriend's to make. She chose. And maybe she chose right; we'll never know because Nita and he just did not work out well after that. But there was one good thing about Ian Anderson and Jethro Tull coming to the bar in Salisbury, Maryland, that night where he worked: he did meet a beautiful and precious girl that night, and they left together at closing.

Then Came the Night

Someone was sleeping facedown on the bar. He thought, *No harm, no foul.* The manager came over and said, "They gotta go."

He said to the manager, "He isn't hurting anyone. Leave the guy be."

The manager said, "It's against the law. Do your job and get him out of here."

He thought, *Okay, easy does it. Just gently wake the guy up and tell him he's got to go. We'll work out a ride or something.* He walked over and gently put a hand on the guy's shoulder, and the guy lifted off the stool and came at him like a lion. He just reacted. They guy's feet never touched the floor, and as the guy's back hit the door, it sprung open. He keep going till the guy was planted, lying on the hood of someone's car or truck. He actually didn't know and didn't care.

The guy said, "Hey, you can't do this to me. I'm a brown belt in karate."

From his peripherals, he realized he was surrounded by four or five of the guy's friends. They were saying stuff like, "Stop. Let him go." He had the guy still by the collar, completely immobile and without the guy's feet touching the ground. He said, "Look, I don't care what color your belt is. You're barred for the night, and you're not coming back in."

He let him go. There was much grumbling, but he just turned and went back in. The place was a madhouse. He could not figure out what happened. The bartender looked at him in sheer terror and said, "Help." He didn't know where to begin. Then the crowd was forced out the door, taking him with it. Then he saw and heard.

The owner started getting pummeled. He started to do what he had to do then learned the manager of the bar sprayed mace in a customer's face. During the bar's melee, he found out the girl whose face the manager sprayed mace into was pregnant, and since he was one of the bouncers, he had to face the oncoming onslaught. It was absolutely unbelievable! He would have to support his manager after he did something so terribly wrong? No wonder the whole bar turned on the four of them—the manager, the owner, the other bouncer, and him. Then the guy he had just thrown out and his buddies now wanted action. It was all he could do to survive. He thought it sad he was on the side that was going to get what they deserved. On this night, after all had subsided, he had handled himself well. He fared okay, better than the others anyway. Then that made the other bouncer mad because he wasn't beaten as badly as they, so he left.

After returning home in the very early hours, he walked to the backyard. Feeling desperation in a life heading nowhere, he looked up to the heavens and stars—a moonless night free from light pollution. After noticing a falling star and with honest want, longing, and an open heart, he asked out loud, "My life is going nowhere. I ask that I go as far west as imaginable or possible and meet a most wonderful girl or woman." Then feeling a need to be sincere, he began correcting vagueness with specifics: a beautiful woman inside and out that he would fall in love with and would love him. Feeling he was starting to ask too much of anyone or anything, his request continued to fade while asking for children. He wasn't really sleepy but noticed it was getting very late now or very early, as it were; the color the of the night sky was changing. It was soon to be a beautiful twilight as the sun slowly came out with brilliant shades of colors pushing away the darkness. It was very quiet.

As he awoke and headed downstairs, he saw his dad was heading to town. It was a Saturday, probably the once-a-week grocery run. He said, "Hey, Dad, drop me off on your way." He sensed his dad felt the dread of possibly contributing to what a twenty-three-year-old does next.

"All right, son."

"Can you drop me at the intersection of Routes 13 and 50 toward the center of town? I'll be okay from there."

Very quietly the dad, checking over at the mom for approval, gave one nod as his dad tended to do often in the affirmative or gave a slow steady longer one to display approval. This time, it was a short nod.

It was a quiet ten-minute ride. He was still a little tired from the night before. Slowly feeling his parents' anxiousness or puzzlement over where he was going or what he was going to do caused him to snap back from daydreaming. Just prior to the intersection, with the light green and from the back seat, he announced, "Drop me off there, just past the intersection on the right. I'm going into the Navy recruiting office."

Since it was a weekend, it was a little busy. In consideration for his parents, as his dad pulled over, he jumped out. Traffic was clear, so he took off jogging across the street, looking back for approval. His dad, looking in approval, gave a slightly quizzical smile. His mom stared, probably worried and trying not to get her hopes too high. Might he have steady work mixed with? What if our country returned to war again? Would he be safe? It would be many years until he reflected back upon the night he looked up toward the heavens and made those life-changing requests. It came to him because invariably, that question would arise: "So anyway, why did you join the Navy?" He always answered, "Because I could wear bell-bottom jeans and grow a beard." That answer had some truth to it and would sometimes get a laugh. But what exactly did make him join, though? Was it a wish on a falling star and a wish come true, or was his request to the heavens a prayer heard and answered? Today he knows the truth.

THE MAN ARRIVES

The day began with great difficulty finding a place to park his truck. Parking was extremely limited in the large city. He thought it strange. Such an important city to have very limited parking options for the disabled. For some reason, there weren't considerations for the disabled as there was in most cities throughout the country. Maybe responsibility for consideration of parking for the disabled was never really clearly identified as a job responsibility when determining parking requirements. Or maybe whoever was in charge of designating parking limitations, rules and requirements never saw a need to differentiate between the handicapped and those fully physically capable. *No matter*, he thought. This was just one very small oddity in a city whose complex oddities were extremely vast and seemingly endless. He would just have to continue to carry his burdens a long way, at least one more time.

Both his visible burdens and his unseen burdens weighed heavily upon him. The visible burden he carried was obvious. Its weight combined with its bulkiness made the load oddly cumbersome. Especially for an elderly man. This time he would carry the burden, over two miles. As originally intended, he arrived at the very old, ginormous man-made structure. He stopped. Standing still a moment taking it all in. Arching his back a little, he looked up as the sun was beginning to peek over the statue of a woman at the top of the building. Freedom? Her odd attire appeared dingy in the sunlight. Surely a sight. Made of bronze, the statue at one time probably shimmered in sunlight. Now it was mostly an odd brownish green. From his view, it appeared black. He thought, *Oh well, the government loves its statues and idols.* This was the building known all over

167

the world as the place where the people had a voice. A building where the people of a nation were to have a say in the laws legislated and enacted which govern them. Many did not clearly understand ideals as first intended were no longer true today. Most people are conditioned to think they choose "leaders to make decisions for them." Originally, representatives were "chosen to represent the people." Throughout the years, original intent had eroded and was corroded to the point of brokenness.

The building was built in 1792. To him, he noticed, there sure were a lot of steps to get to the main entrance of the building. He thought, *Why?* He looked down and noticed what many would not've have noticed. There were odd cracks in the stone steps. How many steps? As he looked up the many steps, there seemed to be about fifty-nine to sixty. He thought there were sixty-four. He pondered for a moment. *Why so high? Why so many steps? Was he in a flood zone? Were the surrounding buildings built on wetlands? Strange,* he thought. *Was someone interested in grandness when this was built?* He thought, *Whose money was used to build this house?* Most of the people he grew up with worked hard all their lives, but none had this kind of money. He counted. There were sixty-four steps.

Although people were everywhere, he was seemingly alone. Some only noticed the man because he seemed odd or out of place. As if he did not fit in their world. Gathered in groups, many with electronic equipment. Phones, iPads, laptops, even media groups with cables, satellite feeds, large cameras, and other associated equipment. Many people walked in groups. Some groups walked on by. Some were shouted at by media. If someone leading a group stopped, someone ran over and placed a microphone in front of their face. Then other media would swarm. He thought it was a very unusual sight indeed. Many of the groups had what seemed some kind of leader. Most common among the groups was a special one, carrying a water bottle. Many of the special ones carried a cup of coffee. He thought it was kind of late in the morning for coffee. Especially for him. He had just walked over two miles.

He definitely did not need coffee. His heart was pounding pretty hard. A bulky handmade wooden book carefully wrapped in an American flag was slung over his shoulder, banded with three brown belts. As the man approached the entrance, his attention was drawn to a guard. The guard was standing his watch. The man understood not to disturb the stone faced guard. The man had compassion toward the guard knowing the guard was doing a difficult, unrecognized job. Most think that the guard is there for looks. He is not! The guard represents the sacrifices made by many to ensure the protection of the American Constitution. And the people know that the Constitution is still protected today. The man walked over and stood near the guard, looking in the same direction and straight ahead as him. The man knew this would not be accepted as appropriate very long by anyone. Especially not the guard. It would be considered awkward. Looking straight ahead, kind of at attention, the man spoke softly and sincerely. "Thank you," followed quickly with "I want to personally tell you that I am truly grateful for what you do. Thank you."

Realizing that this particular moment could not last, the man stepped forward. Then in front, he made eye contact, ensuring he was not in the guard's space or face and continued, "May God bless you." The man pressed on. Not many would notice. The guard changed slightly as to gather more from his peripheral of the man. The guard would not forget for a long time the feeling that just overwhelmed his entire being. No thoughts, just a good, overwhelming feeling. A feeling that makes water well in the eyes. Sometimes the person never knows why.

The load he did bear was bulky and heavy for him. He certainly did not need coffee. Not after being awake over five to six hours. He noticed the "special people" seemed to have just started their day at about 9:00 a.m. Oh well. The big meeting wasn't till 10:00 a.m. The work the House was built for does not get started prior to ten o'clock real early except for those who are prepping for the special people to start at ten. The people required to prep for the representatives would've started as early or earlier than he. Those who did the cleaning, provided water, ice water, and did electronic checks, were the people he came for. They would be why he needed to stay focused. Oh well. He just needed to relax. No real focus needed. He did not have what he was about to say memorized. There was no need. He was told over and over that he would be told what to say at the moment he was to say it. No worries.

Many did not care that he was there. But as usual, there were many that would stare at him. Was it because he was so odd-looking and didn't fit in? Was it because they were special and he was not? Was it because he struggled when he walked? His appearance did not portray any evidence he should struggle as he walked, no reason the man should stagger a little. No reason the man should struggle at each step. Why did he walk with such a strange-looking stick? The man looked fine. Except for his peculiarity. The man did not fit in. He was not clean shaven. His clothes did not fit perfectly. His clothes may have seemed odd to many. No suit. No tie? Slung over his shoulder was something he carried covered by an American flag. Is that why they stared at him?

He was used to it. All his life, he had been in preparation for this generation, this day, this time. He had always been starred at. There were times in his life when he had broken the armor of the elite. Some loved the opportunity. Some would love and welcome the occurrence of the few moments in a time when reality consumed them both. For some, he just had to cut the kite string. Some, once the grounding was disconnected, floated off, back into the world. So today was really no different for him than any other. He always could. He always would. He would share a moment of kindness. He would create a smile. He would spread happiness if it were for only one. He would do it. So what was different about today? The man possibly carried with him tangible hope of restoration and balance necessary to unify a nation as he walked up the steps.

The persons at the MRI, X-ray, and electronic scanning machines called their coworkers over. They had seen bizarre things before, but this was different. Security had to be cool, professional, and calm. As if they had seen it all. There had to be one. They waited. Finally, there was one who knew the day wouldn't end if he didn't ask. So he asked, "Is there anything explosive or dangerous? Is there a gun or any other type weapon?"

The man said, "Nah. Uh, sorry. No, sir."

Security then said, "Do you mind if I pat you down?"

The man paused. Then he shyly smiled and said, "Well, just a little. It's not a problem. It's just that I prefer women not men."

The security guard narrowed his eyes. The man innocently and shyly smirked, then the guard shook his head a little and chuckled. The guard paused, thought, then said, "Well, hold on a minute." Then he called out, "Marge! Can you come here?"

A guard who seemed bothered since she was busy came, saying, "What?" She seemed to be about in her late forties, maybe early fifties, probably looking forward to retirement. She must've been Marge, he figured.

The guard said, "This guy says he prefers to be patted down by a woman. Says he prefers women. You want to pat him down?"

She looked at the guard a moment then carefully with an odd scrutiny, scanned the man up and down, looked back at the guard, and quickly responded, "No." She briskly walked back to her checkpoint duties.

The man said, "Well, you tried." The guard patted him down. Still amused, the guard said, "That was the first time I heard that one. But since what you got there won't fit through the X-ray machines, we're going to have to open it. You understand right? By the way, what's in it?"

Their conversation very relaxed now, the man said, "Not much really. Some cedar, some bark, a little incense too."

The guard listened intently but never took his eyes off the flag-covered object. The guard was very careful. Then the man asked, "Can I help?"

The guard said, "Sorry, no." The man said if you loosen the belt, it opens very easily. Other different branches of government security were a little curious and helped spread out the few items. They marveled at the pieces of bark. The bark was engraved with words.

The man slightly interjected, "Honestly, it's rarely been opened. Not many have shown interest, so not many have seen its contents. Opening it here, there is really not much to see. Here, it does not matter. Here its contents have no meaning. It's the same contents that you see here, accompanied with a message which matters. The message, once brought to the Chambers, has the potential to unify *America*." Some staffers who knew why the man was there came over to the guards and asked if everything was okay.

One said, "This man really has to hurry in. He is expected."

Security said, "Yes, all good."

The guard seemed a little uneasy about putting the contents back. Without words, the man quickly offered assistance to help the guard close it up and ready it for carrying it again. Without words, the guard acknowledged the man's assistance was welcome. There seemed to be a mutual acknowledgment between the two that the guard's job was to inspect the contents, not put it all back together. The kindness of the guard trying to be careful with the contents did not go unnoticed by the elderly man. Many simply stepped back. The man felt the fuss and anxiety of others being held up in line. But still the man paused as he started to leave the guard and enter. The guard was already beginning to screen another. The man moved in close to read the guard's name tag. Both the person being screened and the guard noticed. The man called the guard by his name. "Officer Gillet or Officer Gill-lay, how do you pronounce your name?" The man needed reading glasses to read up close.

The officer now a little puzzled and with a very slight, almost noticeable frown, responded, "Gil-lee."

The man said, "Oh, sorry, Officer Gillee, just wanted to make sure I pronounced your name right." The man smiled broadly. "Thank you, Officer Gillee. You're a good man. I enjoyed the time spent with you. Have a great day. And may God's Grace be with you and your family."

Officer Gillee beamed back, "May God's peace be with you too." The man continued through the Chamber doors, now meshed with the rest but cautious. Cautious for courtesy, letting people who seemed in a hurry, pass through the doors before him. Some didn't even notice and strutted through the doors like peacocks. Many looked down at their phones as they entered. He then made eye contact.

The woman who beamed from within smiled and put her hand forward as if to gesture, "This way, you first."

The man paused and nodded graciously, accepting the kind gesture. He smiled back saying, "Thank you. You are very kind."

As he walked forward, being shown where he was to sit, his thoughts wandered. Could he do this? For a moment, he thought he couldn't. That uneasiness was always accompanied by a physical weight on his body that no one else could see. It made the arthritis in his back hurt. There was pressure in his chest. He would try to stretch his back a little. To someone else, it might seem weird. To others, it would look as if he were anxious. Then what others thought about him would bother him. Is this the medical condition referred to as anxiety? He knew it was not really anxiety. It was a physical condition stemming from spiritual interference or spiritual influences. *This is the time*, he thought. *It's actually one of the hardest times. It is in this moment one should ask.* He calmly thought to himself, *Help?* Then he thought in the form of a request, *Help me.* Then he whispered it ever so slightly: "Help me, Jesus." He slowly and calmly looked upward. Maybe someone would actually physically come? The feeling he had was combined with hope. He waited. Nothing. No one came through the window he happened to be looking at. Nothing but the sunlight beaming through the window. His eyes curiously followed the light. Nothing but dust milling about in the stream of light which ended on the wall, leaving a pattern of a window just above the northernmost gallery door. He noticed the light through the window emboldened the relief portrait of Moses to him, shining in a manner of brilliance. At first, he was so amazed he looked to see if anyone else noticed the same thing he was seeing. Searching for confirmation, there was none to be had. So it would be once again, as it was many times before in his life. No one else would see what he saw.

Oh, he could point it out. But of course, the phenomena would not be shared as unusual. To them it would be the normal occurrence of everyday shadows and reflections caused by light. Not to be deterred, he thought of how hard it was for Moses to have been given such an important mission to free a people from an all-powerful grip of government. He thought of how Moses must've felt having been given such an impossible task. Oh, he knew full and well he wasn't

Moses. But he was not here representing himself. This was actually the last place in the world he wanted to be. He was here for the people. He loved people. He cared for all people.

After being ushered to his seat he noticed there wasn't any windows. The light on the carving had faded. As he sat waiting to get started, he still wondered about something in specific though. He understood that it was God that moved Moses to act against insurmountable odds. Even more than that, Moses was moved to lead a people for *forty years* in the Wilderness. No one can lead a people who were once slaves and now free through incredible hardships of the unknown. Each day and night would bring hardships and put people under extreme duress. Usually people panic, allowing fight or flight to take over, or people turn on one another, trying to ferret out who the best leader would be to lead them to food and water. These people that thought they were led to freedom and paradise were not in a paradise they imagined. We might be able to relate if we were to put ourselves in their sandals, walking on hot rock or blistering hot sand. Basically, they were camping in a desert where food was negligible and water a rarity for one, let alone three million men, women, and children. Unbearable blistering heat was present during the day, and it was cold enough at night that if flesh were left exposed to the elements, a person could die from hypothermia. This was not something modern man, who is often borderline diabetic, could endure easily. But these people had survived four hundred years of physically demanding labor and intensive work in extreme elements without plentiful food sources. The weak died while the strong survived. Everyone would've gotten used to seeing people die. A very hard people, a very tough people—these people were often described as having hard hearts. This is from years of conditioning where death becomes an escape. These people were promised freedom and a land full of milk and honey, a bountiful *promised land*, only to learn of *unbelievable* challenges and obstacles ahead.

Many children would cry from hunger. Wives would complain to husbands. Then there would be a horrendous and incredible amount of complaining coming from four hundred thousand men probably wanting to kill whoever brought them into this situation in life, very quick to forget the incredible divinity and miracles that had brought them to this point, probably willing to turn to any god or anyone for help, and even forgetting a unique giant cloud that would change to a pillar of fire at night was ever present. Although a description of the cloud escaped the people of that generation which is suitable for this generation, even this generation lacks proper terminology to explain divine creation that traverses from heaven to Earth. Without the wisdom to discern, today's experts still declare both good and evil phenomena as unidentified flying objects UFOs and aliens from other worlds. The people are not ever to know *Divine intervention* unless we soften and open our hearts for God's love. So we might come to understand the type of love and devotion Moses had for a people that were almost every day ready to revolt and kill him. Faith and belief would have to be cultivated in the people. It would take years. It would take forty years.

For an example of one of the many divine interventions and demonstrations God would reveal to the people, large amounts of refreshing water *sprang forth* from a rock. The term 'sprang forth' became a parable to understand *life water from the rock* but, eventually was somewhat diluted unintentionally by euphoric use describing the beauty of *fresh water springs* moving along rocks. Unbeknownst to the people at the time, this amazing gift of grace was also a message or prophecy of much deeper meaning about what would come in the future for the people. The *water from a rock* was a seed of great importance intentionally planted, meant to grow for consumable fruit for people in the future.

On one occasion, the Lord commanded Moses to speak to the rock that it would give water to the people. This command from Adonai (God) can be found in the "Book of Going out of Egypt" also known as Genesis, which many believe to be written by Moses himself. This simple command would be to prepare for the *rock* (church of Jesus Christ) that we speak through today that the Father would provide all that we need and more, the only problem being the command was to be followed as spoken by Adonai. Moses was not to deviate, and many times he did not. But we need to understand as our Father does that we are human. So what happened?

Found in Exodus 17:6, Moses struck the rock with his rod that water would spring forth for the people and their herds who were probably experiencing dehydration, and maybe some were experiencing heat exhaustion or maybe even heatstroke. Now, these four hundred thousand men were ex-slaves and were probably a very tough, strong, and hardened people. After all, they had been building and were construction workers under brutal conditions, being whipped and not fed properly. Without the same medical care and food the Egyptians would've enjoyed, these people were much tougher and harder than today's people. They were probably dying of thirst, shouting and hollering at Moses, ready to kill him, and saying horrible things. Moses knew that God had divinely intervened on numerous occasions through this staff to free the people from Egypt. Moses was probably seriously frustrated by a people having doubts, lacking faith, trust, and confidence, and being brutally nasty including threats of death to Moses and Aaron. So Moses actually struck the *rock* when all that was required was to speak with the *rock*. In the "Fifth of the Musterings" another name for the book known as Genesis, after Moses was remembered as saying, "Hear ye rebels; are we to bring you forth water out of this rock," it was then Moses struck the rock with the staff to produce water for life. This would become prophetic that the rock would be struck dead so that life water could spring forth for future generations of people that they, too, could be adopted as God's children for eternal life. The Lord was there to witness what would come to be required of Him in the future. The place where from the rock came water for life is known as *Massah* or also *Meribah*.

Today we come to know that after the battle at Hormah in which the nomads defeated the army of King Arad south of Canaan, Moses organized his people at Kadesh-barnea and sent men to explore into the heart of Canaan. The majority of men came back in terror and horror that the Amorites were of Nephilim and known as Anakim for that generation even unto this generation. Once again, rebellious angels known as fallen angels had been fornicating with women, producing offspring—Anakim. Man's wicked ways and his willingness to work with fallen angels was what caused the punishment and destruction of the earth during the great flood in AM 1656. God promised He would not destroy the earth again by flood, but God will not allow the seed of fallen angel into heaven. It is an abomination to creation to mix that which cannot be mixed. The mixture of fallen angel and man that produces a soul that cannot have eternal life or escape to another planet. So fallen angels try to take over heaven that their seed (children) will know eternal life. This is the goal of fallen angels. Fallen angels want to do anything on their own to make their plan work, changing life and the eternal energy of the universe, and our Creator who has created everything knows it will not mix and won't work, ultimately causing the destruction of the entire universe. After God learned of their plan, knowing it won't work, He wants man to try and stop their planetary destruction plans instead of continuing to work with fallen angels. God wanted the children of Adam (man), the line of Adam and Noah, to rise and convince people to step away from those who aligned with the fallen angels toward their goals. Moses's people were not ready. This type of battle for the *Promised Land* included secrets of the ultimate war. The ultimate war is fought with much having to be secret, for in the spiritual world or among the unseen, there is no place to hide and no secrets once the Word has been or is spoken. God's children were not ready for this type of war. His *chosen* would have to be taken into a secret area inaccessible to anyone or anything other than God's will. On their long journey consisting of cleansing and spiritual training, they would need protection and have to be led to safe places. Moses and his brethren were not ready to war with offspring of angels or fallen angels that were known to be sons of gods. This war includes the unseen and the dead. The dead born of a fallen angel and human is left to roam the earth forevermore or until judgment day. So from the beginning and after the flood, there were many left to roam the earth forever. And every so often (as is numbered in the Book of Daniel), with the help of man, fallen angels begin to mate with humans again. When they do, God intervenes or has man rise. So since Moses and his people weren't ready, they were once again led away by a *cloud* for continued purpose. The cloud is an atmospheric capable traveling vessel or aerial craft by day. When the esoteric or spiritual leave the less dense atmospheric conditions of the heavens (the unseen) and enter earth's more dense molecular structure, they can or must change to be seen. Moses and his people followed a *pillar of cloud* by day, and the people were protected by a *pillar of fire* at night. Both were called pillars because of their shape, probably one and the same from descriptions and only changing appearance for visibility reasons and for the people's benefit of assurance and as a warning to *others*. A very long cylindrical shape yet slightly tapered, becoming oblong in nature, could easily stand and travel vertically, travel horizontally, or become stationary. It really had no limitations known to man. This cloud was at God's direction but commanded by our Lord.

In most cases, the Lord was present, but God did speak to Moses and Aaron regularly. And fifty days after Passover, God spoke to three million people from heaven at Mt Sinai. At one time God spoke to three million people in person but the original firmament shattering event was so terribly disturbing and frightening His gifts would eventually need to be given more tenderly through individuals. Christians have come to know the original firmament shattering event that happened around AM 2513 as Pentecost. About 1,281 years later or AM 3794, on the celebratory date of Pentecost, a major change in the way God would help each individual find the path back home to a new beginning would be revealed. This is a continuation of prophetic word as a gift from God so that man can fight the spiritual war he is to face and faces every day. When God realized the people needed more faith and belief to be better prepared for spiritual warfare combined with physical fighting, Moses, Aaron, and the people were led by the pillar of cloud by day and the pillar of fire by night into *Bedimar. Bedimar* is translated by all accounts into "wilderness." It is time we come to know that it is true they went into the desert of sand and rock, but probably without the masses knowing it, they were also led through a window or what this generation knows as a portal. Although the people walked in the wilderness, they were also led into Bedimar, one of the heavens that was originally written and described as a wilderness by its first human visitor: a man.

This man would never see his great-grandson Noah yet would be shown all that Noah would do and more. This wilderness is one of the lower heavens, which is accessible through middle earth. Bedimar is also where some of the lower living creatures of God's creation live. These are the life-forms created by God from the Angel Archas. Archas came forth from the spiritual world (the unseen) unto earth's atmosphere and became undone at the God's word, becoming a brilliance of light. Archas is to be their foundation unto this day.

Moses along with God's chosen people were not only led by the *pillar of a cloud* through the desert but also through a window or portal with most of the four hundred thousand men to three million people, including women and children, not knowing they had left an earthly wilderness and entered a heavenly wilderness. Only the *seventy* or so chiefs chosen by the Lord and assigned by Moses and Aaron for specific assignments of leadership and communication to the people probably knew. As written it was in Bedimar for forty years the *chosen* would receive their trials, tribulations, sufferings, and their seed would receive additional basic training to become the *select* to return and overcome the Amorites and Anakim, the children of fallen angels also known as sons of gods. Why is this story of Moses in this book? So that you know your purpose and also know that the drafters of America's Constitution at the founding of the United States understood much of this, and that is exactly why the United States was to be a nation where man had authority, just as God gifts authority. Not only did man have authority but the right to govern themselves. Even though the truth was revealed the path would come to be hidden or blocked from man's knowledge. For this generation many believe that man must find his own way beyond the boundaries of this world or through the firmament to everlasting life. Sadly, man was being deceived and misled once again. And so God's plan quietly continues that those who rise have authority and will eventually govern in His government when Christ returns.

THE MAN SEEMED TO BE
ALONE; HE WAS NOT

People were reluctant to be seated, and many stared at the man while many wanted to intentionally ignore his presence as to not recognize the power and possible importance of his message gifted by God. The different cliques and gaggles banded with bonds of certain works were obvious. Sometimes the man smiled. Then he looked back to the boy. Why was a boy there? The gavel pounded again. Yup, for sure it was maple. His thoughts drifted again. Moses led a people to *freedom*. Which would be harder? Freeing the people from the king of one of the most powerful nations in the known world or leading a people through unimaginable hardship and sacrifice to the founding of a new nation? While he looked at the relief portrait, he knew Moses wrote of a time in which men lived about 1656 years before the Great Flood. But how was it that Moses wrote of a period ending some eight hundred to one thousand years before his own life? Today, not many know that writings of man's earliest times ever existed. A highly educated man who had been an Egyptian prince for about thirty to forty years. A prince of Egypt who would've had access to the greatest scholars of the time. A prince who would've had access to almost all known writings. Undoubtedly, Moses would've had access to the Book of Admonition. The same book or most likely a transcribed copy of the *Book of Admonition*. Noah was specifically instructed to take with him on the Ark that not only descendants of Adam would survive the Great Flood, but also the written Word of God would accompany man so that man would know it even to this day.

Who would take the time to write in the earliest of days? Basically, he was documenting observations of what he understood and knew of such things he saw. Most other people in those times were probably extremely busy trying to survive. The difficulty of writing during man's earliest of days should be obvious. How was a communicable language even developed? The sounding of words, lettering *for those words, grammar,* what to write with and write on, only to name a few obstacles. If one were to read his book, these questions would be answered. It would become very clear, and they would come to know the development of communicable languages. In the earliest of known times, who would devote his entire life to research then try to articulate in writing so that one day others would know the same truths of what he saw? It must've been extremely difficult for him, his wife, and their children. It wasn't like he was going to earn a living from writing. In those days, the family required the man for leadership, strength, and his survival skills to live. Not many would think of a man who spent his life writing as important. Not many today would think of God's First Scribe as a hero. He was more than a hero. A man who would devote his entire life to serving God's purpose. He wouldn't know that many years later his writings would enlighten man's pathway to freedom and salvation. There was a time when this man's writings were highly valued. Very few in today's modern times know of him or his writings. Throughout the life of God's First Scribe, he would be shown all the secrets of heaven. The Scribe would have to live those secrets so as to describe the secrets better than any man. He would have to be very special. He would have to know God better than any man so that he could transcribe God's ultimate purpose for man. So that God's Written Word and truth would be carried by God's messengers even unto the end of man. He would have to have walked with God.

He wondered, was the life of the First Scribe as a boy really that much different than his own life when he was a boy? Was the life of the First Scribe as he grew into adulthood really that much different than his life as he grew into adulthood? Would the end of their lives be different? He wondered. Through his mind ran the many questions. Then one question stood alone: What brought me here today? In his head, he heard "Here."

The house speaker smacked the gavel. Wood on wood. He heard the wood sound echo. *A hard wood*, he thought. Quite probably a maple. He looked to the origin of the sound. His thoughts drifted to its origin.

A Global, Cataclysmic, Life-Ending Event

It seemed as if the Earth had opened up disproportionally globally, releasing fountains of water with such force and in such amounts that the comparison can only be made with current unknown events possibly happening on other planets in our galaxy like Jupiter. Although the cataclysmic event would seem as disproportionate to scientist and geologist for this generation; the earth's poisoning by man and fallen angels actually required the Earth's consummation by heaven's waters combined with waters from the fountains of the deep. The combination of the two waters would drown and destroy the Earth and its inhabitants yet cleanse the Earth prepping it for its transformation. The Earth's rebirth was proportional and considered good towards the Creator's desires that man and the earth should continue to live as man as its caretaker once again. Although the appearance of fountains shooting upward and filling the heavens then falling to the Earth seemed like a randomness of violence; the release of waters from both the skies and the Earth were by appointment. There were also a series of windows in the heavens and the Earth that were specifically placed and opened by appointment. These windows are numbered. They may move. They may be guarded. If any of these windows failed to open or close at their appointed time, the guard would be immediately replaced. The force of replacement would be overwhelming, for the command would come from the Creator. There are a number of windows between heaven and Earth that remain and are used to this day.

The torrents of water and the force that propelled underground rivers, seas, and oceans of fresh and salt water once held tightly somewhere in various locations between the planet's outer core, mantle, and crust—also known as middle Earth—spewed upward into the stratosphere at an exact force; that force cannot be calculated. Before this cataclysmic event, the Earth was a planet that had never experienced rain from above. The planet's watering was only from light and moderate to heavy clouds of mist, sometimes a very thick mist as dense as today's dense fogs. Seismologists, geologists, and scientists could collaborate, compiling data of the known and giving an estimate of the unknown, but only provide an estimate. A force, once applied somewhat uniformly, that could squeeze a planet and pop it like a water balloon that might pop if squeezed enough is hard to envision. Although the Earth has nowhere near the elasticity of a rubber balloon when considered in scale and in comparison to the metallic Rockwell and Brinell hardness standards of measurement, the Earth does have somewhat elastic qualities.

When the great deep burst open and gushed skyward the windows of heaven opened, releasing their appointed portions of water. No one that lived on the planet could have ever anticipated or imagined the Earth could experience a phenomenon that would bring the end of life for all species and alter the lives of many more, altering and adjusting the evolution processes of nature itself. But some were warned. There was one chosen by God for that purpose. This one came from generations of men who walked and sought the one true ever-living God. Of the millions that lived on Earth, for each generation, there is at least one who is called by God. If they who are called answer and remain faithful it is they that become an elect for that generation. And then at least another or unknown quantity for the millions of people in the next generation. Among the very first, there were those who sought a return to their Creator. This was in the AM, anno mundi ("in the year of the world")—the period before the Great Flood. These were not pious and self-seeking men. Some referred to the men of certain isles, groups, or families in the beginning as prodigies. If the term is not liked, they could just be referred to as faithful. They were wanderers, for they moved with livestock, living under the skies of day and stars of night. These days, moving with livestock or herds like the cattlemen or like the American Natives did with buffalo is frowned upon and not respected, for land is claimed by one entity or another, transferred to the powerful and mighty. Others struggle to maintain a home or rental. But these men were humble and recognized the beauty in God's gracious gifts as precious life resources to be valued and shared. These men knew and shared love. The rest of the world ignored the gift and secrets of wisdom unless it was toward self-gain and self-purpose. But some listened to the warning from the one. Some watchers hearkened in wonderment and curiosity, always preparing for their own self-sustainment, desires, and wants. The intensity of the rain and water upon the Earth at the end of the beginning has never been matched on Earth since. It rained for forty days and forty nights. That was but a small part of the calamity. The worldwide cataclysmic event continued.

The windows of the deep were not fully closed. The water flowing from the deep was very slowly subsiding from its original burst. Water still gushed upward from beneath the surface of the globe. Earth's surface was still swirling and bubbling upward violently in regions. The water was still rising with only the tallest mountains visible. Even the tallest were disappearing. When the rains ceased, it was a twilight sky, and the sky began to reveal stars. The firmament of heaven remained. The sky began to reflect a turquoise color. Was the sun finally beginning to rise after forty days and forty nights? Would there still be night and day? But the waters were still rising across the globe.

Earlier a fleet of vessels with sophisticated equipment headed in the direction the commanders and navigators, which was known to be westward. The sky was a mix of blackness, greens, and purples with extremely large rivers of electricity streaming across the sky and fading into the tiniest of thousands of branches, appearing like giant snakes shrinking unto little worms crawling across blackness. It would be the only light available. The strobe-light-like effect mixed with the strobe lighting effects of a bluish-green energy in the giant waterspouts had a strangely odd, eerie, terrible, and terrifying effect.

Visibility at times was blackened preventing the hand to be seen when held in front of one's face. Waterspouts miles in diameter were all around. Fountains of water sixty miles in diameter and walls of water as far as the eye could see gushed upward above 3000 ft per second breaching the speed of sound in water. These were not normal vessels as one might imagine being built prior to the year AM 1656. These vessels appeared as giant ships with technology and designs even more advanced than this generation's advanced technology but combined with ancient technology. These ocean-going ships were of and on Earth. But they were actually trying to escape the boundaries of the surface of the Earth. These ships did have sails, but they were not necessarily used during the storm of forty days and nights. Using wind in sails to move a ship or vessel in the water is never a bad idea unless there are storms such as of this event; a storm of such ferocity as to rip sails made of near-invincible materials. Or, if the winds and seas are ever changing with rogue waves higher than hills crashing over the peaks of mountains, and winds approaching a thousand miles per hour. Winds exceeding hundreds of miles per hour in one direction then quickly shifting to come from another. These vessels were built and commandeered for such a world-altering event. Some listened to the one, for they knew from whom he walked with.

During the storm, it was hard to tell the difference between heavens of water and the water the vessels traveled in. Honestly, at times there was no difference. The vessels only returned to the water of the Earth pulled downward by gravity. After heading into the one-hundred-foot swells, the lead vessel's commander ordered the ship to turn away from an approaching horrendous wall of water. There was a large creature whose skin was a combination of smooth flesh and armored scales in appropriate areas and whose snout appeared half-alligator and half some type of horse, yet it was clearly humanoid in giant stature. He shouted to his navigator, who appeared half-leopard and half-human, of same qualities, only slightly smaller in size yet still giant, "What are the coordinates of the window?" The language seemed a type of Sumerian as they spoke, but the crew that overheard the two understood what they said in languages of their own speaking. The crew was an extremely diverse mix of humanoid giants, large men, somewhat normal men seemingly of great agility and prowess, other diverse, living creatures, men as slaves, and extremely beautiful women. All these women were extremely beautiful, almost perfect in endowments and with colored eyelids. There are very few women to this day that match this beauty. There were also large hairy beasts, some white, some dark brown and light brown. Some seemed docile while some snarled. Those that visibly seemed less agile were very strong and proved extremely capable when performing duties. Very odd creatures were about the ship, performing tasks such as pushing slaves out of the way or killing them. These acts of brutality would sometimes generate discipline by an authoritative figure. Slaves were highly valued. These odd-looking living creatures were the lower creatures God formed from the angel Archas. God had previously opened Archas, and his being became the lower creatures. They have since been given names such as grigori, gargoyles, trolls, Bigfoot, Abominable Snowman, Yeti, gremlins, hobgoblins, winged serpents and even more unnamed as yet by man. Then Archas was given the command by God to unfix himself and become the foundation for the lower things. All were God's creation, and to Him, they were His living creatures. And some in the vessels were sons of God or angels. Thousands were sons of angels and humans.

What was left of an entire fleet of ships with some two hundred special passengers was now becoming visible in the very troubled waters. Rough seas remained, and from a small portion of the brightly lit night sky, the vessels could all be seen still being tossed about. It was then the navigator shouted, "The window is set to close!" The commander shot his eyes westward, proclaiming, "It is now or never!" The commander gave the order, "To chariots!" The commander and navigator disappeared belowdecks along with some hairy beasts, grigori, gargoyles, trolls, and hobgoblins. Giant hatches began opening on the other ships, and shiny vessels began to lift out of the ships from belowdecks and up into the twilight above. Some glowed and emitted light. Some glistened in the starlight. Some turned on lights. Some started lifting off, seemingly unstable at first. Some seemed to regain stability after being tossed by crosswinds. Some shot straight up. Some were circular and disklike. Some were spherically shaped or oblong. Some looked almost like spinning top hats. They seemed like shiny or fiery chariots, around twenty in total. As they all steadied and gathered in formations of flying *V*s, an area westward in the sky began to spin in a circular motion. One vessel different from the others lifted from one of the ships. It was shaped as a cylinder (when the prophet Zechariah saw it, he referred to it as a volume, parchment, or scroll) about twenty yards in length by about ten yards in width. As the cylinder lifted skyward, two women on the deck suddenly looked up, unfurling wings reptilian in nature—pterodactyl like, bat like, or as the prophet Zachariah noted, "wings of a kite"—and swooped upward into the cylinder-shaped flying craft.

It was as if the forces that held our atmosphere together became almost fluidlike and began to spin. A pattern formed. It was a window. It was circle with the bottom half in the water. All the flying aerial crafts (what we call today as UFOs or aerial phenomena) zipped toward the window. Some passed through and disappeared above the surface of the water. Others dove into the water, and their glows could be seen moving through the water and disappearing through the bottom portion of the window. It was a gateway to a lower heaven. Of course, God knew not all would be destroyed; all but a few surviving living creatures and entities entered the middle Earth through windows. These windows were accessible only through Earth's windows; they led through Earth and into Earth. Once entered, some of these windows simply led to middle Earth and separated regions known as heavens. As the aerial crafts departed, shouts and screams could be heard from the many left behind. Some ships did not close the giant hatches in time through which the aerial chariots departed, and they were swamped by waves. Those seagoing vessels with deck hatches that couldn't close in time sank, sending their crews to the deep to drown in dark turbulent waters.

It seemed like months when finally the water started to recede. The vessels had no choice but to be pulled by the current. Unable to turn around in time, some sank. It was if someone pulled hundreds of plugs. Some of the openings in the Earth seemed as if they could've been a hundred miles in diameter. Some smaller openings pulled water through with such force as to shake the planet in those regions, making incredible, thunderous roaring sounds caused by rushing water and vibrating rock in those areas. The vibrations could be felt in heaven. It had been many days since the rain stopped, and this day was brilliantly sunny. The receding waters turned out to be just as catastrophic as when the rain came; as horrendously and furiously as the waters came, the waters returned in thundering, roaring torrents, rip currents, and undertows. Some of the seagoing vessels were just pulled under by spinning vortices of water known as whirlpools. The largest rapids began to form, unknown to man even to this day, some of which formed the Grand Canyon. There were still large Earthquakes from the deep and aftershocks. Sucked downward by whirlpools and undertows created by the receding waters and left leaderless, other vessels began breaking apart even when the crew did organize quickly and tried to come about. Even the largest oars manned by the strongest of beasts had no effect or snapped. It was then someone hollered, "Land!"

Becoming visible, the land in the distance was actually tops of mountains. A few giants and men of unimaginable agility and strength dove into the water and began swimming. The beastly giants swam like powerful tugboats cutting through the rapids. The large men of uncommon strength could be seen swimming because of the rooster-tail-like waves shooting in the air as they kicked while swimming. Some men were half-fish and purposed through the water. The women panicked. Some screamed and desperately clawed at the men to take them. Some men seemed to care and did allow some women to hold on. Most didn't. One woman of unusual size and strength began to fight a giant, forcing him into taking her with him. She stabbed him with a sword. The giant picked her up and disassembled her tossing the remains into the water. It was a mistake. The mistake was foreseen. Tens of thousands abandoned the vessels. Then in the distance, the seemingly impossible began. In the distance were giants held above the water by the many tentacles of much bigger octopuses and giant squid without shells. These squid were extremely fast and powerful in the water. The sharks smelled blood in the water. They came. Then the real battles began. Some engaged in hand-to-hand combat. Some had weapons. Of course, there were feeding frenzies, and then killer whales joined in. The killer whales were not frenzied. They attacked with strategy, taking limbs and forcing giants under, drowning them, so that their young might eat. Just as many of great strength or size were almost to land, the largest dorsal fin ever seen rose to the surface. The fin could be seen cutting the water like a large naval combatant. Then came more giant fins, hundreds—then thousands.

The megalodon sharks must've smelled the blood in the water. Or were they called to feast? Or were they called for their purpose? The megalodon covered hundreds of miles of water in minutes, traveling with the current but able to steer toward their prey while following the path of the receding waters. Some of the water was clear, and the blue blood of the Nephilim was easy to see. None made it to land, not even the half-man-half-fish.

The waters cut crevices and canyons across thousands of miles receding towards lower ground. The erosion churned rock into fine sand, creating continental shelves several hundreds of miles into the oceans. Some waters just dropped off cliffs like waterfalls filling the giant basin. Sadly, millions of fish of unknown species, serpents, water beasts, giant octopuses, giant squid, sharks, the megalodons, and even some killer whales got trapped in what we call tidal pools that drained through small creek-type openings and flowed back into the seas. Some young serpents, sharks, and fish of thousands of different species slipped through the tiny waterways, but the openings were too small for the larger species. Giant rapids were too turbulent for many species to survive. There are many species of fish and birds that try to return to their places of origin. The monarch butterfly travels form North America to South America. The beautiful albatross flies to Midway Island from around the globe to nest. It's also known as the gooney bird, for it seems as though it wasn't meant to land. The gooney bird crashes upon landing in water or on land. The striped bass or rockfish travels inland to breed and spawn. When these striped bass are caught in lakes, they're referred to as hybrid striped bass. The salmon run, whales travel great distances, and many other species do the same.

As the waters receded from the great flood, pools were left filled with thousands of species. Without beasts to eat the flesh as it decayed, some fossilized. Much of the plants, animals, and Nephilim were covered in silt, and over the years of trapped gases and chemical reactions by Earth's former life, it is believed by some that this became fossil fuel, also known as crude oil. The megalodon shark teeth are being found even in this generation, in the year 2021 hundreds of miles inland in South Carolina. The giant shark teeth are fossilized and black, sometimes larger than a human hand. Not many fossilized bones of fish or birds are found these days unless there were very usual circumstances causing preservation, for the bones of fish and birds are much less dense or more hollow and thinner than the bones of larger land animals that carried heavy body weight on the ground. All bones are hollow; it becomes a matter of thickness and the bonding of molecular structures, which we call density. When the fountains of the deep released, the force cracked the outer core and mantle in rugged and jagged paths around the planet. The seemingly disproportionate nature of the cracks, fissures, hot springs, and geysers are left as evidence to this day. The geysers at the beginning of man were unusually large and under a great deal of pressure anyway. There began a cooling period after this major event, creating polar caps with volcanoes releasing hot molten lava and gases into the air. The new mix provided just the right balance required for life anew. After this unimaginable event, the Earth was a much different place for life. Today's experts call it evolution. The Earth has constantly shifted in its balance of gases, warming and cooling. If the Earth of this day is coming to a climatic ending, that would be because the Creator allows or decides so be it.

While all this was happening on one side of the planet, on the other side, a very strange large tar-soaked wooden object bobbed in the waters with only its upper structure visible. A very crudely made seagoing structure but actually perfect for it designed purpose was mostly submerged as it floated in turbulent and violent seas. Its dimensions would have it float over and pass through the largest of waves. It is calculated the highest wave could reach ninety-eight to ninety-nine feet before it breaks. Of course today's calculations can not replicate oceanographic and atmospheric conditions which existed in the beginning. But undoubtedly waves during the great flood would've been of unfathomable magnitude during the Great Flood. This ark's design had a ratio of dimensions that took into account greater global forces than those known to today's man. Besides the ark was sealed by God and therefore impregnable. Escorting this strange vessel were beautiful humpback, sperm, gray, and white whales—whales of all species. Many of today's ocean mammals could be seen swimming with the vessel as if escorting or accompanying the odd large wooden box. Dolphins and porpoises repeatedly porpoised high in the air and low in the water all about seemingly escorting the Ark. A white dove could be seen bringing a green-leafed branch to a bearded man in an open window.

There was a man that was actually shown that this great flood with all its ramifications would happen. This man was shown in a way that no matter who you are or were, you would know the reality of the future event and that there would be no mistaking its occurrence. Thousands of years later, there would be men to *know* this great flood really did happen and that there was at least one family that *knew* beforehand. These men would be shown more in ways that would leave life-altering impacts, and there was no mistaking the reality that what was being shown to them was real and would happen. They would come to *know*. Of the many that come to *know* in this generation, there is at least one more that would answer the call. The man was simply answering his call.

God's First Scribe Begins His Life as a Boy

The Log and Branch.

Blessed are the pure in heart: for they shall see God.

—Matthew 5:8 (KJV)

Wood on wood. A sharp strike with skilled intent. An intent to replicate a specific sound. Again, the little boy smacked the log he was sitting on with a hard strike. He started slow, gradually increasing the frequency of hits. He jumped up, spinning around in the air, continuing to strike the log. Soft brown curly locks of hair partially blocked his face. His hair was well-groomed, but at the moment, his somewhat lengthy curly locks seemed unkept, as his hair waved and flowed with his overly animated moves. The boy was shirtless, and his muscles were extremely well-toned. His upper body moved rhythmically in direct sync with his blows yet; at other times, he moved his feet and body setting a type of timing for the strikes. The boy had selected about a three-foot length of a branch from a nearby tree for his purpose. His selection was specific. He had chosen a very hard piece of wood. He noticed the sound as he tested for sounds produced from two different types of wood on wood. He also noticed a vibration traveling into his body as he struck the log. He heard, and he felt the sound. There were some hollow spots in the log. He smiled. And quickly hit the log again. And again. Different sounds were produced? Increasing the impact strikes of wood on wood. Hardly missing a beat, he quickly leaned the branch against the log. He took a step back then leaped almost as high as he could. Funneling his inner core for additional strength, he brought his foot down hard. He followed through with an extra thrust to ensure the branch broke. Almost exactly in half. It did. Just as he knew it would. The stick broke exactly in half. One piece he grabbed with his hand. The other he flipped in the air with his foot. He caught it with his left hand. The grip did not suit him. So as a quick method to compare the lengths and weight of his two sticks. At the same time, he flipped them in the air. Same height. Both sticks took the same number of end over end turns in the air. The "sticks" landed in each hand. He had held his hands with open palms at his waist awaiting their return. He immediately continued "playing," but this time, varying the softness and rhythm at a more peaceful, pleasing pace. He enjoyed the deep-sounding thunks. The boy put a hand on the log, jumped up and over the log, stopping himself by grabbing a branch of the log. He struck the branch a good distance from where he had his hand. He noticed it sounded and felt different than the log. He observed the sound and noticed the vibration he felt in his hand then stuck the branch much closer to his hand. Ouch. Not only was that a sharper sound or higher pitch, it hurt. All the way to his shoulder? *Wow*, he thought. Then he tried striking in various locations a little fast, then slow. He tried again to make a pleasing rhythmic sound.

To us, we might say, he was playing the log like today's drummers might play the drum. Bass or snare drums are considered percussion instruments and are of a large family of other percussion instruments like the xylophone, triangle and chimes just to name a few. A good percussionist requires practicing their skills to hit, rub, or shake the instrument with speed, strength, placement and timing. A drummer commonly sets the rhythm for a song. Various percussions can be used to keep rhythm in an orchestra and can be uniquely timed to add excitement or to reinforce emotional exclamations in a play. We might say the boy was practicing playing a musical instrument. Except his instrument was not technically man made.

He tested sounds from different areas of the log combining skills, agility, and ability. He paused. Now what sound to play? He stopped and stared straight ahead. Then he began to study his surroundings. The little boy looked around at everything—yet nothing. He listened. He thought, *I want to give love. Where does love come from?* The answer came back, "The heart." He listened as felt his own: *Bump-bump. Bump-bump.* He matched the sound on the log. *Thump-thump. Thump-thump.* A type of acknowledgment appeared in his face. A visible realization. He repositioned his stance. He steadied. Bent slightly at the knees. Refashioned his grip holding the "sticks," now balanced in his hands. Then continued. Both hands at the same time. *Thump-thump.* And again. He kept the same rhythm but raised each arm high in the air. Having to quicken speed to match the beat. Then he began alternating arms matching the slightly different sound of his heart as it sends blood and receives. *Thump-thump.* He began to hit harder. *Thump-thump.* Then hard and harder. Bark flew. Tiny chips of wood from the log and pieces of bark flew. Still, he hit harder. His heart was beating harder. He matched the intensity.

He didn't notice, but the mist that surrounded the area cleared. The Sun glistened more brilliantly upon him. He seemed aglow, in broad daylight. He eventually did notice, yet he was unfazed. He continued. His beat varying from hollow parts of the log to solid areas. As he continued, he heard water dripping from trees. Nearby mist had laid heavily on leaves until in ran off. To match the sound, he hit a branch with a clack. Now he mixed in a *clickity-clack* by smacking the sticks together and hitting the branch. He slid his sticks across knobs on the log. He repeated all with rhythm. Now adding a type of xylophone. Finally, he returned to an area of the log with one stick landing on a solid part of the log. The other stick landing on the hollow part. Arms high in the air now, landing extremely hard blows. His muscles bulged; his face grimaced with pleasure. He began to stomp his feet. Stomping in place. Like marching. He didn't see the cloud of mist swirl into a form. Almost human? It seemed to move and march in place too? Too focused, the boy did not notice. Now every part of him was intensely driven into playing this sound. Suddenly he stopped. He raked one of the sticks across the knobs of wood protruding from the log. Finishing with a clack on the branch. Unexpectedly, he jumped, spun in the air landing like an animal in defensive posture. Just before landing, he threw the stick at a nearby rock. He had the follow-through of a professional baseball player with his head tilted to the side. The stick struck the rock and ricocheted. The stick angled off toward a tree? His head was perfectly tilted where he thought the stick would've headed for the tree. It zinged past a cloud of mist that was now recoiling from once being fully enthralled to the boy's playing and actually marching in place. The cloud of mist was even rocking arms timed with its steps. His eyes widened. It was as if the mist noticed him see it. It quickly dissipated. He thought he saw a face? He stood. The mist spun like whirlwind of water. A mini water spout? Then it dissipated into the air in every direction. *What was that?* he thought? Did he see that? Was it real? He knew what he saw it was real! He stood for a moment. He looked. It all happened peaceful enough. Harmless. Could he do that again when it mattered?

No one else would've possibly known the internal emotions he felt as he played. No one would've noticed the overwhelming feeling which caused his eyes to well with water. The sensation throughout his body. The boy could not ever explain what just happened along with what he felt at the time it happened to anyone. He wanted so much to give to One who has everything yet he had nothing to give. Time to go then. He threw the other stick at the same rock. This time the stick bounced back in his direction. He had to step to catch it. The return was intentional. The curvature of the rock did not allow for a direct return. He knew it. But what was that cloud of mist? That, he did not know. In this boy's days, what was seen as normal would not be considered normal today. Some of what was seen in this boy's generation are not seen today but remain in earth or in this world. They are referred to as the unseen. This boy's generation in earth's beginning had many technological advancements. Today we think of earth's beginning as men barely in animal-skin clothing. And when they first left Eden, they were. It was the first time being clothed to step into the elements of a harsh world. But there were other reasons Adam and Eve were clothed in animal skin the day they left Eden. But those in this boy's generation were direct descendants of God's creation with knowledge, intellect, and wisdom far beyond today's man. Some of what is unseen today was unseen for this boy's generation too, but this boy's generation was not that far from God. So spiritual connections with the unseen were more easily recognizable, relatable, and acceptable. Most of today's generation is so far removed from God that when the unseen become seen, more and more people are really going to be in for a rude awakening. Although people are being prepared in movies and in the gaming world, it is not going to be the same as TV and the computer at all.

Many nearby animals took notice. Gathered in places just beyond his notice. Different species of animals. Some species that do not exist today. Beautiful multicolored birds with long feathers were tilting their head from side to side while he hit the log. These birds were a little different than the birds you see today. Varying from large cockatoo-type birds to large hummingbirds the size of today's eagles. It was if some of the birds and other animals were curious at what this one was just doing. Larger animals came close also to see this unusual noise. Many beasts. It was as if they were being drawn to him. Was it because of the similarities between many animals and very young children; both knowing no sin? Certainly many animals see and sense things man cannot see. This boy's intensity, innate abilities, combined with a deep, emotional, desirous motivation to please God was unparalleled with any other of his day. Let alone his age. Something inside caused him to be beyond his years in maturity. Yet no one would ever know. And how could they? No one knows what the spirit of another is truly like. Plus, no one else was there to hear. Or was there? There were birds nesting in trees over three hundred feet in the air. He headed home.

America's Four Branches Sprout From a Seed

The foliage was quite different when this boy lived on earth. There are trees today which were similar to trees this boy saw as com-

197

mon but not very many. For example, the *T. nudiflora* in Thailand and the red tingle in Australia. The United States has the redwood tree (*Sequoia sempervirens*), giant sequoia, and the dawn redwood. All three are of the same family of tree. These three trees are the last of their species today, currently located along the west coast, Washington, Oregon, and California. The Live Oak's natural range stretches along the south eastern cost of from Virginia through the Carolina's, Georgia and Florida, then on to Texas and Oklahoma. Some of these states protect the Live Oak also known as the Angel Oak, by law. All these various trees, most extremely large trees, lived extremely long lives—nine hundred to eleven hundred or even eighteen hundred to possibly twenty-two hundred years old—but unfortunately, many of the trees that existed or lived during this boy's generation would end or die before reaching old age. When the waters of the Great Flood receded some seeds of these magnificent trees were carried and deposited near coastal regions.

Known to live 1,500 years or more, the Live Oak's branches can reach up to 80 feet in height, spreading outward of over 100 feet or more, making its crown 150 feet in diameter or more. Its picturesque shape with large branches helped to contribute to its nickname, "Angel Oak." In America's early beginnings as a nation, the Live Oak was recognized as one of America's most precious natural resources by experts in the shipbuilding industry. When Congress authorized six frigates to be built as America's first official United States Navy, the Live Oak was used in the frigate's construction. The grain of the oak's branches seem to run through the branches in an entangled manner, making it a very difficult wood to work with. Especially, with the tools available to wood workers and ship builders of the late 1700s. The seeming "entanglement" of the oak's grains not only made it a difficult wood to work with, but the unique grain of the Live Oak or Angel Oak's wood cured into an extremely hard and long-lasting element-resistant wood. This was perfect for ships. The USS Constitution was launched October 21, 1797.

On August 19, 1812, the USS Constitution and the British frigate *Guerriere*, barely fifty yards apart, unleashed deadly cannon fire on each other. Eye witnesses gave accounts of cannon balls bouncing off the Constitution's oak sides, giving her the nickname "Ironsides." Today, her name "Old Ironsides" gives respect to her age and toughness, at the same time honoring the dignity and integrity to America's Constitution of which she was originally named after. Live Oak trees destined to be destroyed during the construction of an expressway near Charleston, South Carolina, and Live Oak's severely damaged during Hurricane Hugo found their way towards the 1992–1995 restoration of the USS Constitution. Replacing fife and pin rails, hatch coamings, sheet bitts, and futtocks on the US Navy's oldest active duty ship.

Why is it important to deviate so from a story of a little boy's life in early history with descriptions of the importance of trees and wood? We should consider that trees and wood would have been a highly valuable resource and would've played a critical role in almost every aspect of man's endeavors and his survival in his earliest of days. Only to name a few. His housing, his tools, and weapons, much of which consisted of wooden components in their construction. We could consider that the quantity and variety of trees in early times may have been in greater abundances of foliage than today. Like the Brazilian rain forest once contained a large variety of trees. In the early days, it seems there were some very special trees. This boy would come to learn why cities were constructed of specially honed rock or a hewn stone to exactly match at placement, ensuring an impenetrable seal. The walls also required a minimum thickness; they were extremely thick rock walls. There are things that exist that can pass through walls and cracks of almost all building materials but not through a certain thickness of rock. The walls of the city required at least a certain height too because there were things that could simply go over some of the smoothest and tallest of walls. Many of these living creatures still exist to this day but are of the unseen.

As it turns out, the Vikings living in inhospitable wintry conditions in the far Northern regions of Northern Europe and were seemingly disconnected from the rest of the civilized world in the late 700s to early 800s and prior. There would be language barriers for exchange of ideas over hundreds of years. Vast distances between lands would require dietary differences. Communal living would require laws and differences of those in neighboring regions eventually causing conflict. Unfortunately, Vikings didn't find much need for writing and documenting their historical culture. Most documentation of the Vikings began with the raids west instead of eastward into what we call Russia today. It was the people of what became known as the British Isles who wrote of the Vikings and their raids. The Vikings had greater successes acquiring wealth and land when they headed west into the Isles of Britain. Their desires to raise their children and commitments to family life helped them to integrate into England, eventually becoming some of England, Scotland, and Ireland's greatest of patriots. Some of the Viking custom of laws were of extremely high moral fiber and fit in nicely with some of England, eventually forming some of America's founding principles. It would also be assuredly safe to say that the founding principles of rights, freedom, the people having authority within their government, and the precious gift of self-governance were taken from processes of what historically did and didn't work from thousands of years of extremely diverse nations all over the world. But this was a time of separate kingdoms made up of noblemen or barons within a small group of isles that would unite to become a great nation of vast wealth and power. No matter the reasons when seeking to repair a disconnect of huge differences between Viking religion and the majority Christian religion of eighth to ninth century of England; instead, it might be worthy to notice the similarities.

There are important similarities in religious worship of the Hebrews documented by Moses in the Book of Bereshith or Genesis and the Viking justice system and religion.

Abraham had two sons, Ishmael and Issac. From Ishmael was born Islam and Muslim faiths which look to Allah. From Issac came Israel (Jacob) or Hebrew and Jewish faiths looking to Adonay. Allah and Adonay are one in the same. Issac and Ishmael were raised in different regions each dominated with very different challenges and diverse languages. So God built a personal relationship with both sons of Abraham and their decedents in a very personal way that each "isle," group or nation would come to know Him. Both "isles" and their decedents would need to become great warriors.

Moses was a decedent of Issac. Moses married the daughter of a descendant of Ishmael. This might seem unusual today but God desires that we should learn His wisdom. When Moses's father-in-law witnessed that Moses spent almost every waking moment administering, deciding, and rendering justice in all manner of God's law, all diverse disputes even unto marital spats and divorce; his father-in-law made a recommendation. He recommended Moses select Elders from groups, isles, or clans to administer law and justice within their tribes. Moses decided on twelve. Thus the twelve tribes of Israel were born each with their own banner. The elders or leaders would bring cases that they could not decide to Moses periodically. Elders became *representatives* of their people.

Even some of the Viking linage could be of the nine and a half to ten tribes of Israel that were taken into captivity, sold as slaves, or what has become to be known as *scattered* after Israel's 300 year Civil War. It is written that Spartans who became part of a united Greece most certainly descended from the original tribes of Israel that were of these *scattered* tribes. These scattered children had to leave home without the Ark with God's presence and Livitical Priesthood that were proficient in God's Word and law. Although knowledge of God's law would weaken down through generations, the ten tribes that were scattered were specifically raised by God as warriors to fight. Not just any warriors, these warriors were physically, mentally and spiritually conditioned from birth to fight sons of fallen angels. Fallen angles were once known as watchers, eventually worshiped as gods, and for this generation known as aliens from other galaxies, planets, or worlds. To defeat their children and resist the fallen angels required belief in life after death. So there would be those that were *chosen* generation after generation and shown proof of life after death. So that others would believe there were those to whom truth (the Word) would be revealed until the *last day*. The Spartans and Vikings certainly fit the description of fierce warriors and both isles believed strongly in life after death.

Although the Vikings looked to false gods, their gods all seemed to be sons of gods with unusually long lives. For example: One-eyed Odin, Thor and Loki all sought an *apple* from a *tree* so they could live another thousand years. The Vikings also believed in lower or lessor heavens with one heaven above all called Valhalla. It was in this heaven that after death they would have ever lasting life. Their justice system was of clans with annual group gatherings called "Things." At these gatherings were festive celebrations, religious ceremonies to include sacrifice. It was at these gatherings Elders also met to discuss law, difficult cases to decide, issues between clans, trade and conflicts with other cultures. Similar to America's Legislative Branches, Supreme Court, and similar to the original twelve tribes of the nation Israel. In any case it should be well known that the once the Vikings (Norse or Northerners) were fully established in Great Britain helping to form independent kingdoms they eventually united under one banner bringing much of their culture and important principles of the common man governing with them to Great Britain. There were other Vikings which integrated with the French. The Viking Chieftain Rollo changed his name to Robert after he was baptized a Christian and went on to be the first ruler of Normandy in 911 AD. Many Vikings became baptized as if finally hearing the call of One True Ever Living God; Our Father's call through Jesus Christ. So, can someone who worshiped another God be saved? Oh sure, there would be much delight in heaven over that transformation.

Some similarities also existed with the Egyptian worship of their gods, and the worshiping practices of the Incas, Aztecs, and Mayan empires of the third to sixteenth century. The many similarities all seem to relate to the knowledge of the sons of God, but they are somehow mistaken or misinterpreted to mean the sons of God were to be worshiped or idolized.

Many did not know that the similarities were purposeful. Fallen angels who ruled were copying what they had seen from the One on Most High that seem to work with man. But when man looked to fallen angels, *their guidance only led to ramifications and consequences which required fixes or remedies. Then solutions only seemed to compound problems which soon would require fixing only to complicate things further that eventually would build chaos without remedy. The framers of the United States Constitution warned of this outcome and referred to this ultimate failure as despotism. Many of the framers there-*

fore made strong recommendations that the only way for the nation's success and continued happiness for citizens was that the nation's children should be taught to know of Jesus Christ and God.

None seemed to know the Creator, the one true God, or the Father of all things. Except for Moses and the Hebrews (Israelites) who lived in God's presence through some generations. Moses's father-in-law did witness and testified truthfully and later decedents of Ishmael were rewarded with testimony from Muhammad (PBUH). Muhammad's testimonies were later written in the Quran.

In both the Hebrew and Norse religion, there were several important trees. In the Norse religion, there was an ash tree (Yggdrasil) that connected three realms, worlds, or heavenly bodies, of which there are actually more than three. The Norse knew of a realm below the middle world where the dead gathered. Both the Hebrew and Norse religion knew of this middle earth, heavenly body as where the dead rest in Earth. The souls of giants (Nephilim or Anakim) are left to roam on earth forever. Could Vikings have adopted or accepted some of the Hebrew people into clans, or could the Norsemen who would eventually become the Normans of England actually be from one of the lost tribes of the Hebrews (Israel) who migrated northward, only to drift somewhat from their original one true God and be snared by the fowler once again, drawn into worshiping fallen angels? Without the ark of the covenant, the necessity of survival would permit the highly trained in combat to overtake leadership from any Levites or priest. Seers would flourish more easily, at first pleasing leadership with whispers from fallen angels or sons of God. In the Book of Genesis, there were Sons of God or angels, which came to earth to live among men. The Norse referred to these angels as gods, which by the way would be completely understandable. These Angels or gods would have great powers and intellect far beyond mans. Both religions consisted of a tree of life, which bore fruit. In the Norse religion, the Norse gods relied on a "magic fruit" for longevity of life. These similarities made it much easier for the Normans to be baptized, many becoming Christians. The Norse Christians would go on to play major roles in England's leaders. The Norse not only became accepted as kings and rulers of Normandy but even became great rulers in England and France.

An armed conflict inflicting many causalities in 1188 at Gisor resulted in the cutting down of a very special elm tree. The conflict became known as the "cutting of the Elm," bringing about the permanent split of the Ordre de Sion originating from Abbey on Mount Zion and the Knights Templar (Order of the Temple). It seems to be unknown as to why the meeting between King Henry II of England and King Phillip of France took place. Henry II, accompanied with his son Richard I Couer de Lion and Templars fought against Phillip and a large military force. It was said that Richard and the Templars greatly outnumbered, fought bravely spilling much blood of the French, but in the end, it is documented after King Phillip's victory, he ordered his French carpenters and wood cutters to cut down the over eight-hundred-year-old tree. It was said to be over fifty-four feet in diameter at its base. For some reason King Richard and his men arriving at the tree first had even built iron around its base to protect it.

There are several moments in history, which at the time were felt to be so important that many sacrifices were made. Thousands upon thousands thought that these values and principles so important they must be made permanent for all men. Forever enduring, no matter what. Precious were the lives lost. Every bit as much as your own. Men and woman lost everything they owned and had. Many sent to brutally die in prisons. Many were tortured to death that the sun would shine forth on lands where liberty, freedoms, and rights could be enjoyed so that everyone would have the right to pursue happiness. There are several of these times documented. From these examples came the foundation of this generation's greatest tree. The following are just two examples which laid some of the most important frameworks of the United States of America's Constitution. So important were these ideals and principles that just didn't seem to fit in the framework of a governmental structure that the ratification of the Constitution was jeopardized. Opposition from the representatives chosen for the task of establishing the framework for America's government was so great, several of the large states insisted in not becoming part of the new Union. Only when George Washington and some others suggested allowing the First Amendment to be included in the Constitution was there agreement toward the states ratifying the Constitution. These First Amendments were called the Bill of Rights. So strong was the insistence that the people had irrevocable rights that the states almost never unified. For the people to have rights, authority, self-governance, and freedom that could never be taken away, certain principles had to be rock-solid. Assurance of freedom and the right to pursue happiness could only be ensured for the people if the principles and ideals were to be based upon God's Word. The United States would have to be built upon a rock. This boy had no clue he would be a critical component in sharing forward God's Word on earth and the formation of a stone that, in turn, would also become the rock upon which the United States was built. Without this boy, God's gift of freedom would not have been included in the formation of the United States and its Constitution. So powerful are the principles and wording of the Constitution, including its Bill of Rights, that it became a model for many nations to emulate almost verbatim.

Not only the right to gather but the right to protect yourself, your wife, your children, your property, your neighbor and your community can be found in the Book of Esther within the pages of the Old Testament of the Bible. Not to mention the *freedom of religion*. But little is known in truth of additional intellectual consideration of the right of self-defense from ancient history passed forward and implemented in the days of Assuerus, King Artaxerxes, Mardochai, and Esther, which was around 450–480 BC. The Book of Esther KJV 16:2–6 clearly espouses the abuses of goodness of some regional leaders, the oppression of people, and the breakout of madness (despotism) by lies and crafty fraud, deceiving those who would listen and then having them judged by persons deriving justice from their own nature and standards, not judged by people who live as the defendant. Freedom and equity did not exist. And drafters of the Bill of Rights considered Esther 16:4 as seen in the phrases "violation of the laws of humanity" and "the justice of God." Finally, in reference to Esther 16:20 is the right of self-defense unto death, even against regional authority who seeks to revoke the rights of man endowed by His Creator. This type of defense could only be achieved with equal weaponry. Obviously, the drafters of our Constitution relied heavily on God's Word and the Book of Esther when drafting the Second Amendment in the Bill of Rights for each citizen.

The king of Persia during these days would often accompany his army in war. During the period of about fifty years, the king of Persia, Xerxes, and his father fought four major battles with Greece. During one of these battles, King Xerxes (Ahasue'rus) left a Jew named Mordecai to rule in his stead or while he was gone. Mordecai, as acting king, sent a written decree carried by posts (couriers) throughout all the land that the Jews were entitled to the right to defend themselves.

> Wherein the king granted the Jews which were in every city to "gather themselves together"" and to stand for their life, to destroy, to slay and to cause to perish, all the power of the people and province that would assault them, …(Esther 8:11 KJV)
>
> The copy of the writing for a commandment to be given in every province was published unto all people, and that the Jews should be ready against that day to avenge themselves on their enemies. (Esther 8:13, KJV)

The right to gather, have meetings, and express your freedoms, including religion, would be adopted as some of America's most treasured principles. But the ideals would not simply carry forward. It seems despite the principle of freedom and the right for one to protect property, family, and oneself, after Esther and her uncle Mordecai had proven the model throughout Asia for citizens; wars and loss of life would have to happen for freedom to be won from tyranny over and over. This was finally well recognized and well-documented almost 1,700 years later. Recognizing citizens' rights would not come easily, with known abuses of trials without a jury of their peers and the citizens' own government military quartering troops, seizing food and personal belongings from its own citizens. Preventing the seizing of property and protection of privacy became a must! A search warrant from the Judicial branch approved by peer group became a requirement before entry. Millions upon millions sacrificed everything they had unto death that others might live in freedom.

In England, beginning with what would become known as the Magna Carta 1215, a series of charters in 1216, 1217, and 1225 followed. England's Norman barons were a critical component forcing King John under threat of Civil War to sign the Magna Carta of 1215 and the ideals contained therein. Many of these ideals, principles, and values were so treasured as to be enumerated and encapsulated in America's Constitution that American citizens could enjoy their life and liberties in a land in which freedom would endure forever. A few of these are as follows:

1. *Government would fall under the Rule of Law.* Known then as jurisprudence. Prior to the Magna Carta, the king was the law, the ruler. The king was independent of law.

2. *No delay or denial of justice.*

3. *Habeas corpus.* A person did not have to pay for a writ of inquisition (pretrial hearing). A request for justice was free and could not be refused. *Habeas corpus* was so important a principle of judicial law it was embedded into American judicial system. The only place it can be found in America's Constitution is for "its protection." Article 1, section 9, Clause 2: "It takes an act of congress to suspend writ of *habeas corpus* and only in a time of rebellion or invasion and the public safety may *require it.*"[*] Once *habeas corpus* is suspended, we know it as "martial law." Ironically, the judicial branch throughout every state in United States has abused the original intent of *habeas corpus* in American law.

4. *A widow could not be forced to be married and could keep her inheritance.*

5. *The church was free.* Prior to Magna Carta, kings were appointing bishops.

---

[*] The Making of America The Substance and Meaning of the Constitution, W. Cleon Skousen NCCS, 1985

6. *Freemen were no longer to be arrested, jailed, without lawful sentence of their peers.*
7. *Liberty* or *liberties* and the term *free man* is repeated throughout the sixty-three clauses in the Magna Carta bringing forth to this day ideas and principles supporting life, liberty, and the pursuit of happiness.

For this generation, this is referred to as freedom and rights. The lifeblood of people over thousands of years has been drained, as has Lake Meade over a hundred years, all to decrescendo from which was once a rock-solid Constitutional foundation of law supporting self-governance, freedom, and authority to ensure governmental support of freedom. From a Constitutional structure, it somehow turned to looking to "spirits" and pursuing "dreams," with Lady Liberty as the spirit, symbol, or idol of freedom and Lady Justice as the spirit and ministrant of law, justice, and fairness. There is one in New York Harbor and one in front of the Supreme Court of the United States, holding a magistrate in her hand. A spirit is everywhere—the American spirit. On top of the Capitol Building is another statue of a female spirit of freedom. So too in Nashville, Tennessee, she stands—a giant Athena, the goddess of wisdom—in a large Parthenon, and ironically, she holds the goddess of victory Nike in her hand.

For this generation, God began pouring His spirit out like rain across the entire land upon the heads of everyone, everybody, and anybody. What an awesome gift and offer. So people began pulling down statues, but sadly, they could not hear God clearly. The people look to a metal woman, the wrong spirits, the color of their skin or, to their choice of reproductive identity. God granting freedoms to find ways toward Him through His only begotten Son was a gift to aid in going back to Eden or heaven and eternal life, but turning to a lady who provides pathways of reckless abandonment in the ministration of justice supported by a morality that shifts as the wind blows for each generation and worshipping a statue of a woman who offers freedom of sexual immorality and offers the loss of identity toward a seemingly happy death all lead to a very sad ending indeed.

Vines can be good for nurturing soil, but too many vines strangle the weaker trees. And even too many vines destroy much-needed vegetation required for ongoing life and necessary trees that produce life-sustaining fruits.

Trees certainly are not to be worshiped but valued as precious life-sustaining critical components of life. Trees and branches (not unwanted vines) are such an important physical part of life on earth that can be considered as flesh or skin that one cannot live without. The tree is an organ of the earth similar to the lung of a human. The earth would become barren and void of life without its various and special trees. This is why important parables and analogies have been made in comparison to a tree, its roots, its leaves, its seeds, its canopy, and the fruit it bears. For enlightenment, one does not need to know the tree, but it would certainly aide man's life to know the tree is alive, is a form of life, and the importance the tree and its branches forever enduring. Eventually, men and women will come to know the entire universe is alive. It's just not a life-form easily understood by man. Because of the magnitude of the universe and the infinitesimal manner men and women think; men and women were distracted from their purpose despite originally being created to be caretakers of a world with ultimate goals of universal caretakers. It seems the first step was an immediate misstep—a slip, a fall, a wrong turn on major intergalactic confluences of forces not easily seen or understood. We could easily just skip to the boy's life without some seemingly digressive descriptions of the importance of this boy who only seems to be seeking boyhood curiosities but, is actually driven by deep desires of love. Not love just for himself and his family but for everybody and everything. As he grows and is still young, he just doesn't understand why he is driven or why he seeks answers to many questions. After all, he is just another boy, as are millions of others.

It was men not unlike this boy that thought of similarities of original man and trees that lived to be a thousand years old, which bore seeds, and some even edible fruit. This principle of a tree which bears fruit was thought so highly of we have actually worded in our constitution a framework built like a tree. With its three branches. Some might think of our Constitution's roots as its people. But consider that which was planned not long after the beginning. America was built and resides on a rock. The rock being its Constitution meant to be forever enduring and surely made to be amended but not changed and not stood on to make lofty decrees of destructive and hateful behaviors toward the end of loving neighbors as you would love yourself. So how do the people fit in to this tree? The framers **intended that** *the people are to be the fourth branch* of government.

The three branches were named Executive, Legislative, and Judicial. *The fourth branch* is implied as was *habeas corpus. The fourth branch* was assumed as an unspoken truth, just as checks and balances were implied, assumed, and built into the Constitution as unspoken truths. Although a word search of the Constitution will never produce the words *checks and balances* as a result. The people were to perform their duty by voting. The very first step in the *checks and balances* formula for success. Finally, the people were to perform their duty as a "jurist." The people performing jury duty service (a duty to serve) were not only to determine guilt or innocence or, an award; the *common law jury* was created as the final check of **Legislative Branch law, the** Supreme Court's ruling of constitutionality of the newly created law, and the Executive Branch disposition to carry out the law. The *common law jury* was to determine if the law was applicable within their community, thereby creating the balance required between the governed and the governing body. In the 1930s, the judicial branches throughout each state became furious at the people for knowing they had authority to nullify a law that was not applicable or applied a ministration of inequity or injustice within in their community. They felt the people were usurping law and instituted what became known as *jury nullification*. Virtually eliminating the people's right to determine if the law was applicable or not. But make no mistake, the people were to be the first step and final check in the *check and balance* formula of America's constitution. Therefore, the *people* were always meant to be the *fourth branch* of America's government. As their duty to serve, performing as our government's most critical branch of the tree. This boy had no idea that he was to become a major step or gift toward the many gifts and opportunities for the people. He was just a boy with a loving heart.

This boy's family tree would be written of and translated into more languages than any other family tree. That is because God would ensure His word was carried forward by man and passed on even unto this generation and the next generations to come. As with all families, trials, rifts, and tribulations would bring stressors that can rip families apart. As with all families, devotion, trust, and love would hold many family members together. There was one key ingredient that if man was not careful to avoid would cause the end of everything: envy and jealousy, also known as covetousness. Seeking what another has would come to destroy nations and kingdoms. This family that grew into groups of peoples also known as isles, thriving communities, and bustling cities are written of in a book known as *Sefer Maaseh Bereshith*, the "Book of Creation." The book is believed to be written by Moses. *Bereshith* means "in the beginning," and when the book was translated into Greek, the word *origin* seemed to work for creation. So the Greek word for origin is *Genesis*.

The boy that was making music on a *fallen tree* with a *broken branch* was trying with all his heart to reach out and please who he knew to be the Father of all things.

THE BOY'S FAMILY BEGINS WITH THE UNIVERSE AS A LIFE-FORM NOT UNDERSTOOD BY MAN

The planet earth has at least three life-forms since its beginning that have never been fully understood or completely explored but have caused rousing curiosity and vividly stirred the imagination of many. That which has a *face* or a *mouth* is alive. From the Book of Creation, the "*face* of the *deep*, the *face* of the *waters*, the *ground* opened its *mouth*."

The complete body of man including a brain and mind that the body would function as living being began with that which was created with *three* major ingredients. *Water* flowed upward from the *ground*. What would eventually come to be known as *life water* flowed upward from the midst of the earth as a *mist*, which in turn would cover ground. Has one ever seen a geyser that its water eventually turns into mist? Now imagine the unimaginable of earth: giant geysers possibly shooting water thousands of feet in the air; large bodies of water becoming heated by the sun, causing evaporation; cooler air at night forcing water downward; condensation forming around warmer areas, creating fog and mist; and live trees storing the sun's radiation and attracting the condensation or mist as a cup with cool water forms condensation on the outside from warmer air. Of the different materials containing water, one might notice a *clay* cup allows less condensation or water to roll and drip away or escape.

God formed man with *dust* "as a potter fashioning a cup, chalice, or bowl from clay" *with a mist nearby*. The third major ingredient was *God's breath*. God breathed *His spirit* into man.

Over the centuries some would be led astray in search of a "Holy Grail (clay cup) or Fountain of Youth (life water)." When all along it was actually Jesus Christ they longed for. Jesus showed us that he was the divine *clay cup* and if we drink of *his life* water (blood) and eat of *his flesh* (his word) from him (a clay cup), then once again we too can become as the first man of clay (Adam) ready to receive God's Breath as in the beginning. And for us overcoming our own continuations of down fall with forgiveness and life water we can be blessed with eternal life.

The first man would be named Adam by his Father. In the beginning, man and animals communicated easily in similar fashions with sounds of clicks and whistles, guttural grunts and growls, and rolls of the tongue combined with spiritual, soulful, heartfelt, connections and other physical techniques. This communication would sound alien to us today. Since man was made in the image of God and Elohim, so Adam would learn from his father and Elohim a heavenly manner of communication. Of course Adam would come to relate to his Father in a very personal way as all children do when coming to know their father. But for this generation the differences in communication, physical and spiritual requirements of then and now is by far too great for us to replicate God's name as in the beginning. The original pronunciation is very powerful and meaningful, and it becomes a humbling experience to try and replicate it, especially when delivered by the Creator of all that exists Himself. It would be God and Elohim to teach man to use these sounds or speak respectfully with dignity skillfully and artfully but all in ways to suggest transference of messaging or communication with respect.

When one so powerful, mighty, and righteous says His own name, the sound and pronunciation develops a breath as a gust of wind, and it becomes an unforgettable life experience. The sound and effects accompanying the acoustic energy, which would have had effects on surrounding elements, can and will contain a life-altering experience. It was the sound and name Moses could not replicate. While in Egypt Moses had been a prince in Egypt for forty years he probably attended worship services of Egyptian Gods before coming to know God personally and intimately on Mt Sinai. The Gods of Egypt were actually fallen angels. Moses was so humiliated and humbled after hearing God pronounce his own name; Moses would not dare utter God's name ever again. For humans who have sinned, being in God's presence causes immediate death. It was only through esoteric and metaphysical transfiguration could a physical presence be on earth with man. For man to stand in that presence without dying, requirements still had to be met. Because of their relationship, being in the presence of God, and the importance of who Moses would be required to be for God's purpose, messaging and leading the people required life-altering physical changes inner and outwardly, which became clearly visible to others. For this and other reasons such as Aaron being way more righteous and priestly than Moses, God told Moses to get Aaron to replicate God's name and to have himself be a messenger to the people. Basically Moses became a living conduit or what some refer to a religious relic. This probably required Moses to be very careful around people. All was easier for Aaron because Aaron was priestly and mostly incapable of sin, especially when compared to the way Moses had to be brought forward, being the only one capable for what God would need for the coming generation and generations to come.

The life of Moses had for forty years been one of royalty and utter sin, even killing. Hopefully, this helps the reader understand God's name cannot just be tossed about but, when building personal relationships it can be very respectful to try and pronounce someone's name as pleases them.

God's presence would transfer from afar through a window. To meet scientific explanations, scientist call it a wormhole because there is transference and transfiguration from where time may not be relative to an earthly world to where time is present because of planetary axial spinning, solar orbits, and satellite orbits—all which spin, creating magnetic fields, gravitational forces, solar light spectrum frequencies called radiation, and rays of the sun. So it is a transfer from where the forces that affect time to a place where forces that affect time are not the same. It's like saying different time zones are not close.

When God's presence passes through, there is an alteration of physical barriers. The Bible calls these barriers a firmament. The barrier has to be firm because the barrier separates in some cases less dense matter, a different time relevancy, and living creatures of pure forms of energy from a world dependent upon dense matter and the bonding of molecules and molecular structures. Man calls the passages, pathways, or windows between the heavens and earth portals, wormholes, or time warps between dimensions. That way, man steers others away from the explanations of the different heavenly bodies that were written from over three thousand years ago, giving credit to man's knowledge of discovery and not God's shared wisdom of divinity and divine nature.

It might be easier for this generation to understand if heavenly bodies are likened to platforms of the internet universe. Where traversing platforms is protected by codes and coding (like how Xbox and PlayStation are not compatible), compatibility between the two (Xbox and PlayStation) is possible but requires agreement from the two different owners and recoding or hacking. Entry into heaven can only be done by agreement with God and by God's Word. For this generation God's Word walked with us in the flesh and showed the only way permissible for us. Any other way is a violation of heaven's secrets. Punishment for revealing heavenly secrets makes even son's of God terrified, tremble, and shake with fear.

Code violations or hacking by man trying to back door heaven since the beginning or trying to find windows for access or ways through the firmaments between heavenly bodies are similar to platform hacking. Of important note: these secrets were revealed to man by the fallen. God knows it. They know Him as their Father, and God knows them as His sons. But just as when some grow older at home in their dad's house and break curfew, only to come home and find the doors locked from the coming and going of a child as they please does not bode well at their dad's house, neither will sons of God coming and going as they please throughout their Father's house. God will not allow it to continue much longer. This generation is to see some major changes.

Even for this generation and until the end and even the worst of the wicked and evildoers must be told and know there is opportunity to be saved along with the most casual of sinners that may not even know clearly they are sinning. All can be forgiven and seek salvation. And so that you may come to know God better, one still must try to understand that it is very important to know that science and scientific explanations will never match or equalize divinity and God's power. Much will remain unexplained until each individual comes to know God. As an individual builds a closer and more personal relationship with God, He will pour out His wisdom unto each child as their very personal and intimate relationship grows. Wisdom will abound and pour like rain but never more than the individual can handle.

Let's continue with the story of the boy's family beginning with the father:

Enoch wrote of God as The Holy Great One, The Eternal God, Lord of Majesty,& King of Ages Abraham, Jacob, Issac knew God as *El Shaddai* or God Almighty God shared with Moses & Aaron a much more personal name 'YHWH or YHVH' which only Aaron used YaH'-WeH, YaH'-VeH Yah'-Weh, Yah'weh, Yahweh (I Am 'power & authority who gives life, breath & spirit') Follow on Rabbi's changed YHWH or YHVH to Adonay or Adonai Known as God or Jehovah today or Allah by children of Ishmael or as Jesus taught "Our Father in Heaven"						
First Children: Elohim, Son's of God, Angels, & Watchers (Son's of God)						
Adam		First man		Created Ø AM Died 930 *AM		
Eve		Created from the rib of man		Meaning "The Mother of All the Living" Age unknown		
Children of Adam of Eve Cain's Descendants				Prodigies	Birth	Death
Cain	Age unknown	Able (Killed by Cain)	Age unknown	Seth	130 AM-1042 AM*	
Enoch	Age unknown			Enos	235 AM-1140 AM	
Irad	Age unknown			Kenan	325 AM-1235 AM	
Mehujael	Age unknown			Mahalalel	390 AM-1285 AM	
Methusael	Age unknown			Jared	460 AM-1422 AM	
Lamech (2 wives) 4 children	Adah (1st wife) 2 sons	Zillah (2nd wife) 1 son 1 daughter	Ages unknown	Enoch	622 AM-987 AM	
	Jabal	Tubal-cain	Ages unknown	Methuselah	687 AM-1656 AM	
	Jubal	Naamah Meaning: pleasant, gracious (Noah's wife)	Ages unknown	Lamech	874 AM-1651 AM	
The Great Flood	1656 AM*			Noah (Married Naamah) 3 sons	1056 AM-2006 AM	
		Shem (white)	Japheth (red)	Ham (black)		

*AM *Anno Mundi*: In the Year of the World. The years of *Anno Mundi* and the Hebrew Calendar are the same.

The first children were sons of God or angels and not meant to reproduce. Sons of God were commonly referred to as stars, mountains, or angels. It is not *known by man* if God's next creation (man) was meant to reproduce. What is known is that man disobeyed God, which caused the Father to tell his children they must leave home and build their own home. God clothed His children before they left home, and we learn it was after this then came their first offspring. What is slowly learned over the many years of man is that there is a longing of the Father that his children return home, and many of his children want to return home to their father.

Cain murdered his brother Abel from jealousy. Cain sought forgiveness, fearing death from others for murdering his brother. God heard Cain's cries of regret. God promised none would kill Cain for fear of God's wrath of vengeance. To ensure Fulfillment of His promise God marked Cain so that Cain would be unique and unmistakably different than any other man. So much so, none would mistake him. Try to imagine marked Cain's skin or flesh becoming a remarkable mix of colors, even possibly ever changing in front of man's eyes—a shifting, changing mix of a bright white, scarlet red, and a dark black. The first thought might be one of a distasteful appearance, but in actuality, it was quite the opposite. It was so unique as to be striking and hard to look away. Cain's fleshly and physical appearance would actually be extremely beautiful. Undoubtedly, Cain's offspring would bear some kind of fleshly difference from others, if not the same as their father, Cain. Noah and Naamah, a descendant of Cain, married, and it was after this mix of linage that God informed man of the reduction of life longevity. But the reduction in life expectancy was certainly from a huge change in the global climate but probably mostly due to the change in soil content after the flood. The fruit was so nutritious and high in proteins before the flood, man and animals did not have to eat meat. Many summations could be ventured about the descendants of Cain and the mix. God's second written example of forgiveness of sin. With each occurrence came change. With sin comes change. First Adam and Eve then Cain.

Obviously, it's love that over the years produces a continued mix just as in Noah and Naamah overlooked their obvious differences of fleshly appearance. Naamah was no doubt striking and extremely beautiful in physical appearance and in all aspects of character. Cain was quite possibly a remarkably attractive and good-looking man in all aspects. Noah was probably, well, Noah. Because when Noah was born and first opened his eyes, blue light shot from them and across the room. Still wet from the water of the mother's womb, Noah immediately jumped up with arms held high and began singing glorious praises to God. His son's actions at birth horribly frightened his da, Lamech, so much so that he ran from the room, crying out for his da, Methuselah, for answers. Once Lamech found his da, his da knew there could be only one way to know. Methuselah knew and was told never to do what he did next. The fear was too much to overcome. Methuselah called out to his da who had translated into heaven as Jesus would thousands of years later. Methuselah's da explained Noah was a critical part of God's plan and not to worry. Noah was special, all right, but toward God's purpose. None knew then, but many would come to know that Noah walked with God. Many would just stay clear. Noah would come to need the gifts he was given at birth. But this is not the story of Noah, not yet. It's the story of his great-grandfather as a boy.

Once consumed can a word and a piece of fruit do very similar things to the human body?

Some trees and fruit might not be available today that were bountiful on earth in the beginning. But there was fruit which was not available in the earliest of days, which was made available today, intended to be available today from the beginning. This boy did not know he would be part of all that. But he would grow to be shown.

During this boy's life, not only was the vegetation and foliage on earth vastly different than today. In addition to today's plant life, there were a variety of different species that went extinct or might we say, many went dormant. And as there are geological changes happening to earth for this generation, new species of plants, animals, and other living creatures are to be discovered. These new species are not new but merely lay hidden or dormant. Climate and terrain weren't totally different than today. There were similarities, but this boy grew up among the earliest of man and the earth was like a new car never driven by anyone yet. These are the days when the earth still had that "new car smell." The soil was greatly different than today. Much of the earth was covered in extremely rich soil. The plants thrived in a manner almost unimaginable. For example, additives such as nitrogen that today's farmers add to the soil for corn to grow was not necessary during this boy's lifetime. In other words, in early times using fecal matter as fertilizer for agriculture was not necessary. After the great flood, many geological changes, including the richness and nutrients of the soil, caused many agricultural changes. Many things have changed.

The birds that built their nest over 300 feet high in the trees stood, on average, ten to twelve feet tall. The wing span was about twenty-eight to thirty-two feet. Once mature, the difference in size of these particular birds was based upon sex. The slightly smaller birds were females and were of a lighter shade but both of the exact pattern and color. Extremely difficult to see in the trees they nested in. These birds had feathers that were a red and green almost, a tiger stripe pattern. Red legs and green claws. The same color of the wood of the tree. Its beak was a camouflaged perfect blend of greens matching the tree. The size of these birds forced them to attack down sun (opposing the sun) to prevent casting a shadow on its prey. While the little boy had banged away, just before creating a likable, percussive tune, he had snuck a glance over his shoulder. There was one these birds clearly watching him with great interest. This one was on a low branch about thirty feet in the air. Its head tilted and moved for a clear view of the boy. The boy had noticed its interest in him. Now it was after the boy had finished, retrieved his stick in midair, and began walking home, the bird made its move.

Suddenly, it launched in his direction. The boy recognized the bird was not attacking from the usual "opposing sun strike," which the birds were known for. Surely that did not matter right now. There was no time for hesitation. First dipping. Starting slow but gained speed with its muscular thirty-foot wing span quickly. Dirt, blades of grass, and small twigs lifted off the ground to create force of lift required for a bird this size and weight for flight. Without hesitating, the boy leaped, ducked, tucked, and rolled down into a slight hillside cove surrounded by some boulders. He finished his roll by planting himself into a defensive posture. Beyond his years, he revealed innate abilities, agility, and physical preparedness. This boy was of linage from men and women who were just a little lower than angels. These men and women were in the image of God and Elohim, meaning not only were they of God's creation but were created to look like God, be like God, be God's children, and to be taught by God and Elohim. These men and woman had knowledge of God-like character and being, but because they were misled and disobeyed their Father, they had to leave home (Eden). One way to explain the ramifications of their early departure from their Father's house and His protection was they weren't ready. Man and woman weren't finished nurturing. They weren't finished with all their training and mentoring, and although hundreds of years in age, essentially they left home before they were completely mature. They weren't ready. So this boy's abilities, some call instinct. Not really instinct. These were gifts he had sought. His pursuits had been internal. No one would've or could've have known. None other possessed the aspects of this boy's curiosities, desires, and motivation. He was extremely different from others of his generation. His only defense now being a small branch. He quickly visually assessed his surroundings. This small grassy hole or, more like an indent in the ground, partially surrounded by boulders would only temporarily keep him out of reach of the bird's claws. If the bird's wings remained extended. He knew if this bird really wanted him, it would land near the boulders and reach downward with its long neck to get him. Or just jump in from the side. He was easy prey for this size of bird.

A bird this size could easily pick up a man and carry the man high in the air. High enough to drop a man from a deadly height easily. Even if the man didn't die from the injuries, a man falling from such a height would be in no shape for worthwhile resistance. After the drop, the bird would simply return to feast.

As the bird closed quickly, strangely enough, the sun darkened. *Why?* he thought. He looked up. A different giant bird was attacking from directly above. Its claws already outreached. These claws looked like rugged, red, slightly curved swords. He moved his branch with both hands in a position to protect his chest and face. Then came an indescribable impact just above him. Giant feathers went everywhere. It happened too fast to see. Did the two birds just collide directly above him? Feathers went everywhere. So many he was completely covered. He paused long enough that he could feel that the feathers were warm. *The body temperature of the bird,* he thought.

The squawking noises were loud. He'd heard it before. Just not this close! Regaining his composure, he climbed the boulders just enough to peek over. One was flying away, while one had its back to him with its wings spread wide. Head held high in the air squawking, changing to a chirp-like chant. Clearly watching the other fly away. For some reason, the boy could tell. He knew. The boy slowly walked from behind the extremely large bird toward its front, carrying an extremely large feather.

The boy had traded his only defense, now carrying a feather. The boy's stance was extremely confident but humble. He looked at the bird's chest and saw some blood. A lot of blood. The boy slowly tried to put the feather over the blood and hold it there to stop the bleeding. The bird looked at the boy and lowered its head to curling its neck around the boy and enveloped him with its wings. Deep inside the giant ball of feathers could be heard "I will call you whistling air." After a moment, the bird straightened up, backed up, and began shuffling the feathers over its entire body. The feather which had previously stuck to its blood, lay on the ground now. The bleeding had stopped. The bird did look and notice this. The bird picked it up with its beak, high stepped to the boy, leaning in as if the bird wanted the boy to take it. The boy did. The bird turned its head straight up to the sky, making a very loud-pitched, whistling sound shaking its head. The boy did too. The boy mimicked the bird. The bird noticed. But the boy's whistle was rather weak. As the bird lifted into the air, the boy kept trying to whistle. Always improving. Why did this bird save him? Why was this relationship built? There will always be "experts" in almost every aspect of life that will provide an answer. When in reality, they will really not know. For the answer, we have to look even further back in this boy's life. His earlier years.

This was a very curious fellow, as most children are, but his questions weren't the same as the other little children. Exactly like most children, his playing was driven by observations, curiosity, and questions that he had. Many others seemed to accept voluminous information or happenings as "It is what it is." This boy had a different knowledge, and he agreed that "it is what it is," unless God says, "It is not," or, "It is as he wills." He wondered about even the simplest of things, like why does a snail leave a trail? Not only why does a snail leave a trail, but why is the trail shiny? Why the kind of fluid or oil secreted by the snail might reflect beautiful colors? The reflection even more so under a light at night. Was it because the snail had no legs and it slid on bodily fluids? But why so beautiful? So it was no surprise that while laying at bed at night with the moon shining bright in his window, he began to wonder. The light of the full moon enveloped him as he lay. The light seemed to give him energy, making it hard to sleep. He thought it wasn't the moon making it hard to sleep but the energy in the light of the moon giving, like, one-seventh the energy of the light from the sun. The light was not hot like the sun. In the dark of night, he could look around the room and be able to clearly see all his sleeping brothers and sisters. Was it the light of the moon which kept him awake, or was it the fullness of the moon which gave him energy? Making hard it to sleep. It was said during training that God lifted the spirit of man and gave man energy. He longed to feel that energy or the power of God. Did it feel like the energy he felt now? What did God look like? He so longed to actually see God. It was on many occasions part of the moon could not be seen leaving a curvature or an arch. It was not a straight line. Enoch wondered so many things about the moon and the stars. So many questions. Who could he ask? These were not questions he would ask his brothers and sister. He couldn't even ask adults. They didn't have time. Everyone was so busy. Most seemed annoyed or indifferent to his curiosities. So he usually played by himself.

Not really by himself. His curiosities led him to see very differently than many others. He remembered during training on the Holy Day, that man was master of the animals and could rule them. He learned animals had souls. Now of course, he really didn't know what a soul was. He was only five years old. But when he observed the many kinds of animals, even though some were the same species, they behaved differently. What we call today personalities. He noticed that of course, the males and females of the same kind acted differently toward one another. He also noticed animals would behave differently when he talked with them. There were some he had to give stern commands to, but others would simply come to him when he called. He also noticed some animals would not pay him any attention. Many liked him to touch them and hold them. Many liked to be stroked, even caressed and loved, the same as when he saw his mother hold and care for and give life milk to his baby brother. Some just liked to spend time with him. Play with him. Some were really characters and would make him laugh. Sometimes he rolled on the ground laughing so hard water would come from his eyes. Once he was on the ground, some would rush in, climbing on him and rolling on top of him.

Some of the animals like bears and great beasts with horns were too big and realized they could hurt others. They would be so gentle, just wanting to be nearby while their cubs or little ones would play with Enoch. Some were scared of each other and for good reason, but when Enoch was with them, they would abandon their fears and come near. Enoch loved being in the water with the fish. Some would come to his hand. He would even momentarily hold onto big ones, and they would speed off through the water together as one. It was fun. Some animals were really close with Enoch like family. It was Enoch's curiosity which led him to understand there were differences. Enoch was even more curious who God was. The one that could breathe life and gift the soul. The one that created everything. Everything that is seen and everything that was not seen. Where was God? Could he ever be with him?

He loved to practice skills. When family work was done, Enoch could practice his physical skills running, jumping, and climbing rocks and trees. His parents knew how their boy spent his time. He was told when he got older that his training would be quite different. He would have to leave the village and head into the trees to practice. Older men had an area they practiced in. Sure, the men took time to train together with coordination of self-defense, but this was not all the family of this boy trained in. Over the many years, since the beginning, things had been changing. Many men and women had become wicked, and violence began. These men also began to look to God for forgiveness of many wrongs over the years and began to cry for him to be a part of their lives and for his help. God would answer. They learned from Adam, Abel's offering, and the mistakes of Cain.

The boy was longing for what they knew and what they were doing, but he was too little, too young. So he would run off and throw rocks, testing his accuracy, picking the right sizes, and bouncing a rock off a tree, utilizing the ricochet method to knock a branch off a different tree with another rock. It was such a young age to actually practice the art of using angles and strategic methods of using the energy derived from objects gaining acceleration from certain materials and deceleration from other material after the ricochet. To gain distance or gain an advantage of hitting something not clearly visible by using something like a rock or a tree to hit something difficult to see. Skipping stones on water was fun practice. But usually, angular strategies were very difficult to explain. He was too young to know the words to transfer the information or share the knowledge, but he knew the strategy. Now how to really study it?

After some throws, Enoch grabbed a short hard stick and lay on his belly, making markings in the dirt of the angles he had worked on. Of course there were some that didn't. He pondered why. When satisfied, whether the rock was misshapen or not a precise hit, he would simply move the dirt to cover the angle that didn't work. Then he drew angles, envisioning distances lost or gained after ricochets. Enoch was too young to understand that at merely four or five years old, what he was doing was very advanced for his age, even advanced in comparison to many adults. Not that others couldn't do what he was doing or that others didn't imagine and utilize angular loading for advantage because there were elders who after many, many years of life experiences and mainly through trial and error were able to share advice or teach how to use angular loading toward advantage. It is precisely because angular loading causes mathematical disadvantages that the block and tackle or pulley was used. Each pulley wheel gained two times the lift or pull ability. There were also those who relied on the teachings and directions from the fallen angels for construction. Those who relied on the fallen angels got what they thought they wanted. But those who relied on the fallen angels did not gain wisdom, only knowledge. But the fallen angels would definitely get what they wanted unless there would be one who stood with God. Even at four or five years old, Enoch was probably not the first human to write, but certainly for a boy his age he was clearly demonstrating some advanced skills. Maybe any child could do what Enoch was currently doing, but Enoch was extremely confident in what he was doing. Enoch knew what he was doing. He stood and took in what he had just done, then looking off the drawing, his demeanor changed to a more serious focus into the distance. Sighting a branch that seemed strong yet breakable if he could hit it right, he knew he could break it.

Scanning the ground quickly as if some day there would be need for speed, he spotted the right rock. His motions were steady and fluid. No muscle was in a turgid state. He stepped quickly scooped the rock with the left hand, tossed the rock to his right. Knowing the flip of the rock according to its shape was critical. While his right arm was reeling like a fly fisherman casting a fly rod, he could feel the shape of the rock and maneuvered the rock for perfect placement in his finger's grip. The rock fit slightly loose before it was released. His eyes locked only momentarily on the precise spot which the rock was to hit. The distanced required a slight curvature. The curvature was quickly envisioned in his mind. The force of impact which was required to snap the branch, required the strength in his feet, legs, and back transferred to and through his arm to the rock's path. The rest of the rock's path would be guided by will if the boy would only release and allow transference. It was at precisely the right moment that only the intricate connection of tendons, ligaments, and muscles required reacted as if each were commanded by a general step by step to a perfect military strike. But Enoch's brain did not send a signal to each bodily part required for the perfect in less than 25,000,000 inches/sec apart (speed of light). All that was required to happen in unison or in sequence within Enoch's body happened as one instantaneously. Why? Because Enoch *knew* he was going to break the branch. There was no doubt. Not a measurement of impurity. Enoch *knew*.

The strike was perfect. Invisible to the eye, the rock produced damage at precisely the right depth. Weakening the branch just enough. The *thunk* sound of the rock hitting the branch sent sound waves and vibrations deep into the main body of the tree.

The resultant small crack produced was so small, almost impossible to be heard by the human ear. The branch was strong. The branch had lamented, bending and twisting in many storms. Its sinews and strands, bonded with glue like sap, provided the branches elasticity and strength to remain intact to the main body and trunk of the tree during the many storms. But today, after being struck by a small rock and as if in slow motion, gravity, which is always present, began gaining advantage over the branch. It was as if gravity now threw a net up and over all the leaves at the end of the branch and began pulling down harder. The cracking sounds, at first quietly long, increased in intensity and frequency. Now the sounds carried loudly into the forest. Then came the loud snap.

He retrieved the branch. Using different techniques of leverage of strength over length, he began breaking the branches that he could. He varied his braced stances which were required for full body leverage to pull some branches till they broke. Some would break with a loud snap. Placing small rocks under branches, he would stomp some smaller branches. Some he would leap in the air landing with full body weight and both feet breaking some of the unneeded smaller branches. After approximating the right length, he placed the larger part of the branch across two rocks separated by the chosen length. Enoch selected carefully a rock nicely tapered with a good working weight suitable for Enoch's manipulation. One end of the branch was cracked and splintered. The other long and tapered with many sharp chards sticking off from the smaller limbs he had broken off. Now braced on rocks, he began to strike the branch with his tapered rock. On both ends. Enoch would turn the branch, striking the branch making a weakened point at the branch's chosen length. The length was purposely chosen to be a little longer than Enoch's height. Enoch stood back and surveyed his work and the next step. He climbed to a larger rock, leaping down this time with legs slightly spread for correct weight distribution. Both ends broke off simultaneously. Or close enough that the separation of time in both breaks could not be ascertained. Enoch was now set to grind and ground both ends. One flat and one end bluntly rounded. Enoch could now use his branch as a walking stick. He now had a staff like the ones he had seen his father, Jared, with. Unbeknownst to Enoch, he had just performed one the best isometric workouts contrived by man. Every muscle in his body was used isometrically with his senses—hearing, eyesight, and touch—emotion, heart, soul, and brain. He sat for a moment surveying flaws over satisfactions. Holding the stick upright, his eyes flowed to the angle of the shadow cast from the stick on the ground. The shadow was long. Enoch quickly whipped his head toward home. The shadow was long because the sun was sinking. The angle of the shadow gave him an immediate reverse direction of the sun, and he immediately calculated the direction home. Once he saw the signs of the shadow, he knew immediately which way was home. More importantly, he had to hurry.

The next day, after some completed chores, he was practicing with his stick. Sometimes he would practice swinging it and maneuvering the staff into different positions to stretch and use muscles normally not used in such manners. Although he was actually doing some great isometric exercises, the movements could be interpreted as offensive meant to deliver bodily damage. Plainly put, it looked like he was practicing fighting. In truth, maybe so. But it was actually fun to practice theses skills. Plus it felt good taking his muscles to limits and a little beyond. He could tell the exercise made him stronger. He actually noticed muscular change. Of course, seeing this from a boy so young troubled his mother. One day while he was doing this, his father called to him, "Son, come sit with me a minute."

He saw his mother watching. But she turned and walked away. The boy said, "Am I in trouble, Da?"

Jared said, "No, of course not, son. It is natural that you would practice that way with your staff. Let me see it. Walk with me a minute." The boy handed his father the stick. Jared walked to where the different herds were kept by the village. Jared walked with the stick and closed the gate once they both were in. "You see, son, sometimes the animals we keep, are afraid. Sometimes they do not understand us. They may even hurt each other when we approach for, they know not what we are about to do." It's like we speak a different language. But we can still communicate with them in different ways. I see you with animals, son. You do understand more than most about animals. And seem to be able to build relationships with them. But there is always more we can learn from others. Now open the gate. Watch. Learn."

Jared used the stick to gently wave at the animals. Pointing in a direction, he wanted them to move. Some resisted. He would very gently tap or touch their legs with the stick. Those would leap into the direction the herd was moving. He did not hit them or hurt them. Then Jared simply walked toward the open gate, and the herd followed him. He exited into an open area. When his father moved about the area, they followed. On occasion, one or two would be bumped or jostled by the others and would stray. Jared would simply tap the ground with the staff, and the stray would look toward the tall staff and run back toward the group, following Jared. His father walked back toward the gate. Jared stood to the side as the herd hustled in, and he closed the gate. Then Jared said to his boy, "Now open the gate, son, and you try to lead them about. Just over there, toward that tree and back." Naturally, after what the boy just learned, he made his way toward his freshly made stick. Jared said, "No, son. Try it as you always have done in the past." The boy confidently opened the gate and led the way, stepping aside once the herd was in the right direction. The boy was actually more serious than usual. He had done this before with no problem but now was being scrutinized. When Jared saw all was good, he picked up a small stone and tossed it near one in the herd. Once the woolly animal spooked, they all began to scatter. Some even climbed on top of each other. The boy was actually doing pretty good at calming them, but it was time; Jared called out, "Son. Your staff!" The boy looked in his father's direction just in time to reach up and catch his stick his father had sent sailing through the air. Jared said, "Now use it." The boy held the staff high at an angle with one arm and with the other arm low but at an angle. The boy began gently talking and telling a story of how he made a stick. He slowly began walking while talking, changing into a rhythmic type of singing while walking in a small circular motion. His voice was very pleasing and soothing.

The herd was a strange mix, ranging from very large beast with horns, some with antlers, to the smaller woolly animals. In the beginning, the different breeds needed no separation. Normally, the large animals were careful not to hurt one another or the small ones. Parents of animals seemed to care for offspring of other animals. It does happen in the wild to this day, but in the beginning, it was more common. They seemed to learn about caring for one another from man. Sure, God had given animals a direct connection and relationship with him. And the animals had a deep loyalty and devotion to God, for they had not eaten the wrong fruit—yet. God had commanded that the animals would know they were to be subject to man. So they looked to man. It was hard for the average person to notice, but all beasts watched and studied man very carefully. In the herd, the various sizes of the beasts blocked the vision of other animals, preventing them from seeing the boy. The ones in the back of the herd were able to look at a high angle and see the *staff*. Some were comfortable in following the boy's voice. Younger ones were staying close to parents while astutely studying the various techniques of the leader who they would grow to trust—the one who would protect them with a *rod* when needed. So they all began to regain composure and be at peace, and they mustered together nicely to follow their leader. The boy then easily corralled the herd back with his staff now upright and used as a walking stick as he closed the gate behind. Both he and his father smiled. Jared actually admired his son's abilities at such a young age. *Something is different about this son of mine,* he thought. But he really gave it not much other thought at all. He loved all his children—each one no more, no less. Jared said, "They will look toward your staff and *rod* for protection if a serpent strikes. It may be difficult for them to see you, so hold your staff high when in danger. It's not really the rod or staff you carry. It is you they look to, but sometimes you are hard for them to see."

"Now let's go sit, Enoch," his father said. Enoch watched as how his da walked with the staff and saw him differently this day.

Jared began, "Sometimes the herds cannot see you or hear very well for they get confused. The staff is taller than you. When you tap the ground with it, they can feel the vibration through the ground of the earth. They recognize you as authority with your staff."

Enoch said, "What is authority, Da?"

Jared said, "It is like the ability to command. Every man was gifted authority by God, but some are not taught or shown or do not ask how to use it. So if man is not careful, others may take authority from man and use it over him. The animals learn this and recognize authority. The animals recognize the one with a staff has authority."

Enoch said, "I see, Da."

Jared followed with, "Yes, Enoch, the word has authority when spoken, but you have very much to learn before you can command such authority. When we have God's commanded Day of Rest, you will learn more of His wisdom. You will learn to ask for wisdom and the spirit before the word should be spoken with complete authority. Son, you ask many questions. This is good. You will learn much at the training sessions on the Holy Day. For now, son, know this. I saw this in a vision that this should be important to you. Here son, I made this for you. Your staff is sharpened."

His new staff was tapered with beveled edges near its rounded tip. The staff was wood without its bark. The wood this staff was made of was considered to be an unbreakable wood. Almost everything will eventually break if set in the right circumstances, but breaking this wood was not yet known to the common man. The wood was very difficult to cut or work into a usable tool. Most avoided working with this wood because it was very time consuming. Only men who walked in the spirit of God worked this wood.

The boy asked, "What's a vision, Da?"

His father replied, "It is the way God shows or reveals something to us without harming us."

Raising his head excitedly, the boy asked, "Da, God asked you to make me a gift?"

Jared said, "Yes, son."

"Why?" asked the boy.

Jared said, "That part remains a secret. It is another way he protects us, by not showing us too much at once. It will have many uses, son."

The little boy was so very proud and happy that his father gave him such a gift. The boy's head was facing the ground while he listened intently. With his eyes angled toward the staff, the boy asked, "What is a serpent?"

His father took the staff and stood. He took the tip drawing an oval almost like an almond. Then began to walk from the oval with the tip still on the ground, making a swerving line. Jared walked about ten steps then lifted the staff and began walking back to the point where he started. Putting the staff down at the very beginning, he said, "This is its head."

Then he drew a line from its head, saying, "This is its tongue." Then he drew two different lines from the end of the one. Jared began, "Its tongue…"

Before Jared could finish, the boy was so excited that he knew that he blurted out, "Its tongue is split?"

"Yes," said his dad. "Almost all serpents will respect a man with a staff. For they know the man can strike its head. But a man must be careful because the snake hides and will bite at the man's heels."

Jared continued, "Not all speak. If it does, you can never trust or believe what it says. It lies almost all the time. When it does speak truth, the serpent will only speak truth to deceive or trick man. Its tongue is split to speak deceit."

While the boy was absorbing this, his father quickly drew another smaller one. His son was still thinking, wondering, *If? If it ever speaks?*

Before the boy could ask, his father was quickly drawing another one. Another one, a lot smaller. Then he said, "Son, not all of them are bad."

His son asked, "Father, how will I know which are not bad?"

His father replied, "Son, you truly ask many questions. For now, son, know this: the serpent who will not leave when you approach, is likely to strike at you. You could die if it bites you."

"If the serpent speaks to you, never believe or trust it. This is the one that must be commanded with authority. It only knows authority." It was then Jared seemed to stand beside the staff and looked as if to study the length of the staff in comparison to his own height. Once satisfied, Jared laid the staff on the ground, noticing its length. Walking the length of the staff, Jared set it down again, this time turning it straight up at ninety degrees. Then he picked it up and, using the angle on the ground, drew in the sand a snake that crawled on its belly but stood upright about halfway. It had the head of a dragon or an alligator-type head and a long tongue split at the end.

"Son, since Enos, the son of Seth, has cried unto God that God's breath stays with us, we have authority with God's word to command this serpent. By God's breath, his spirit, lives inside us that we have authority. He taught us to speak his word, so it is by the gift of life we have his spirit inside us. When we speak, we speak his words, and when we speak, we speak with his authority. It is for this reason we are careful when speaking. But son, you are too young to fully understand these things. This is why you must listen carefully on the day of rest and at the gatherings when Adam and the other elders speak. While your days are young, stay close with your family."

"Yes, Da," the boy replied, earnestly thirsting for more.

"Son, I must return to work. You must learn more on the Day of Life of the Spirit." The little boy knew this as Holy Day. A day of training. A day of rest because he didn't have chores or work to do. The little boy loved this day. It was opportunity he could learn more of God.

Jared said, "Now, son, go to Mother. You must have fallen behind on your work by now. Tell her you spoke with me and ask her which work you must do now."

Enoch said, "Yes, Father." Enoch grabbed his staff and quickly ran toward their house, to his mother. Enoch was so excited to have learned so much he almost forgot. Enoch skidded to a stop with dirt flying up. Enoch turned to his father and said, "Thank you, Father." Then he turned around and ran just as fast as he could to his father's house. To his mother. Some of the animals came out of the nearby woods to run with him. They could barely keep up. Enoch was so excited. He just learned so much. Jared watched Enoch as he ran. Thoroughly amused. Smiling. Even allowing himself to laugh a little. Then a little wind kicked up and blew as if it seemed only on Jared. He noticed because he looked at the trees, and the trees were still. Jared became worried for Enoch. There was horrible evil in the world. Too much. Too much evil and wickedness to even begin to explain to such a little boy. Even if Enoch was more curious and different than others. They needed time.

Enoch needed to know of the serpent's ability to change. That there was pure evil in the world. That there were fallen angels and fallen angels, which were planting their offspring; the Nephilim. The Nephilim were sewing much wickedness everywhere. Fallen angels seemed to be helping men, but they were in actuality leading men further from God to more of a reliance on them and man. Enoch was too young to explain such difficult concepts. Jared started to become deeply troubled. Then Jared remembered the wind was there. God's spirit was with him. Many would not notice, but Jared did. The soft breeze began to soothe him. Jared faced into the wind, lifted his head a little, and took a deep breath. Some called it the breath of life. He was taught by his father, Mahalalel, and his father's father, Kenan. Jared was taught by Adam himself to know God's Spirit. God's Breathe. God's Wind. Jared knew it was His Spirit. The spirit of God. Jared could feel it. Inside, Jared could hear and feel it. His Spirit spoke to Jared. "Your son will be all right." Jared began to feel good all over. Jared believed. The wind slowly died, then the leaves in trees began to softly sway. Jared felt good as he headed off to work.

Even though Enoch was young, he had many tasks. Much of it was helping his mother gather water for different uses. Enoch would also care for the animals they kept. Animals were kept for many uses. Some of the larger beasts helped greatly with manipulating vary large boulders and logs. Some animals would protect the village from other dangerous animals. It was that some animals only became dangerous after learning Nephilim would eat them and knowing fallen angels. The animals were good at sounding the alarm when danger was near. He loved caring for and tending to the many different animals and the tasks around the house he did for his mother. Enoch loved being with his mother. She would teach him things and tell him about other things many others didn't talk about. Enoch loved hearing his mother talk about God.

Enoch ran up to their home. Right up to the front entrance. Enoch stopped quickly sliding up to the front door, kicking up some dirt from under his sandals. Suddenly remembering what his mother had taught him and what his father had told him too. Enoch had to jump in the water before entering the house. The roof was made of leaves. The mist, which hung in the air much heavier at night, would run off the top of the house into different gathering pools and barrels. The water was purposely directed through careful planning during construction of the homes. Some for drinking water and a container or pool not too far from the entrance for cleaning. None knew of rain. In those days, it was yet to rain. The water came from mist, sometimes forming like heavy, thick fog. The view from their homes was strikingly beautiful. Everyone was busy, but it seemed as though with long rest periods, it made it easier sometimes to take in the beauty and possibly allow for understanding. Many simply ignored the beauty, but not Enoch; it was almost every occasion when he came home that he would astutely study his surroundings. This gave the young boy an advantage not many others had when he was away from home. Cleaning up, again he studied the mist. One could see it hang around mountain tops. Sometimes it hung around very tall trees. In some areas, one could see water spewing from the earth like constant gushers or geysers extremely high into the sky then float with wind down to earth. Like giant sprinklers, only controlled by wind. These were the mist and rivers born from life water from *the deep* of which the earth was formed.

Cleaning the body was an everyday task. His mother made sure Enoch knew to clean himself before the sun began to warm and when the sun departed. His mother used to help him. Then his mother showed what must be done. They used a substance from a mix of herbs. It was squishy. It smelled good, though. His mother and father had said it helped to wash the grime but also of the bad which could not be seen by the eye. Enoch did not know what this meant yet. Was it tiny stuff? Too small to see or really stuff that can't be seen? Father had showed what he said, "how a man cleans himself." It was pretty much as Enoch's mother had showed him. Almost. He took off all, but his undergarment and jumped in the pool. The water was cold. So cold sometimes the water could take one's breath away. Enoch loved it. Such an eye opener.

Enoch came in the house, announcing himself: "Ma, I am here."

"Come, Enoch, are you hungry?" his mother asked.

Enoch loved every opportunity to eat his mother's food. "Yes, Mother." She always had fruit on the table and the large grapes and other fruits were special, almost like desserts. Enoch enjoyed helping to gather the different large fruits. His mother brought over some vegetables fresh from a fire. The vegetables were still on the unique type of wood they were cooked upon with some greens on the side. Cooking using this particular wood added seasoning and valuable nutrients, also making the cooked vegetables smell deliciously yummy. As she handed it to Enoch at the table, he asked his mother, "Will The Holy One (he didn't pronounce the name correctly) be at our training on the Holy Day?"

His mother said: "No, son. The Most Holy One (as if to punctuate the correct pronunciation) will not be there. We cannot see Him. But He will be there in Spirit."

"Does he really love us?" asked the boy.

"Yes, he really does. He created Adam and Eve. You know them, right? God is like a father to us all," the boy said rather contritely and sadly but also steadfastly. "If he loves us, we should be able to see Him and be with Him."

His mother saw the conversation as harmless curiosity. Her boy was serious. And, knew what he was saying was true. His mother turned from cleaning and noticed her son was a little distraught. She walked over and hugged him lovingly, saying, "Son, I know you want to know everything at once, but it's just not possible. You will learn much more on the next Holy Day. It's only a few days away." Pulling away from the hug but still holding on, his mother said, "Here, son. When you finish that, I need for you to repair something for me."

"Yes, Mother," he replied.

Enoch was always taught to thank God. At least three times a day. So before he ate was a good time. Enoch began, "God, I thank you for making us, the sun and the moon, that we would know the seasons. And thank you, God, for making all the animals and this world so beautiful for us to live in." His mother had turned to retrieve something by the household water container. She looked out the window and saw her husband, Jared. He had finished packing some tools and was heading toward Kenan's place to help with roof and water run off repair work. He felt her and looked back toward the window. They made eye contact. They both had a very serious and intent look. They both knew the world was changing. Ever since the Fallen Angels had begun their teachings toward the benefit of man, horrible wickedness had been growing. The city had been growing in size. The bigger the city grew, the greater its wants. The people in the city could not toil the ground. The city could not produce its own food. It was only a matter of time. Their concerns reflected in their traded looks. Jared broke the tension with a reassuring smile. With the smile, he was also reassuring he would be back. She returned a genuinely loving smile.

She said Enoch, "Did your father talk with you?"

Enoch replied, "Yes, Mother. He gave me the staff and showed me how to use it. It's really nice. See, Ma?"

As she admired the staff, Enoch's mother said, "You know, Enoch, a woman cannot tell a man how to be a man. This is why I am glad your father teaches you. But as your mother, I can teach you some things that will help you as you become a man. Here, Enoch, put these skins together that they will look like this." She set down an outer garment down made of animal's skin. "Enoch, these help us stay warm at night after we travel through the mist. I do not expect you to make one. I want you to learn to repair outer garments. Then if you ever need you can repair or even make one for yourself. This hole in this little bone is for the yarn. The sharp bone makes the hole in the two skins like this. Then pull through the yarn through, again and again. Cut it and tie it. See?"

Enoch said, "Yes, Ma."

His mother continued, "Make the first knot your father showed to put on your sandal. But twice. Make two knots. Like these. Tight."

Enoch grew a little concerned. Enoch asked, "Mother, which animal are these skins from?"

His mother immediately understood. "Enoch, I know you love animals. These are from the cattle we keep. The cattle actually know their purpose. God clothed Adam and Eve with skin when they left the garden many years ago. The clothing was for Adam and his woman's protection, providing the skins showed what they were to do on their own. Providing the skins also demonstrated a continuing relationship with God. It is God that provides all for us. Enoch, you must learn that as God provides for you, it is the same as a father must provide for his family too."

Enoch was thinking. After some deep thought he replied, "I understand, Mother. A father must provide for his family." Of course, as Enoch always did, he asked a question: "Is the Garden real?"

His mother replied, "Yes, Enoch."

"Is the garden still there?" asked Enoch.

"Yes," said his mother.

"Can I go there?" he asked.

His mother answered with a very firm "No."

Enoch asked, "Why?"

His mother stated, "Because the entrance is guarded by a Cherubim with a flaming sword. This Guard will kill man and even destroy which is not supposed to enter." Adam and Eve were tricked by the serpent into defying God's commands, and everything changed. Now no one is allowed back against God's commands. As she glanced out of the window, his mother noticed Mahalalel's wife approaching with a basket and her two daughters. She remembered they had arranged to make some more suitable garments for the girls.

His mother quickly said, "Son, you have too many questions for me to answer. If you can't wait for the training sessions to find out more, you can try and ask Seth. I am sure it will be fine if you go to Seth. I am sorry, son, I have some work to do."

Enoch said, "It's okay, Ma. Can I go to Seth now?"

She said, "Yes, son." He ran for the door and slid to a stop, immediately spun around running back to his mother. Grabbing her around the waist, hugging her tightly, he said, "Bye, Mother. I love you," as he laid his head just above her belly a moment and giving his mom time to put both hands on him. She caressed his head and ran her hands through his hair. She said, "I love you too, son. I will tell your father where you went." Then he took off again. But sliding to a stop at the door again this time because the mother and two girls were at the door. It was Criggy and her little sister.

Note that something like the idea of cousins was not something that existed in the beginning. In the beginning, men and women lived to be one thousand years of age after leaving Eden. In the beginning, men and women did not have quite the same functioning body systems as the men and women of today. Some major changes have taken place. But all were family though. Almost like a thinning of the herd except no longer the almost angelic breeding in the beginning to man and woman breeding today with some downgrades. These families were groups or isles of thousands with merely the same name of people's of the prodigy or father of the generation. Today's man is quite possibly living with slightly different genetic downgrades, or slightly altered DNA is highly likely. The term *missing link* might better suit the genetic coding downgrades that altered man's DNA from those who would live to be a thousand years old before the flood.

Why is the truth hard to accept?

Man and woman were told by the *one that created all things,* that of everything known to man they could eat except for one fruit. That if they ate of that fruit they would die. Basically they were told of a poison fruit or plant they were not to eat. Like nightshade (belladonna) or the castor bean from which the deadly toxin ricin is produced. No one should really blame their ancestors for being tricked or deceived into eating poison. People have been poisoned for centuries and continue being deceived for profit or by word of mouth to consume things they shouldn't. Some that gather in groups to entice or tempt for profit are called *marketing firms* or news corporations. Try to imagine the original *forbidden fruit* consumed by man actually enabled him to know both good and bad. Before he ate the fruit he only knew that which was good. Nothing that was seen or known to him was bad. Is it really so hard to fathom or believe? Are there not plants which cause temporary hallucinations like mescaline from the peyote cactus and psilocybin mushroom? So powerful is the mind and brain over bodily functions having only good thoughts and eating right would bring longevity of life. This generation has been convinced they've evolved from lower species of neanderthal or ape into higher species always gaining knowledge and intellect. When actually man has greatly devolved from his beginnings of much higher capabilities truly unfathomable today.

So it was sin which wrought actual change in man and woman which resulted in non-divinical, unnatural, or unintended death; much like a mind altering poison with permanent consequences. Direct disobedience of a father's children made in his own image caused great and catastrophic consequences. The results were irreversible. A father and his very own children could not stand in each other's presence without immediate annihilation of his children. The children would have to leave their father's house to survive. But before they left, God revealed there would be a pathway back home to a new beginning. Not many would understand.

After sin and for man's protection, God and man had to stay on each side of a firmament separating heaven and earth. But as a good father would God did what was necessary. God killed an animal innocent of all guilt that the father and his children could be reunited. The blood of innocence had to be spilled upon the ground for it would be the Earth which would would endure much pain and suffering too. The life blood of innocence became an absolution or absorption of sin allowing man to stand in God's presence. Once blood was spilled unto the ground the *good father* physically clothed his children before they left home. But make no mistake, this occasion was all very real and traumatic. An event so shocking as to alter every part of their being. Now knowing good and bad, the good mother and father would have to emphatically warn their children of the bad. That they might always be susceptible to unwanted influences. Warn them in a way that their children would warn their children unto generation after generation.

Warn them of an almost unnoticeable internal conflict of good and bad and that the only way to clearly identify or differentiate between the two is by fasting. Fasting allows the body's natural filtration processes to purify unhealthy nutrients and proteins so that the brain can process to its clearest and fullest potentials; both physical and spiritual. Prayer during this time clears unwanted thoughts allowing for a purer from of communication with our father. This generation might think that we have too many distractions to hear *the good news* but generations in the beginning would've been bombarded with huge amounts of enticements and temptations too. Try to imagine advancements all new and exciting are in each generation unto this day. Advancements *in the beginning were not necessarily all barbaric as we are led to believe. In just a short time man evolved from lightening to an electrical key and on to nuclear fission powering cities. Now try to imagine accomplishments, discoveries and successes of man a little lower than angels that lived for a thousand years. Man's main failures stemming from envy, jealousy and covetousness of man's ability to procreate by those who were not permitted. In the beginning* all advancements would be very exciting, enticing and tempting as for this generation.

The Voice of a Young Boy Raised Up

Now this was awkward. They were so close he almost bumped into her. Even leaned back a little and said, "Hi, Criggy. Uh, I mean Ka'na-deh." Criggy smiled enthusiastically, and her body swayed just a little where she stood. Both women made eye contact and smiled.

Then Criggy's mother looked at Enoch very straightforward and said, "Hi, Enoch."

Enoch looked down, stood erect, and said, "Hi." Enoch tilted his head a little toward the littlest and winked. Enoch poked Criggy in the side as he grabbed his sandals off the wall and ran. He would have to stop and put them on later. *That was too awkward*, he thought.

Keller and Gadder appeared from nowhere, running behind Enoch. They could easily catch him. Both Keller and Gadder were bounding, leaping, and bouncing back and forth. Enoch didn't even look back. 'Cause he knew. Then he said, "Come, Ba'headge." Ba'headge wanted to come. He just needed the formal invite. He galloped acting like he had to go. But truth be told, Ba'headge's feelings would've been hurt if he wasn't called. Enoch knew this. Enoch really did know a lot for a boy his age. For some reason, Enoch was special. Most who met him seemed to sense it. Only the very ignorant could not see it.

During these times, not all wooded areas were of gigantic trees of extremely long life. Trees capable of living up to two thousand years old. There were many areas of trees, which produced very large fruit.

There were also areas, which contained plants which produced large vegetables. Not all fruits and vegetables were large, but the soil was so rich each vegetable or fruit produced was unimaginably rich in nutrients. To the boy, large fruit was common and normal. Carrying one piece of fruit would require him to put it in a pouch he could sling over his shoulder. Or if available, roll one onto a handcart he could pull.

These fruit trees required tilling when young. The various fruit trees also required maintenance towards maturity or the tree could not produce the best quality fruit. These fruits were full of protein and other various nutrients, which were actually so good for one's health man was able to live much longer than he does today. If the trees were not tended to, the tree might still have produced fruit. One might survive eating such wild fruit, but the fruit would not be considered healthy for longevity.

One of the reasons for such bountiful fruit was the soil was much richer during these times. There wasn't a need for fertilization. In certain areas, the soil was so rich in nitrogen and other nutrients a person could smell the soil from great distances. As the plant lives and breathes, it gathers many major and micronutrients through its roots from the soil. Many plants even have reproductive systems and have complex capabilities of "understanding or knowing" a partner is nearby. Certainly not as we understand a reproductive process, but it does exist. Fruit trees produce fruits containing a mix of nutrients and vitamins, providing a healthy growing environment for its seeds.

During pregnancy, a human mother's amniotic fluid is a makeup of various nutrients, proteins, hormones, carbohydrates, infection-fighting antibodies, lipid proteins and other vital components necessary for the development of new born before it enters a world full of diseases and germs.

Is fruit and mother's womb a far stretch for comparison and contrast? The two forms of life are extremely different. Many differences and opposites exist such as the plant gets its nutrients from the soil and humans get their protein and nutrients from the plants. A conversion process exists, if you will. I think we all can agree the taste of a cantaloupe, watermelon, burger, or rib-eye cooked to one's desire is by far much better than a handful of dirt. Man was made from dirt so his body needs the nutrients from the soil he came from. The nutrients just have to go through a filtration process.

In the early 1500s, Ponce de Leon searched for a mystical and mythological fountain of youth. It was believed drinking of the waters from this river or spring would restore youth, extend life, or cure ills. Today, we might refer to the fruits and vegetables grown and available during this boy's life as "Fruits of Youth" sprinkled with mist from *fountains of life water.*

Originally, men and women were physically different than the men and women of today. Their physical stature and structure was created to last a very long time. During these days, the world had available fruits and vegetables which would sustain bone density, a flesh composite, and all other complexities of the human anatomy requiring physical longevity. If the fruit trees and plants were not tended to properly during those times, some would still produce edible byproducts. Maybe good enough for today's anatomy but certainly not yesteryear's times. But these wild fruits would still taste good, be refreshing, and still provide some necessary benefits. Original man just could not live as long if that's all he ate. The boy had heard there was an area where the various fruit and vegetable plants and trees required no maintenance. The boy was also very strictly warned no one was allowed or permitted near those plants. He was told why, but he did not completely understand the reason. He had many unanswered questions as to why they couldn't go there.

The boy was about halfway to Seth's home when he noticed a man in the distance selectively picking a piece of fruit from the trees. The sun had just fully risen. This group of fruit trees were shared between some other families he knew. It would not be unusual if a traveler or passerby was picking a piece of fruit. The boy slowed his stride, maneuvering a bit to get a better view of the man. But even without seeing his face, his stature, mannerisms, and movements; the boy knew it must be Seth. Still quite a distance away, the boy's excitement and joy caused him to shout, waving his arms, "Seth!" The boy loved talking and being with Seth. Seth would answer many of his questions.

Without even looking, Seth smiled broadly and calmly raised his arm high to acknowledge the excitement of the little boy's greeting. Seth absolutely loved this boy's curiosity and innocence. The boy noticed Seth had a very small beautiful lamb, and of course, Seth had a staff. The lamb was leashed although the lamb merely trotted along leaving slack in the leash. The boy also noticed a large bundle of wood bounded tightly together that Seth carried on his back. On the ground were two smaller bundles.

The boy ran the rest of the way to Seth. When he got to Seth, the impact of the collision was so hard it knocked Seth off balance a little. The boy reached as high as he could for a solid hug. He loved and admired Seth greatly. He felt like an outsider to others. But not when he was with Seth. Seth reached down with a soft caress. Seth couldn't help himself; he surely loved this boy. It was almost as if this boy was his only beloved son. Seth had other children. Of course Seth loved his other boys and girls as much as this little boy, even more so. But those relationships were not as this. This was like a father who for some unknown reason had to be a teacher to this boy, and the boy unknown to himself had to seek this mentor as if he were his father, master even. Seth quickly changed the hug into a manly pat, pushing softly, at arm's length, to make eye contact. Make no mistake, the love was obvious between the two in eye contact. Can't let the boy grow up to be mushy. But this little boy knew he cared for no other like this.

Laughing a little, Seth said, "Careful, little one. I have a gift for God. How to give gifts to Yahweh was revealed to Enos from what Abel had started." Seth reached into a pouch sewn into the front his clothing. Reaching into one side with one hand slowly and the other side with the other hand just as carefully, he brought both hands out gently to show the boy. Seth held them both very close to the young boy's face.

The boy smiled enthusiastically, asking, "Can I touch them?"

Seth said, "Sure." He knew how much this boy loved and knew he'd be careful, there was no need for further instructions after saying he could. He knew of this boy's special relationships and understanding of animals. Seth didn't know why. But he knew it was real. He carefully set his cheek on one while caressing and cupping it. Looking the other dove in its eye, he stroked it softly. Then moved his nose to the top of its head, making the cooing sound of a dove.

Both doves seemed to make a purring sound that only a dove can do. It was no surprise to Seth, only a reflection of curiosity, when the boy replicated the sound that only the dove makes.

Seth handed him a small bundle and said, "Here, carry this bundle of wood. We will need this for later tonight. Grab the other one too. It has some food in it." The boy quickly grabbed the bundle and slung it across his shoulder, shifting the weight for balance and ease of walking while grabbing the other.

Seth followed with, "Do you need water before we start? We have long travels ahead."

As the boy drank juice from the skin flask, he asked, "Where are we going?" Pointing with barely a glance as if he was used to this journey. The young lad's eyes followed the gesture. He then stopped and stood with awe. "Come, boy, we have a long way. I know you have many questions. You can ask your questions along the way. I will try to answer your questions. Come. Let us be quick and diligent making our way, for speed and accuracy in our steps are necessary. We have a long way to go." Seth had pointed to a mountain that had a thick cloud of mist wrapped around the base of the top. There was also a very large fissure of water spouting out the side of the mountain as if it had sprung a leak. Or it seemed as though the water shot out from the side of the mountain.

The boy drank quickly, more interested in asking his next question than drinking the juice. The juice was very good though. Too good not to drink. "God wants these doves as gifts? There are too many birds to count. Birds are everywhere. I don't understand. Why would He want these? Are these two special?"

It was harder to talk while walking. Seth knew eventually the questions would fade. "Yes. These two are messengers," replied Seth. Then Seth got on one knee, unfastened the leash and held on to the little lamb and said, "Go on to your purpose little one for God has plans for you at a much later time." As the lamb trotted off they boy asked, "What's the little one's purpose?" Seth replied, "Only God knows. I completed what was intended." The boy marveled.

The boy wanted to ask another question, but Seth interrupted and finished by saying, "Because they represent what's in our heart, mind and soul, and they are from us. They represent that we are grateful. A gift of gratitude if from the heart is truth, and He will know that truth. The type of truth that is as real as life itself. We will talk more later. For now, let us go. Talking is slowing us down, and we really need to be up there before sunset. We must hurry." Seth referenced where they needed to be by looking in the direction in which they were to go. This time, he was gearing up and moving with greater intensity and quickness.

Seth gave the young boy much to carry. It was a load appropriate for his stature and ability. A small bundle of kindling to start a fire, a pouch of vegetables, and water. The boy trotted behind then passed Seth, never failing to amuse Seth. "Does where we are going have a name, Seth?" It really didn't matter. The boy loved being with Seth.

It was merely the curiosity, which caused him to ask, "Mount Hermon," then came the return rather matter-of-factly while looking at its peak.

The boy's eyes followed Seth's gaze. Now with his head tilted high, the boy said, "Wow. All the way up there?"

Seth said, "Not actually all the way to the top of Mount Hermon. We are going over there." Seth's gaze changed direction to mountains, which were still part of same mountain range as Mount Hermon. The boy's eyes followed, but quickly changed back to the top of Mount Hermon. "Why does the mountain shimmer and glow white light like the sun at the top?"

"That is ice. It is so cold up there the mist becomes very still and freezes, becoming ice. The ice reflects the light of the sun."

Seth added, "We will not have time to go to the top of that very cold mountain. Besides Mt Hermon has been defiled by those who have rebelled against God. Mount Hermon will be cleansed but not by us this evening. God's voice does not tell me to go there. Not yet beloved. He calls me to that peak." Seth's eyes shifted back to the peak he had previously referred the boy to.

Puzzled, the boy asked, "He talks to you?"

"Yes," Seth said.

The boy looked around and said, "Can you see Him?"

"No," Seth said.

"Why not?" the boy asked.

Seth responded, "His existence is not as you imagine, beloved. You will see this even. We are going to that mount there." The boy looked. It was not as high as Mount Hermon. No ice or maybe just a little. The boy was not sure that the glistening near the top was rock, ice, or something else. It looked different than the glow of Mount Hermon. "Beloved, although it is not as cold as Mount Hermon, it will be cold. Wrap these extra skins I have brought for you. You will need them this night." The boy took the skins and ran slightly ahead. He was very excited. For tonight, it appeared he was to see something special. He was to see what cannot be seen; he was to see God.

They were in the shade as they both neared the top. The sun had lowered just enough that the light was blocked by the mount's peak. The boy could see his breath. He knew it was cold, but his body was warm. They had kept on the move and were walking a tough rocky trail. Burning the energy required getting to the top caused his body temp to rise a little. Kept him warm as long as he was moving. During the times he was behind Seth, he admired Seth's agility and quickness. As he followed, he copied some steps Seth made. At other times, he would jump from rock to rock. The boy kept up well. Of course, Seth intermittently slowed and checked to make sure the boy was all right.

Once they peaked the top, the boy's eyes widened. The top was still bright. In situations like this, it does seem that the sun moves more quickly than the noonday sun. At the top, there were very shiny rocks shaped like a big table. In the rock of the mount nearby was a pool. Seth removed his clothes down to the bare minimum then stepped slowly into the pool up to his chest.

"Come, beloved. Slowly now. This cleansing is done with respect and earnest." They both cleansed completely. All must be washed away. The water was warm. A little steam seemed to rise.

This was a little surprising to the boy. He thought it would be cold. So he asked, "The water is warm?"

Seth said, "This water is fed up to this pool from the earth. The sun helps warm this rock during the light of day. In turn, the rock helps warm the water. The mist which forms to ice from above toward the north melts in the light and warmth of day. Then it flows down the rocky mount to this pool of water. So this *water* comes from the *mist of heavens* and *water* from the *deep*."

Seth knew the boy's level of curiosity and intelligence could grasp these concepts. These concepts would stick. The boy loved knowing. Seth continued, "The warmth will be leaving now." Seth pointed to the setting sun. Come beloved, we have more to do." The boy looked. It seemed the sun was gaining speed?

Although the boy knew the sun was setting over the distant land as it did every night, on this night, the sun was settling into a very thick mist that stretched for miles. The color was a magnificent orange and red. The colors in the mist also were of brilliant reds with orange. The colors bled to some yellows outward to the fringes of the mist. There, near the edges of the mist, even a wider variety of colors like purple, violet, blue, and magenta. The boy had never seen anything like this before. Suddenly, he was stunned by something very unusual. He was in awe. He had seen sunsets, and this one was truly more radiant than any ever seen before. Even more stunning, from this vantage point, he could now see a very bright light in the midst of very tall trees. West of Mount Hermon, there in that clearing of the mist was an extremely brilliant golden light. On the side of the bright light, he could see a flame, the colors of fire, that shot straight and narrow into the air. Not difficult at all to see. Only difficult to describe because of its great distance from where the boy stood. It appeared the fire turned in a circle. Like a lighthouse, it's brightest when its direction is directly facing the one looking. When its fiery brilliance struck his face, he had to cover his eyes. As he squinted and covered his eyes, he couldn't help but blurt out an emotionally perturbed yet exuberant exclamation: "*What is that!*"

Seth didn't even have to look, but still, he glanced over to satisfy his own inner being before replying, "That is the guardian God has placed at the entrance of the Garden of Eden to prevent anyone from entering. Beloved, these guardians are cherubim. Cherubim are angels of destruction. Seeing this cherub means God's presence is near."

Quickly the boy said, "Does that means God is there?" Finally, he looked at Seth. Now he noticed Seth had a glow about his face. "Can we see Him?"

"He is not as you think," replied Seth.

"But are we not in His image?" The boy immediately followed with more questions, "So we are like Him?" Honestly, the boy had been taking in so much he'd forgotten he should've been helping. It was way too much for anyone to take in, let alone a boy of such innocence and youth.

The boy looked to the east of Mount Hermon and saw a very large soft glow and two smaller ones in the distance. "What is that over there?" the boy asked.

Seth replied, "That is the city of Enoch." The boy exclaimed, "That is my name! The city has my name!"

"Yes, the Marked Murderer. Cain named the first city after his son. Enoch that city has nothing to do with you, and you have nothing to do with that city. That city gives birth to new evils every day. Enoch, beloved, you are the complete opposite of the goings-on in that city. You represent all that is good. Seek God, and you will know this. Beloved, you will learn more of the evil of cities later. For now, know man sacrifices his freedom to live there. The city was built by a murderer and is now ruled by fallen angels who demand to be known as gods."

"But why is my name the same as something so bad?" asked the boy.

"Enoch, that is complicated. Evil works its best with opposites. For now know that all the secrets of heaven are not completely revealed when God plans His works towards man's benefit. The watchers observe, plot and scheme against good and the relationship between God and man, for the fallen angels are truly covetous. Enoch, you are too young to understand that sometimes those who are good have to work much harder to overcome challenges than others who submit to the fallen angels and the evil one."

Now in complete astonishment, the boy looked over at Seth and asked, "Then God could stop all the evil or bad?"

Seth said, "Yes. But think of it as something like this. Evil does a preemptive maneuver, like naming a large, modern, and sophisticated city your name before you're even born. It would be to reduce the importance of your name because God looks for us to *overcome adversities* like jealousy or envy. God wants us to overcome the simplest intrusions that a mere name can cause and, in that manner, strengthen all our vulnerabilities and weaknesses, preparing us for our most major conflicts. Fallen angels have taught men to be like them, how to be cruel and attack when man is at his weakest, least expecting, or most vulnerable."

The boy asked, "But if the city had my name before I was named, why is not the name more important than me?"

Seth replied to the boy, portraying confidence, "We don't know yet. Until the One on Most High gifts us Wisdom many secrets remain with Him."

The boy became a little frustrated, and it showed. Then he replied, "So how did Da know what to name me?"

Watching the rapidly setting sun, Seth began to speak with urgency, "Before your mother carried you as one with her, it was a night of the first moon, and your father was sleeping. A vision of a *Holy One* came to your father in his sleep to awaken him and deliver a message from living creature to living creature from God. The Holy One walked outside under the stars with your father while all slept. It was as if all were set into a deeper sleep, even the animals, for it was a secret and a very personal conversation of many things, one being your name."

Enoch was abuzz with curiosity. There was so much to ask. What a revelation. He didn't know any of this and wanted more, much more truth. To Enoch, truth was the most valuable of all, even more valuable than the tangibles like his home and the herd. The boy started to ask, "What about—"

Seth had to cut him off by saying, "Enoch, it is late, but I will tell you truth. There is much truth from God that must remain secret until it's time to be revealed. Come, boy, we must ready the eve."

Seth was preparing the wood for the fire. The color of Seth's face was the same of the many colors of this sunset. The table glowed and reflected the colors with rays shooting off the table in many directions. The rays seemed as beams. As if the rays of light could pierce what they hit. In a very calm, soft, but firm voice, Seth caught his attention. "Come, beloved. Its time you know how to present a gift to God." The first step was cleansing the field *stripped* birds with the two waters combined, as they themselves had just done.

They both prepared the doves. Although these doves seem innocent and benign to many, as they are, the boy was used to skinning animals. Their demeanor was calm, solemn, respectful, heartfelt, but deliberate. The doves seemed at ease. To the average, this may've seemed cruel. As hard as it is for us to understand, the two doves understood their purpose. They felt and knew the love shared and that they were chosen to be the ones to personally deliver the message to their creator. Seth could easily tell it was important that he reinforce this concept to the boy. Seth began, "The animal has great pride being a gift to God for us. You know, beloved, God's Spirit fills the doves with the knowledge of His purpose. The dove is extremely proud in knowing he has been chosen to deliver a special message. The dove also knows that many doves and pigeons deliver messages, but rarely are they chosen to deliver a message to their creator from man. They had a special purpose. Just as you have a special purpose."

The boy said, "Seth, what is my special purpose?"

"This I do not know, beloved. But the day will come when you are told. You have a long life to live. But you must always be listening, for there will be a day when you are shown. It is on that day you should be proud yet very humble. Trust me, boy, that is a very hard combination to achieve." As the fire burned, the sun still had a fiery glow barely visible. The smells of the doves combined with a soft smoke drifted upward, bending toward the soft glow of the setting sun. The aromas actually smelled really good to the boy. The wood. The meat.

Seth turned to the boy until eye contact was returned. "Beloved, as I call to God, there is something you must know. There are others that will hear." The boy looked around. This was a mystery to the boy. He responded as such: "Who?"

Seth followed. "We may or may not see them. But they will know, they will hear us. They usually don't really care what we say. But there are times that when man has the potential to do the greatest good. This is when they attack that one with the most ferocity. When we talk to God, this is when they 'watch' most intently. This is why we call them the Watchers. They are always watching everything. Do not ever fear them. Fear God. The Watchers fear God, "God, and they fear us. They fear our relationship with God, for He loves us as his own because we are in His image."

The boy started, "But…"

Seth laid his hand on him. "We have no time left. Sometimes you must accept the gift you are given and work towards your next opportunity. You must listen and look for God. Now listen."

There was now only a glow from a small fire. The millions of stars were starting to create their own light of the night. Enough to see. Yet there were many shadows. Even more than during the day. Now many of the shadows moved and swayed from the light of the fire mixed with the light from the brilliance of the many stars which light the clearest of nights.

"Boy, I know you have many questions." Seth put his finger on the boy's lips. "I know you are too young for all this. Abel, son of Adam, showed us how to please God. The spirit fills me just now to show you this. Sometimes you must be quiet to see."

Seth cried unto God, "Oh, One on Most High, we know we are no longer worthy of your presence. We constantly fail you. But we do not wish to fall so far from you that we might never be near you again. We long to be with you. We long to live with you once again. We ask with the most unworthy but humblest of heart that you would please accept our small gift of thanks. You have given us a world with an unlimited abundance of fruit and food. You have given us all we need. For us to give such a small gift must seem trivial and meaningless to one with such magnificence to have created all, but these doves are to deliver a message from us to you. That we love you. We need you every minute of the day. Without you, we are lost. Please accept our gift, Most Holy One."

Seth was on his knees. His hands clasped together with bowed head, eyes closed. He slowly lifted his head, now eyes open, looking skyward, spreading his arms wide, and simultaneously saying, "Please forgive us, One on Most High."

The boy noticed tears streaming down Seth's cheeks, rolling off the sides of his lightly bearded face and falling on the ground. The boy noticed the ground slightly open and close as the teardrops were received and kept as valuable fruit. Seth did not notice. This was this line of men from Adam that still understood God and sought the connection. It was because the dragon led man into direct disobedience of structure (law) that caused real changes and consequences to unfold. The brilliantly lit and jewel-encrusted one of the heavens was now altered. He was cursed. He no longer could fit in a functioning divine structure because of leading man away into disobedience.

What we think of as molecular structure is not the same in an esoteric world. So we speak what we know: that a Son of God physically and esoterically changed. It still can rebel but only if God allows it. When sons of God rebel, there are ramifications to themselves and even unto man, like the ramification to the ground: because of man's physical changes, technically, the ground had to change *for man's sake (benefit)*. Taking care of what was alive was man's ultimate purpose. For Enoch's generation, the ground had drank man's blood. The ground had also soaked up and drank sweat from man's face. The ground would also drink water from *the mist that dwells deep inside man*, who was now in remorse and communicating regret. And because the ground bore man's curse for his sake, the ground now consumed the salt from the tears of man. This was how forgiveness from God was first sought by man.

In the drift of the smoke began a small swirl. Enoch wondered, *Is there no wind?* The swirl of smoke, already somewhat colorful from its surroundings, earthly and skyward contributions, now began to emanate light and colors of its own. Not outward but inward. The boy stared intently. There now seemed to be a soft glow in what seemed a hundred miles away. A soft golden glow. Slowly, two beautiful purple and magenta-colored outlines of doves lifted from the base of the fire and began to fly. Slowly at first. Once in what almost seemed like a tunnel, they sped up. When they first lifted, they could've gone anywhere they wanted. After lifting off, the pair hovered briefly. Then committed in the direction of the golden glow. As the doves neared the glow, it brightened. The two doves faded into the glow then disappeared. The doves seemed to be consumed. Then the glow faded. A soft wind picked up and blew the smoke into a little whirlwind. The smallest and weakest of smoke tornadoes but really cool. The wind lifted sparks from the flame. The flame grew as the sparks swirled.

Seth turned to the boy and said, "See, God has accepted our gift."

Excitedly, the boy responded, "Yes! I never would've thought the two doves would lift and fly again!"

Seth looked at the boy a little puzzled and said, "What did you see?"

The boy looked back and said, "They appeared differently, but I'm sure that they were of the same doves." The boy paused with a look, wanting confirmation of what he had just seen.

Seth couldn't confirm. Seth did recognize a need, though. Attempting to console him, Seth said, "That's not possible. Animals do have the Breath of Life, but as the breath leaves, we cannot see it. Come, look here, beloved."

They both stood and walked toward the dying flame as Seth said, "Look. Here are the bones of the doves. But God has given us a beautiful sign that He accepted our gifts. Did you not see? The great sparks and the whirlwind of God?"

The boy was frustrated. The boy said, "If we are made in His image, why can't we see Him?" He understood the boy was experiencing a lot.

Seth responded compassionately, "We saw his presence. This was good."

This was a long, long day with much to absorb. Really too much for one so young. Calmly and lovingly, Seth said, "It has been an extremely long day. Enoch, know we both saw His presence and He accepted our humble offering. We must wrap well in the skins we brought and lie near the rock by the pool for it is the warmest area of this mount. Come sleep now. If you are hungry, eat some, but try to rest and sleep. Tomorrow will be a glorious day, for we know for sure God accepted our gift." The boy begrudgingly went for his bedding.

As he lay looking at the glorious night sky through the dwindling smoke, his mind wandered at 100 mph. How could he sleep? He rolled onto his back and looked up. The smoke from the fire faded. They both laid on a mountain top which happened to be situated slightly above most of the mist. They were nearly surrounded by mist. In some areas, the mist appeared to look like pillows or clouds. Some areas like fog. Some mist seemed to stretch to the heavens above. But not where they were. With no clouds and no light pollution, the brilliance of an endless unfiltered sky revealed an infinite number of stars. The heavens lit the ground where he lay. The light, a fully visible Milky Way, emitted a multitude of colors so bright, pristine shadows of boulders and trees were cast, even near where he lay. While on his back, he turned his head and spotted a curved stick nearby. *Perfect*, he thought.

He turned on his side, repositioning his head for comfort. Nestling a little. Without realizing, maybe trying to comfort his unease. A restlessness? He picked up a stick and drew an outline around some of the shadows nearest where he lay. As he reached to select another shadow, he noticed the shadow seemed to be the perfect outline of a dove. And another slightly out of arm's reach. Clearly there were two. Quickly deducing from the angle, he looked for an origin. He looked but could not see what could be blocking the light. Now looking back at the shadows because he knew. Now he could see these two shadows as they were: Dark, self-emitting energy. The shadows started to move. It was as if the shadows knew that he now knew. The one closest first. The two shadows blurred. He realized the shadows were now dissipating. Were those shadows a different form of life? The outlines he drew clearly were visible and firm in the dirt. He was sure what he saw and what he was seeing. Now back into relaxing. Whatever they were, were no longer a threat. Setting his long, curved drawing stick gently on its side, he withdrew his arm, now snuggling back under the skin. He knew the shadows were no longer a concern. Still, he wondered. Would Seth have been able to see them too? Most people would've never known that they were there. Sitting motionless. Hiding in the midst of other shadows. No one would be able to see them unless they knew. Why did he and Seth clearly not see the same thing earlier? How is that possible? He knew what he saw. There was no doubt. Even though he knew he should be amazed at the appearance, the motion and dissipation of the shadows. The shadows were no longer a threat and nowhere near as important as what he'd already seen. His eyes became heavy. He drifted off very peacefully. Even though he didn't know. From necessity, peace was gifted this night, for sometimes our father knows what we need and know not.

The sun began to rise, casting its light along the ground. The light came with an edge; sharp as a sword as the light climbed over rocks and across dirt as it approached steadfastly toward Seth. Seth woke as a bright light from a brilliant sun struck his face. Eyes wide at first, seeking the realization and assurances of location and surroundings. Gathering himself from the very small amount of grass he had used as bedding to a stance, shaking the skins he had used as covering. Folding and rolling the skin used as bedding tightly into something manageable to carry. Without looking, he called over nonchalantly to his traveling companion, "Open the eyes. We must get back. We have quite a trek to get back. Even though it always seems to take longer to get where you're going than the time it takes to return. The time it takes for both trips is about the same unless we run into problems. Right, boy?" He paused and waited. "Right?" Now he looked. The boy was gone.

He ran over to where the boy had set to lay. He looked and called out. Again a little louder this time but not shouting because the boy could simply be going to the bathroom. The thought settled Seth a little. He relieved himself. As he busied himself to gather belongings, Seth began to wonder. His scan of the area became more intense now, looking for footprints on the ground. Quickly filling the water skins without looking at what he was doing. Seth didn't holler but firmly called out, "Boy, where are you? Enoch are you okay?" He looked west. Seth walked to the edge and looked down. He could see the cherub. Of course, in the daylight. Nothing completely blocked the light of the cherub. The sunlight raced across the valley, causing some of the mist to glow multiple colors. Seth then looked northeast from the Cherub at the city. As he examined both he looked for a path. He also looked for foot prints. Broken branches. Anything. A sign? Nothing? Which direction should he focus on? He looked back over his shoulder towards home. Then back west to northeast.

Seth calmed and said, "God, fill me with your breath. Just as you did for Adam in the beginning." Seth took a deep breath. He paused as he exhaled. Seth paused, worried deep into his heart, and thought which would Enoch be most interested in? Which path? A soft wind picked up. Some branches seemed to move in one spot narrowly onward somewhat down the hill. Seth started a slight smile that immediately left his face. He looked up and said, "Thank you, God." He took a quick glance back surveying where they had laid. Then turned back again. His first step was a small leap to build momentum. He would need to hurry. Carefully. Downward. He could not fail.

ENOCH CRIES UNTO GOD

If we tried to analyze today's topographical, geographical, and physical geographical maps looking for historical proof or evidence regarding the Great Garden's location, many geologists would admit we might run into great difficulties. Thousands of years of earthquakes, meteorological events, and changes in atmospheric conditions have altered the face of the earth, at times, let us say dramatically. Just for example: Giant watersheds have become barren, low lying areas have filled with water and some rivers have altered course or disappeared completely. This is not to say these changes cannot be analyzed, proven, and documented. Usually there has to be a reason. Sometimes it takes money and motivation to discover historical information. Sometimes it seems to be luck. Some things are kept secret until revealed. Will we always know why some historical data or something else is revealed? No. Rarely if ever do we know the reason some things are said to be discovered (revealed). Sometimes the most dramatic of events—geological, historical, UFOs, whatever it may be—is just so the one somewhere on earth knows the answer to the question he or she asked God. In any case, the following story's location is as yet to be discovered.

As he paused to take a drink from the river, the boy looked back at the mountain he'd left hours earlier. For a moment, he thought of Seth worrying about him. He hung his head. He did not want to be the cause of sadness. Somehow he would explain to Seth. He had to do this.

He traveled along the side of the river. He had noticed the rivers from the mountain's peak last evening. Their meandering paths and how they merged. He did not memorize every bend, but he stored information from his view available for recall. Because of the trees, he thought this river might be the Pishon. He remembered from one of the great gatherings that Adam spoke of this large river and that the Commiphora tree grows in great numbers along this river. Adam had said the tree was important for the elders. Even the young too. The gum or resin found in the tree was called bdellium. Bdellium, when burned and breathed in, helped reduce the aches and pains which befall the elders. Mainly for the elders, yet he learned it was given to others, no matter their age, when sick or injured. As he looked at the trees, he remembered its sweet, aromatic smell. He scooped up a branch while still trying to keep a fast pace. He broke it and held it to his nose. It smelled so good. Kind of seemed like his quick pace was now physically unnoticeable to himself. *Bedellium* the light stone and *bdelleium* the tree were pronounced similarly for the similitude of effect which benefited man. He loved the sound of the water and being by these trees. He was happy. It was easy to remember the tree. Now he neared where the other three rivers—Gihon, Tigris, and Euphrates—all emerged with the Pishon from one river. This next sight was hard to take in for anyone, especially a boy. This boy merely looked on at what was difficult to behold; far away he could see the head of the river that fed the Garden of Righteousness. The water fell from the sky. The mist that was created was of a magnitude beyond measurement. The mist swirled upward as if to hide the water's entrance from beyond, and it drifted away in all directions. Normally, this emergence created turbulence. Not on this day. On this day, where all four rivers emerged from the river from Eden, the water was as smooth as glass. Not even a ripple in the main river. The water was moving, but today, it seemed slow and quiet.

The Four Branches of the River that *Went Out of Eden*		
The rivers flowed eastward (the boy did not know these rivers yet, only the smells of the Gihon)		
Pishon	Land of Havilah/ hill country, east	bedellium (the light stone) and onyx
Gihon	further east, resin from trees	nectar, styrax/sarara, and galbanum

Tigris/Hiddekel	further east, resin from trees	aloe and full stacte, like almond
Euphrates	the Great River to the sea	fragrant trees of cinnamon and pepper

He could hear wings of birds fluttering all around. Some swooped near him as if curious, even seemingly accompanying and, at times, following him. Some large, some small. Some beautiful, some plain. Fancy-colored large butterflies in the flowers. Butterflies consisting of multiple colors. Some plain. But even the solid-colored butterflies were beautifully floating everywhere. It would've seemed as if an air traffic controller was required that the birds and butterflies didn't hit each other. Some butterflies landed on him, but he was moving somewhat so quickly that the butterflies could not stay with him long. So quiet he heard some very large bees on the large flowers before he saw bees the size of a man's hand. *"Don't bother them, and they won't bother you."* That was an easy one to remember. That would not be the motto for all things seen and unseen which God created. There would be many lessons to learn. Some flowering pedals the size of him. So many colors. So many fish he could not count. All the animals and beasts seemed content to lay beside the water's edge. Some large animals swimming with fish. Some larger animals' predators even stopped and watched him with obvious expressions of curiosity. Smaller animals tilted their heads. Some kind of purple fox looking creature loping beside him until a large catlike animal tackled it, pinned it, and licked it in the face. Then jumped off. Staring back. The "fox" animatedly took chase. The large cat ran as if they were lovingly playing tag. He had to slow down due to laughter, then quickly shook it off with a dead look of seriousness, regaining his former pace. Enoch had never seen such tranquility and peace from the animals, birds, and fish. Oh, how he wanted to stop and frolic as they! But he was in a hurry. He could feel in his heart, a purpose. With several leaps, bounds, and some climbing, he grabbed a quick location referencing view. Even though it was daytime, he could see the light bluish-violet glow and rays of light through the trees from the cherubim. The glow was even reflected off the water. He was close. *Not too much further*, he thought. Reality set in. He was there.

Elders said the cherubim had the face of a child. No one would be fooled by its face. Its face was not like that of an infant still fed from its mother's breast. The face was without blemish, rounded, of righteousness, and the purity that exist only in the infant of a human. The face was of one whose trust has not ever been broken. The face that endured much pain during birth and is quickly recovering to know of its first sights and smells. A face which as yet knows not what thirst is. It does not thirst. Appearing completely satisfied and justified. In a striking addition to the purity and righteousness of its face, the breastplate the cherub adorned was of a swirling flame of fire. A fire of every direction. The fiery breastplate fit comfortably. As if form fitted perfectly and appeared malleable to its body. The armor flexed when the cherub's pectorals flexed. The cherub was very muscular. Its face and head size were symmetrical in size. This cherub had a ten-foot-long sword of flame. The flaming sword could send fire almost as far as the eye could see. The sword was symmetrical to its body size. Although the cherub was large and muscular, the cherub was extremely agile and quick. Cherubs were between twelve to fifteen feet tall. This one was about eighteen feet tall. Movements? Almost fluid and graceful. Earth's gravity seemed to be of no consequence to the cherub's speed and abilities. Its muscle movements and innate inner strengths seemed to chide gravity. As if gravity were not a factor at all. This cherub was all that and more. This cherub was truly special.

There is a supposition that this particular cherub was to protect the Tree of Life from man and that protection was required because of man. This takeaway is certainly a pure truth but not an absolute truth, because man and woman were not alone in their fall and expulsion. There was another creation specified which was expelled. This other expulsion and rebels required a special cherubim to keep or guard the way to the Tree of Life. We will learn some creations would not necessarily want the fruit for themselves but, as the Vikings came to know; sons of God would seek the *fruit* from the *Tree of Life* for their children. This special sword this cherub yielded would've been destructive to more creations than just man and woman. This sword could aid in binding angels or quite probably destroy other angels.

He proceeded to walk so softly for so long his muscles ached and bulged. He crept behind a rock by a small nook in the river. He moved, sure his presence was not physically visible to the cherub. He was so young. How was he to know that cherub knew things seen and unseen? He was extremely thankful the animals no longer seemed to pay attention to him, although he noticed they really did not change in their behaviors or activities. There was relief and gratitude inside as he was keen to his situational awareness. It was as if he was in a heightened state of alertness, yet very calm with purpose. These traits utilized and demonstrated by him are normally not achieved in man until later in maturity and with great mentoring and excellent situational training. Finally, he was so close he could hear the sizzling of the sword's energy, the flickering of its flame. There were distinctly different sounds from the sword and breastplate. The breastplate was of blue, purple, and neon green, but mainly red and orange. The flame of the sword was mainly a golden color and red but consisted of the blue, green, and purple too. The cherub had wings of gold, whose breadth was no doubt large enough to carry this cherub's weight. The boy knew instantly not all cherubs were the same. This one was different. He tried very hard to remain out of the cherubim's view. He noticed from the self-emanating lights and colors it moved. The cherub had moved. Closer? Closer to him. His awareness now heightened, he also noticed dead silence.

No noise. Not a sound. Except for the cherub. Now he saw no animals. They were gone. He saw a beetle scurrying away from his location. It was moving faster than he thought a beetle could. Huh. He thought. Must be inside-the-Garden animals and outside-the-Garden animals? He listened. No sounds except from the cherubim. The sounds emanating from the sword were extreme and intense. Enoch marveled at the way the surrounding trees and foliage seemed to vibrate from the sound of energy emitted from the sword.

Now he could also hear the sound of grass giving way to the weight of the cherub's steps. The sounds were really close? The boy pressed his back hard against the boulder he was behind. The vibrations in the boulder matched the sound. To most, it would've seemed an unusual unseen energy emitting from the sword. Enoch simply accepted what he was taking in. He felt it. He knew. There was a shadow on the ground caused from the boulder he was behind. The boulder blocked light emanating from the Guardian.

The boy could see light flickering in many directions to each side of the rock he was behind. To the boy, this was not an eerie glow at all. It was magnificent. The rays seemed pure. He was not afraid. The boy was in awe. Outward from the center of the boulder's shadow, he could see the light reflecting from the cherub's upper body getting larger. He could make out the cherub's face now reflecting off the grass. The swords distinct reflected image extended onto the water a good distance away. All beginning with the top of the boulder's shadow also centered from his own head. There was no doubt of the power of this sword and the cherub's abilities. He felt internal confirmation. The sword could easily cleave the boulder in half. And him too! The cherub slowed his motion to a stop. *This is it*, he thought.

Maybe he could jump in the nook and swim away, holding his breath underwater. He slowly closed his eyes. Enoch was too young for all this. Of this, it is certain. But what moved Enoch to be here at this moment was far more important to Enoch, outweighing all other ramifications. Merely five years old, it was not bravado that brought him here. It was purity of heart. So great was this throughout his soul, it had to be addressed. He thought, *Trust*. That thought was followed with, *I trust in you, God.* Everything within him changed. There was no time. The time is now. This was it. From his hunched position, arms spread wide behind the boulder. He stepped out from behind the rock. He did not jump. He stepped out.

As he stepped in the open, he simultaneously lowered his arms to his side. Now he was standing beside the rock and facing the cherubim. Although the distance between the two measured in mere feet describing this encounter as face to face seems like a stretch. The boy's neck was awkwardly upward and required a slight arching of the back. Enoch's legs momentarily went weak at the knees. He caught himself, locking his knees, just long enough to prevent himself from crumbling. Then a weakness inside. Enoch unlocked his knees and forced himself to stay. He whispered, "Oh Most Holy One, give me strength." Gradually the boy's fear and weakness noticeably dissipated. He looked up at the cherub's face. Enoch had been told the cherubim's head and face was that of a baby. To Enoch, that was not at all what the face looked like. It was a face of intense innocence. After the quick look, he could no longer look directly at the cherub. The light from it and the sword actually caused great discomfort. A blinding light which forced a natural instinct to try and shade the eyes, mainly from the sword. The cherub prepared to strike.

The cherub quickly raised its sword as it prepared a striking stance. Its wings quickly completely tucked for greater ground maneuverability. The boy looked somewhat in the cherub's direction but clearly beyond where they both stood. The boy extended his arms downward slowly and methodically as he stepped out in the open beside the rock. He now unfolded his hands to open palms then said, "I've come to see you, Most Holy One. If you are real, I can see you." He continued to cry out, "He Who Lives, why can you not forgive? Why will you not show your Face?" The little boy was sincerely reasoning as to why he might be seeking wisdom and answers. Willing to face certain death and totally unaware of other risks and ramifications. The boy didn't fully comprehend that he was asking for forgiveness for all mankind but, that is exactly what Enoch was doing at that very moment. He actually had no clue how bad evil and wickedness was to escalate. How could he? He was just a little boy driven by a need towards resolution. A gust of wind from behind came striking his back and him, throwing his hair forward and upward.

Just as the sword began a downward motion, the wind, accompanied by a shadow hit the Guardian Cherub. The glow was for the boy to see through his own billowing hair, which was raggedly slapping his face. The shadow was very unusual. This translucent light blue shadow was not created by the absence of light. It seemed independent, not really blocking the light from the sun because it did not cast a shadow on the ground. The wind and glow flew upward toward the sword on its downward strike. The flames flickered heavily in the wind, now dimming in intensity. The sword slowed. The sword stopped before it was to devastate its target. The cherub's muscles, which had bulged, now seemed to relax. There was a different activity now. He couldn't hear it. The boy felt it. He knew.

Not instantaneously but the cherub's appearance did change methodically and quickly. Changing from one with a forceful and firm intent, now revealing traits and characteristics. To reveal a kind, compassionate, and caring cherub. The cherub returned to its original guardian pose, all except the angled head, kindly looking down at Enoch. All its brilliance seemed to change in intensity. The cherub's flames seemed to calm and dim a little as the wind accompanied a glowing flow of the lightest of a blue-colored light or like a cloud to us? The boy and the cherub's gaze both followed it upward as it left. The boy turned his head over his right shoulder to look, having to turn to follow the angle of its movement. It continued skyward. No fear. His only thought? Almost a question. *It's not going over the Garden?* It's headed to where the sky was beginning to change. In one area of the sky, the sky began to swirl.

It wasn't like the sky had clouds or a wind swirling. Clouds didn't really exist then as they do today. Clouds of mist lowered to the ground, but foliage was much larger and thicker and were in areas very large and dense, which caused a difference in the mix of carbon dioxide, oxygen, and nitrogen, enabling the atmosphere to hold water differently when this lad was a boy. The boy intently watched. It seemed almost as if the blue sky was like water in one area. The exact area where the light blue glow accompanied by the wind now had a rippling effect that made the sky almost seem fluid or liquid-like. He knew it wasn't water. That was not possible. The sky began to ripple with waves, like the sky was now fluid. The colors of the swirl began several shades of blue. From the lightest, cobalt blue, to the darkest, navy blue. Now the swirl almost looked as if it had depth. Almost like a tunnel where no tunnel existed. The swirl or circular motion did not begin as small but did expand in size greatly. The shape in the sky now seemed almost as if it were a window to an unknown which always existed. An unknown which was very real and always there, just not normally visible. As this revelation solidified in permanence, a very large man simultaneously became clear and visible also. The boy could see His Face. God was accompanied by four large men with wings. Each man was recognizably different in physical attributes than the other and was dressed in garments that would further cause unique distinction of each of the four. Two were at each side. All four seemed as men in all aspects except that each had four wings. There was one that was to the right of the very large man seated at the table of fabulous makings. He smiled at the boy. The smile soothed the anxiety and genuine fear that was building then faded. Dressed in casual attire, the winged man did display a type of liking toward the boy. He wore a long hooded robe with a golden rope around the waist accompanied with an extra bundle of rope. All four had the extra golden rope and carried it different. One had it draped over his shoulder and looked like a mountain climber or traveler. Enoch felt the exchange of warmth in his heart and entire being from the hooded man that smiled and had wings. There was an exchange of equal curiosity and wonderment between the two. What seemed like five to six minutes lasted only a few seconds. The sun stood still, so time was irrelevant. The boy thought it was unbelievable that the boy and the man to the right arm of the large man exchanged similarities at an equal level. One wore the armor of a warrior and was helmeted. All wore the breastplate of fire, but another had the build of a laborer and was adorned with a some type of metal headband that emanated a glow of energy. The traveler had a golden staff and sang soft songs of glorious wonder to God while lightening spewed nondestructively in all directions, accompanied with sounds of ground-shaking thunder from all four. The lightening was electrum and different from the energy of light the boy had witnessed from clouds of mist near mountains.

The wind seemed to dissipate as the separation between heaven and earth opened. The clouds were no longer translucent. They solidified. A large man was seated in the middle, and the boy knew in an instant he was God. His appearance of electrum was a mix of many shades of blue. A little purple and violet seemed to help define His physique. He was not fat nor were all His muscles extremely well-defined. But He was a very large and strong man in appearance. At first, the boy's gaze ignored the fact that He began to look up from what seemed like a table or altar He was sitting at. Slowly, He began to return the look of the boy. The boy's gaze began at the large bulbous toes and feet, which wore the most basic of sandals. His plain garment or robe was past his knee, now jutting into view as He maneuvered. He wore His garment as if it were merely draped to cover His body as casual attire. He turned to lean over and to the side of the table's end. The garment was not made or worn to cover His arms. His forearms and biceps were fully exposed. The boy's gaze quickly traveled upward, noticing the chest half exposed and a little hairy. A staff with the appearance of knotted wood was in His right hand. Suddenly His Face grabbed most of the boy's attention. Burly white curly locks of hair billowing in the wind. Thick white mustache, sideburns and beard fitting well to his face, consisting of locks in length which billowed. He could even see bushy eyebrows billowing in wind. A wind which seemed to blow in His Face more intensely as he was beginning to lean downward. Directly toward the boy. Not a word. The man spoke not a word to the boy but did seem to communicate in spirit to the other *four*. Just a look. A look as if He were busy but now interrupted by the boy. That was quite enough for the boy. He pulled back and away as if he were in a trance. The boy looked back toward the cherub. The cherub was back at its post, guarding the way to Eden.

The next thing the boy knew, he felt some bouncing. What happened? Awareness began to set in. He was flopping around slung over someone's shoulder. The boy lifted his head by pushing with both hands off the back of someone that was running while carrying him. While trying to control the bobbing and weaving, he tried to obtain a look. The cherub was halfheartedly chasing them with the sword. The sword spewed forth flame which extended pretty far outward but not hitting anything. Seth took a giant leap over the fallen tree then did a side-jump to the very large stump from which the tree had fallen. Seth then leaped up and into the tightly fitted seat on the back of a very dark-black five-ton unicorn. The horn of the unicorn seemed like the bone of a narwhal. The flame withdrew to the sword as the cherub returned the sword in a ready to strike position. The cherub slowed and walked. The boy thought he could see the cherub smile? The cherub stopped and turned. The boy was confident the cherub returned to its post. The boy relaxed back into going with the flow. It was easier on both of 'em. The boy tried to steady himself and said, "I saw God."

Seth said, "What?"

"I saw God," came the reply. Seth was concerned about how he found the boy, but obviously, right now, there were more important things to be concerned with.

Seth said, "Do you see the cherubim? Is it upon us? Is it ready to strike?"

The boy said, "No. It went back to its post." This was not of the winged unicorn but was amazingly agile for its giant size and weight. The unicorn was bounding like a gazelle over ravines and fallen trees and even leaping from boulders. How a beast this size was agile on an oddly shaped boulder was amazing. Even more amazing was the understandings between the rider and the unicorn. The unicorn actually knew to get away from the cherub as quickly as possible. The unicorn knew the *fear of God*, as do all animals. This is not to say the unicorn does not or would not passionately obey God's commands, but animals were assigned by God to be subject to man's care, the care being reciprocal. And the unicorn understood the Holy Spirit's compassionate desire that we know and love God but leave or receive God's wrath. Seth turned his body as much as he could to confirm with his own eyes the cherubim was no longer about to end their lives. After looking over the shoulder without the boy, Seth maneuvered his body to look back over the other. The cherub was gone. The glow was back in position near the entrance to the Garden of Righteousness.

Seth calmed and asked, "What were you doing? Were you trying to die?"

The boy said, "I wanted to see God."

Seth said, "Never ever do that again."

Amazed and now a little perturbed. The boy said, "But I saw Him, I saw The Most on High."

TRAINING SESSIONS

At the time Enoch was too young to understand completely all the teachings, memorization and songs, but he loved the time spent together with everyone, and he loved learning. Most of all, he loved learning of God. What he had done, what he could do, and his love for man stirred the little boy deep inside.

The training of the Word would last according to the length of passing of the sun or moon. There was morning, beginning the day of the greater light. There was evening beginning the night with a lesser light. The sign of the beginning of the first training session was the night of the moon when it was its fullest, brightest, and roundest. Enoch was told at the training sessions and shown there were thirty of what they called days and nights in a period. Enoch was told that he had to attend the training sessions every seventh day. He couldn't miss it.

For Enoch was told the signs of the first lights at night were to be the sign which begins the day. During training, it was said, "First, there was darkness then came the light." And that was the beginning and thus the beginning of all the days, nights, periods, and cycles. He didn't know the seasons yet by name but knew there were four. Although there were about twelve full days of rest in each season, there were six daytime training sessions of the cycle and an equal number of night training sessions of each cycle.

Enoch liked the day sessions for those sessions were the greatest of gatherings. The smells of the food and other aromas which were in the air smelled enticing. He would never forget these gatherings. He loved the gatherings so much Enoch would run full speed toward the smells. He learned a lot. Many things. He loved it. At times, certain smells would bring memories of these gatherings. These gatherings were the best of occasions. Everyone was so nice, and he could spend time with people from villages from afar. They would come too. Oh, the different foods were so good. His ma made great meals, but at these gatherings were many different foods that others seemed to enjoy. The day sessions were the longest with meals throughout the day. There were also days they couldn't eat, but the boy didn't mind at all. It was for some reasons these days seemed the longest and he learned the most. He thought people ate too much anyway. The nighttime training sessions were the most interesting to Enoch. Under the stars and moon, the elders would speak. Sometimes beside the glow and intense heat, the elders prepared for their words to be shared. Enoch was told the stuff that looked like dirt was dug from underground entrances. When this valuable powder was added to the glow stone the light became much brighter. The light was a soft or sky blue very bright. The elders would speak at night sharing knowledge that each knew since his own beginning. But at times, there became serious arguments amongst elders. There were times when the oldest, Adam, would speak and all would listen. Enoch could tell some elders did not like Adam. They were mean. Some even evil. But for the most part even though some did not like Adam, they all agreed, Adam was first. They all agreed that "He Who Lives" made Adam. And there was no doubt Adam was the oldest. So he spoke on this night, and this is what he said: "God shows us many things. He has never left us. His Spirit kindles the fire inside us that protects us from those that strike at times deadly blows to our heels. God allowed Jared's boy to survive when approaching the Garden of Righteousness. I caution any of you. The only reason this boy was close was because he is too young to know of *knowledge of the tree*. None of you go there, for it has changed from when Eve and I lived there. It is now to become an extremely deadly area no longer to be at all. He lives with us and among us, and His Spirit dwells inside us. Listen!" Adam's voice reverberated for all to hear. "God sent me an angel whilst I slept. My Lord did awaken me and take me outside without awakening anyone. Mahaleel's noisy, winged, purple-and-blue-feathered kraiets that lay the large blue eggs never even made a peep. My Lord sat with me under the stars and told of future days. He said, 'Tell others that they who believe will know what it means.' Who am I to withhold that which might change another life forever? Now know this."

Story by Adam

The man traveled about as far west as one could go until he was returning home from the east. And the man did travel about as far east as he could go until it seemed he returned home from the west. North and south were traveled about the same as his eastward and westward travels until the directions only mattered for navigational purposes.

It was then the man found himself in a waste and water long metal and stone cave. This very large round metal and stone cave was man-made with sophisticated machinery that used fire for energy with smoke billowing in the air. The cave was used to drain all the human waste and feces from the big city. Houses on top of each were built to reach the heavens. As the man walked, the stench and filth was wretched. He couldn't go back; he wasn't welcome. Where he had come from, he was no longer welcome. It was a dead end. So he pushed forward until the darkness became blindness day after day, month after month. Finally, way in the distance, there seemed a faint light—a difference in the blackness. For a moment, he thought his eyes to be playing tricks on him again. So forward he pressed on. At times invisible smoke filled the round man made cave of metal so thick it would make eyes water and hard to breath. He dared not make fire with wood and rock. He was drenched and covered with feces and filth. Rats ran about in the darkness. He could hear them scurrying about and at times feel them. Some checked him out and even climbed on him. He wasn't sure why. Maybe it was to see if he was edible and willing to fight to survive. He was. He brushed them away. There were thousands of other tiny creatures too—worms with many legs and various species of insects, worms, roaches, beetles, bugs, and many other creepy and crawling things he didn't even know existed. Strange enough, these critters seemed to have adapted and seemed at home. As he closed in on the light, the light from above revealed a ladder up. A way out? The exit at the top of the ladder was blocked. It was very noisy up there. He climbed and struggled a bit but pushed aside the cover and looked around.

The noise was intense. The sounds hurt his head and body. The sounds were maddening. There seemed no rhythm or purpose to the sounds, just bone-jarring noise. The light hurt his eyes. Thousands to tens of thousands of men everywhere. Many men were inside metal things that moved this way and that. Some of these things were the the size which could hold six men yet, with only one inside. Some smaller. Some much larger with twenty to thirty men and women inside. These things were man made but growled with fire inside with smoke coming out the end. They all seemed to be herded by unseen desires and made sounds when angry like the sheep horn when blown. Many looked intently at something in their hand which put a light on their face. There were buildings that reached the sky. There were so many people that they pushed and shoved. If a person stopped before crossing the street, they were pushed from behind. He saw no trees. Back down he went. This was not the place for him. At the bottom, there was a junction. He sat in the muck pondering which way to go. This would be the first time he met a *mud derkel*. The mud derkel popped out from a recess or crack in the wall. It was almost like a frog yet different. It sat, tilted its head, and stared at him. It was greenish gray in color and had smooth skin, except for the bumps all over. It sat in a squatted position, ready to leap. It had yellow catlike eyes. The man and the mud derkel made eye contact. They were both at peace. Although one was home and one was traveling, both seemed at peace and accepting of their fates, destinies, and even more important, God's purpose, mission, and works.

A beam of light from above did shine on the mud derkel. The man heard and watched a fly approach through the air. Unfazed as the fly went by, the mud derkel swung out a long red slimy tongue and *snap*. It captured the fly with its very long tongue, recoiling it to its mouth, the fly as food, before one could blink an eye. This was over and done with in less than half a second. The head barely turned to complete the task, and its eyes barely left the gaze of the man. As the mud derkel sat with an awkward gaze at the man, it slowly reached out to him. Suddenly, a smaller fatter one jumped from the same fissure and snap-cracked its tongue, slicing the man's finger. Strangely, the tiny tongue lash caused a small wound on the man's finger. Now both seemed ready to strike the man again. Before either mud derkel could make its move, a sharp light burned through a tiny hole from above the cover overhead, right where the mud derkels were both perched. Both the smaller rounder mud derkel and the larger slenderer mud derkel slipped back, disappearing into the crack. The man leaned against the wall, puzzled. Then came a voice seemingly alive within the light. The voice said, "You will see a very comely tree. It is not for your consummation, not as yet. Pull and uproot the tree and throw it into the bitter waters of which you cannot drink." The light faded. The man had no idea what this meant. As he looked in the other three directions from whence he came, for some reason, one felt more favorable. So the man pressed on in the most favorable of directions. The tiny wound itched and burned a little. The man paid it no mind.

Day after day, it was the same routine: see an access to what was above, climbing up, peer around (only to feel as if he wouldn't fit in), and return back to the stench and filth of cave. The smell was enough to make someone vomit, but not him. He had now grown used to the smells now. It was not home, but it began to seem as though it might as well be. The tiny wound was festering now with blackness eerily winding up his finger and into his hand and arm. He wondered, "Were those mud derkels poisonous?" Out of the thousands of tiny- to medium-sized living creatures in the cave, why would those two attack him? It was not as if they could eat him. Or was there a way they might devour him? He was sickened and confused. Finally, the man began to talk to himself. Then the man began to talk as if another was there and as if the other had been with him all along. Finally, the man became so comfortable and at peace; the man stated, "If only you will help find the home I need. From then on, I will look to you." The man became particular and added requirements that were more like requested conditions: "Not home I want but a home I need, a companion, a helper, a woman to raise a family," for the man was lonely. Although he wasn't alone, he needed the touch and warmth of another one's breath. Suddenly a soft breeze was felt. The man thought, *From where?*

To him the air was almost too pungent, for it was fresh. He picked up his pace. He could see light in the distance. As he approached, he saw a tree. It was only waist-high, but its leaves shone brilliantly. From its branches was also a fruit of some kind. He hungered. His arm was grotesquely darkening now. He wondered. He pondered. If he were to eat, might it cure his aliments? Then he remembered the light and the voice—the only brightness in a world where he was surely lost. He almost ran forward, his feet splashing. He didn't care. All the living creatures scattered. He grabbed the tree with all his might. His blackened arm, which was no longer of much use, gained amazing strength. He paid that thought no mind and only thought, *Throw the tree into bitter waters.* He did a twirl as if there were room that wasn't available for a hammer throw. The tree sailed through and into the darkness of the cave. It disappeared. He started to hang his head when heard a soft splash. From brick and mortar, everything swirled in fluidity. Suddenly he was there. Just a few steps forward was a noisy babbling brook with water so clear he could see the fish running. The light was excruciatingly bright even though he was shaded by the many trees. The foliage was beautiful and bountiful. Trees, flowers, and fruit were everywhere.

A beauty to sore eyes suddenly appeared almost straight across the brook from him. A woman popped out of an opening similar to his own. They made eye contact, and both looked at their surroundings, thoroughly speechless. They did smile softly at first, then broadly. He stepped into the brook. His shoes were so worn the clean water washed his feet within. A dog burst past the woman, almost knocking her down, running to the man, and it jumped up to greet the man. Obviously, the dog was overwhelmed with emotion; it wanted and desired to be with the man. The woman too. The man and woman both gracefully walked toward each other, meeting in the middle and reaching out open hands then clasping, never to let go. At the same time, they sat in the brook, took a deep breath, and lay back to die and be born again—life anew, heaven on earth all together as one. Who was this man and the woman? Who were they? What am I to do with this?

Adam continued, "Who am I to know all the wisdom and secrets of God? But it is with absolute certainty that I do know I am to carry the message forward. It may be for you to carry, for I do know this. This message is for through this one, God will offer opportunity that will change everything for all the people."

The story made Enoch think. Enoch did not like the mean men. Enoch did not trust all that they said. Enoch knew some of what they said was true because they said the "Watchers" taught them. But many wore evil on their faces and Enoch knew he could not trust those men. Most of them were from a "City." Enoch heard of the "City." The city actually bore his name, Enoch. The city, having the same name as him, stirred a little curiosity in him, but Enoch really wanted nothing to do with the city. Enoch had heard of the many awful things that happened there and of the many rules which had to be followed to live there. Enoch heard everything the people possessed was not their own, even the food. The boy understood sacrifice as gifts to God but to take everything and give it to the ones who had the most; this did not seem right to Enoch. Enoch did not want to live there.

It was good that the men from the city did not always come to the gathering. Because when they did, it was usually sad and upsetting when they argued. They didn't get to learn names of all the animals. There were so many. It was almost impossible for Adam to tell of all he knew. Enoch loved learning about all the animals. There were so many animals. There were animals that were absolute giants. Some were so small and jumped a great distance. Some could climb the smoothest of surfaces. The big beast mainly just ate tree leaves that no one wanted. If the big animals were ever caught eating the roof of their buildings, someone would just run over with a staff and shoo them off. Or if a youngster was busy, he would just throw a rock near it. Didn't have to hit it. The boy showed some kids who didn't know that they did not have to hit it with rocks. They just needed to get its attention. It would obey man's commands if it were taught the commands. Or the animals could be convinced of what a man wanted it to do without hurting it. All animals were smart. But the trust between man and animal was being broken. The trust between man and animal was broken once the fallen angels mated with women because the offspring of fallen angels began to kill the animals to drink their blood and eat their flesh while the animal was still alive.

Not all animals knew of this phenomenon yet. Adam said that this way was not meant from the beginning. Animals began to teach their young of man. It was not easy for their young to tell the difference between Nephilim and man. Some animals could tell. But the trust was still being broken because man was collaborating with Nephilim and eating animals even though there was not such a great need to. The men Enoch knew would only kill that which was a gift towards God's purpose. Many animals seemed to understand this until the Nephilim grew in number. With some animals, the trust did not seem to be broken. So some animals saw man and obeyed man.

They boy loved listening to Adam. Adam displayed great emotion when he spoke and could teach from the very beginning in such a way it was really easy to learn. Adam always stood tall among the rest. Everyone looked up to Adam and many of the other elders would go to Adam with questions. Adam would stand by the glow under the stars at night and tell how all the stars were in their place in abeyance to God. That all was alive. The trees, the seas, all the waters, and the earth were alive and lived in abeyance to He Who Lives. Everyone had to memorize and learn to speak of creation and their line of birth. Some could tell of knowledge and share information much better than others. When they spoke, they seemed to be filled with an energy the boy was finally beginning to understand. The boy knew the energy was real. The boy had seen where it comes from and felt it himself.

Adam was really so kind and loving to children, women, and other men, but Adam was also kind to all the animals, even the flowers and plants they all ate. Adam seemed very different from all other men even Seth, Adam's son. Adam was older than Seth; of course, he was his da. Even though they both looked old, they both looked about the same age. Adam even seemed more agile than his son. All men carried or walked with a staff, but Seth and Enosh (Seth's son) seemed to lean on their staff more than Adam did? Adam was very special. All the Adams were not as Adam. Adam was to have children. One of Adam's offshoots was Seth. Of course, there were more. Seth was to have offspring, one of which was Enosh. This was when after Enosh, a son was born to Seth. We are not sure of when this transition period began. It was probably made clear in one of the 366 books and more that were written and carried on the ark by Noah. But from ages of those men written of, we can ascertain it may have been around three hundred to three hundred and fifty years from man's creation that there were some who had learned from Adam, Eve, and many other unknown ways and that maybe our Lord had been reaching out, calling to, or even communicating with man. For it was in the days of Enosh that men began to call upon our Lord, some say to pray unto Adonai (Adonay) or even cry unto God. These may have been very exciting times for young boys and girls, and sadly, these days would also contain tribulations. No one is to conjecture with certainty, but in most cases, just because a son or daughter has to no longer live at home does not mean the father doesn't love with all his heart and would not do everything he could to help them *if they ask or if they want help from their father.*

It was on this night Adam spoke of the beginning. Adam was the only one there at the beginning of man, so all were quiet and attentive. Adam spoke of how he and Seth's ma, Eve, ate a forbidden fruit and changed. Adam said they both physically changed. They had been warned by He Who Lives that created Adam and Eve that they could not eat the fruit or they would die. Adam said they were tricked by a serpent, that they were lied to and surely they would not die. But it was almost immediate that both their flesh changed. Adam said that even inside their body, they could feel changes like movement inside and that suddenly they knew things they shouldn't. They could tell. They felt awful. They felt horrible. They both felt shameful. They knew what they did was wrong, so they hid from Adonay. It all happened too Fast. They didn't understand. No one would really understand for thousands of years what happened. What happened was too much for man to handle. After he had eaten the fruit man now knew that not only his flesh was naked but man also realized his mind was naked unto God. This was something man was not ready for at all. His thoughts were revealed unto God. And, he was experiencing bad thoughts for the first time. It was all so truly shameful. Now Adam and Eve were truly like children with nowhere to hide from their father.

He Who Lives came, and although He still loved them, they could no longer be in His presence. Since they changed, they could not live with Him anymore. So Adonay told them to stand nearby with the mist then slip into the body of water of the ground nearby. Adam said they did what Adonay said, but now the water seemed cold. They both were cold. Then they both watched in shock and horror as Adonay slaughtered some animals, removing their skin. Adam and Eve had never seen Adonay behave in such a way. They both became very afraid for the very first time. Now they both knew fear. Now they both feared whom they knew loved them. He Who Lives told them both to come out of the water and come to Him in the midst of all the blood from the animals. Then Adonay personally clothed them. Adonay placed the warm skin on their cold bodies. Now warm, Adonay told them they must leave paradise, the Garden of Eden, the only home they had ever known. Without saying a word, they both knew Adonay still loved them but they had to leave. Immediately, they both knew humility. It wasn't just the nakedness of man's flesh he was ashamed of and, not necessarily the good thoughts he experienced was he ashamed but, it was man's bad thoughts which truly brought him shame. They then turned in shame and walked away.

Men like Cain would seek to hide their bad thoughts and shame behind structures of thick stone or rock. Others would seek God and ways to overcome bad thoughts realizing there really was no need to hide their shame anymore. Some would try to live humbly by the sweat of their brow and tilling of the ground. Eventually God would grant a sanctuary built upon a divine cornerstone of love, forgiveness, mercy and grace. But not yet, for man was still too arrogant believing his was like the angels. After all man was in the image of God and God's children as were angels also his children. Man would need to become more humble before man would ever seek forgiveness.

As Adam and Eve headed east, they heard the command for the cherubim to keep the way to the tree of life. They could hear the flame as it came to life as part of the cherub's sword. Holding hands, they both turned to look back toward the west. Even from a great distance, the yellowish light mixed with the red and orange flame was almost too much to behold. Not to mention the pain of expulsion. Now it seemed they were in a world on their own. They would need to get busy building shelter, gathering food, tilling soil for future fruits. They would have to build a home. Their own house. Adam was suddenly interrupted by arguments from the men who came from the great city.

Their eldest one, called Cain, said the sons of God were teaching those of the city many things. Cain was a breathtaking sight to behold. Cain said the children of the sons of God were conspiring to take women, as did their fathers, and kill men who would stand in their way and that all men might need to unify to fight, for surely they planned on killing men. Enoch wondered what children of the sons of God looked like. He didn't get it because man was created by God too. Cain sure was different, but no one cared of his appearance. These men from the city with Cain were dressed very different than the men Enoch lived with. These men wore a type of armor and had weapons that glistened and shimmered by the glow. Enoch tried to stay away from these men because these men made people serve them. Even get them drinks. Enoch did not want to be near them.

One of the men in their group was resting in a small sitting area slightly back from the elders. The man called for Enoch, beckoning Enoch to come to him. Waving him over to his side. Enoch had to obey elders, so he obeyed. The man really wasn't an elder, but he was clearly a man. And it would be rude not to entertain an invitation. The man introduced himself to little Enoch, saying, "I am Lamech, descendant of Cain, whom He Who Lives said no one can kill lest vengeance be brought upon him." Lamech was truly attempting to be friendly to the little boy. Lamech was bragging to gain respect.

As Enoch approached, he noticed the man smelled awful. The man opened his metal garment and handed a sharp, shiny weapon to Enoch, explaining to the little boy the weapon's usefulness. Out of Enoch's peripheral, he saw someone trip carrying a drink and spill some of the drink on the man showing Enoch the weapon. The man quickly turned his attention to the server and grabbed him, who at that very moment was being extremely apologetic and humble. The man from the city pulled from beneath his garment of fighting another sharp weapon. Enoch was close; he could hear the soft sound of metal mesh the man's overgarment was made of as the man revealed a weapon. Another weapon with a handle adorned with bedillium, onyx, and other seemingly precious stones. The weapon was much larger than the one he handed Enoch. But not as long as the very large cutting knife Lamech displayed boldly at his side. Lamech wore jeweled adornment in a gold band around his head. He had much adornment around his neck and even around his wrist. Most men accompanying Lamech and Cain from the city wore much of the same. They even had precious stones on their outer garments.

As quickly as the young server had tripped, slamming into Lamech's side, spilling the drink; Lamech was just as quick to grab the server by the hair. Lamech lifted the man upright by his hair then leaned his head back. Using the weapon, he cut with a quick motion. While the city man still held the server's head, Lamech announced, "I have killed a man for wounding me and now a youngling for bruising me. If Cain is to be avenged seven times over, for any who slay Cain, I, Lamech, tell you truth, I will be avenged seventy-seven times over."

Enoch looked at the blood on the ground. The ground seemed to open a small crack, and after some blood flowed slowly in it closed quickly. The boy looked around, and no one else had noticed the ground open and close. Some applauded; many others focused on the people of the scene. He then looked at the weapon in his own hands. It was a horrible thing. Over spilling a drink? Spillage of a drink is not good, but this was not justice or righteousness. Enoch was not afraid. He searched inside himself. Could he be next? Something was horribly wrong with many men, and he knew it. Enoch determined he was to take a stance of preparedness. Enoch steadied his feet. He slid one foot slightly back, very quietly and gently twisted his foot into the dirt of the ground seeking a good, firm stance. He knew he would need the strength of that leg to strike a blow with the weapon in his hand, already at the ready. Enoch settled within. There was calm; there was peace. Enoch felt sure this was to be the day Enoch died. Still holding the server's head, admiring death, and how the ground drank the blood, he slowly turned his attention down toward the little boy and smiled. Enoch saw wickedness in the man's face and evil in his black eyes. Enoch still knew no fear. Enoch did not smile. They both locked eyes. As the body fell to the ground, people stepped out of the way.

Adam, Enoch's father, Jared, Mahalalel, Kenan, Enosh, and many others did not step away. They all rushed to little Enoch's side. Enoch did not know whose grasp which wrapped around Enoch like a blanket because Enoch remained locked in eye contact with Lamech. Enoch had to look at who had him. It was Seth. Seth pulled Enoch slowly into his body. Caringly, caressingly, but also very tightly. Without saying a word, Seth slowly slid his hand down Enoch's arm to Enoch's tight grip of the mini sword. With a light slide over Enoch's grip, barely touching Enoch, Enoch opened his hand. Then angling his palm downward, he let the mini sword fall to the ground. Enoch felt at ease. He felt peace. Enoch hadn't noticed, but all the men had closed in. Enoch had been very focused. He could now hear all the commotion and loud shouts of commands from other men quieting. Then silence. Then the one called Cain said, "Enough!"

Irad (Cain's grandson) shouted to all, "We did not come for this. We came because the Nephilim are growing in great number and having a thirst which cannot be quenched." Seth slipped Enoch behind him. Leaving Enoch behind, Seth stepped nearest the glow, holding his staff upright.

Cain beckoned loudly that all could hear. Cain shouted, "The sons of God have given us much knowledge in enchantments and roots which heal. They have taught us many skills in working of metals, giving man much advantage to subdue all the earth and rule over all beast, animals, and every living thing that lives on earth. But there is evidence that Smajaza, Azezel, and their Chieftains seek this for themselves and their seed. The sons of God take all the women for themselves. They take even the wives of good men. The sons of gods have killed men and drunk their blood. There is talk we must sacrifice our own, our firstlings, to them. In the years to come, man must unify and prepare for war. The One Who Lives knows, sees all, and does nothing. It is up to man and his weapons to stop what is to come. Together we can rule as intended."

The rest of Cain's clans all snarled, growled, and yelled, banging shields in unison with long, sharp, cutting knives and spears. Enoch heard Cain's words but did not really understand completely how someone or something could possibly do all that Cain said. But Enoch saw the wickedness and how evil men could be. He saw the darkness in their faces. The blackness in their eyes. He knew blackened eyes must match a blackened heart as well. Some of those men seemed scared. This all was very disturbing and troubling, but for some reason, Enoch was not afraid.

Seth looked down at Enoch. Seth placed one hand on Enoch's shoulder and smiled. Seth beamed brightly. There was a very soft glow about him. Enoch could see it. Seth raised his staff high, angled between the stars and earth, and stepped toward the offering altar. Everyone was intently focused on Seth as he walked toward the altar.

The alter was positioned near the center, in front of a very large boulder. Chieftains and elders spoke from the area of the altar because of its location. Very often, those chiefs or elders who shared life's lessons would move table to table as they taught. The stone altar was framed in cedar and black and twilight crape myrtle trees. The altar was positioned on a very large circular flat rock. The walls of the valley were of rock. This valley formed a natural amphitheater perfect for acoustics. The sound would carry and bounce off the walls, permitting sound to travel further. Selected for its usefulness, unique qualities for acoustics (sound), and of course, location. The valley was centrally located from the chieftains' and elders' homes. Making short travel distances for the elders and chieftains, and making it easier for them to attend. Especially since their presence was highly desired. Some people who lived further away were encouraged to stay in houses built nearby. Built for just such reason. These were very well-kept. Some enjoyed staying and visiting with family. Trading, different gatherings such as union of man and woman, festivals, and the training sessions happened here in the valley. At night, the moonlight would be captured and reflect of the shiny rock walls, making it much easier to see. There were many tables and chairs.

His Son, Enosh, stepped up to Seth's side. Seth's voice carried outward to hundreds of men as he spoke. Seth did not shout, but his magnetic charisma still carried through the valley that all could clearly hear. Seth spoke calmly and firmly. Many of you have chosen the ways of fallen angels. You have built massive cities to dwell in that your lives might be easier. Cities with many of man's laws which benefit some and force others into permanent debt, even unto slavery. These laws create inequity (inequality) among men. This is not righteousness.

God created us to till the grounds of His garden. Now because we choose that which was forbidden, to gain the knowledge of good and bad, we were served justice. For that which is just that we are to toil in harsh land and work hard with our hands to tend the ground of the earth. Then work hard we must. For the life of the earth needs man. And man needs earth and all its life. We will seek mercy from He Who Lives. Enosh added, "We will seek to atone for all we have done wrong. We will seek Forgiveness. We will do as God commanded."

Seth continued, "We will do as Abel did to please God. We will take that without flaw from the herd and offer our best to He Who Lives. For it is Him that clothed Adam and the Mother of All the Living, that they and their young would not suffer so greatly unto death. Death from the fire of the sun during the light of day. Or death from the hoar-frost that blackens flesh during the darkness of night. We truly wish no harm unto you all. But we choose life through the Spirit of God. Cain, we will trade with all of yours as long we can."

Again, Cain shouted boisterously, "What is done cannot be undone. The sons of God have shown man many mysteries of heaven. Man can now melt metals to make the sword, knife, and many other tools for easier construct. Now man is strong. Only man can protect man and woman with weapons and his own strength. Yes, Seth we will always trade with you and yours. Now come. We must return to the city together for there are a few Nephilim which were cast from the city who are disillusioned, who roam with much hunger and thirst. When the tree's shadow covers my knife, we leave for the city." People quickly stood aside and made clear a path between Cain and the shadow. Cain pulled his knife, throwing it a great distance, landing it upright in the ground.

Many were gathering belongings, agreeing to head back to the security of the city. Others were dispersing, getting some more food and drink. A young one of an isle from the city around Enoch's age came over to Enoch. He seemed caring. He proudly introduced himself. He said, "I am Tubal-Cain, son of Lamech. From the great city called Enoch. Who are you?"

While Tubal-Cain spoke, he pointed in the direction of the city. Enoch replied, "I am Enoch son of Jared. I live here." Enoch spread both his arms wide.

Tubal-Cain said, "The name of the great city is Enoch. The city is named after the son of Cain. The same Cain, He Who Lives, said, "Vengeance shall be taken sevenfold on whomsoever kills Cain. Come to the city with us. I saw you, Enoch. You are very brave. You will do well in the city. Besides, since your name is the same as the city, all the young women will think the great city is yours. And they will want you. Come. You could become great."

Enoch looked down at the ground. He thought of the earth. The dust beneath his feet. He thought of the work he must do for his family. He thought of all their animals. Ba'headge, Keller, Gidgag, and not to mention, Criggy. Enoch liked Criggy. She was friendly and very nice. He knew he would miss her. Enoch said, "No, I cannot. My family is here. They love me, and I love them. God is our way. Not the way of the city." While Enoch's stance was meager, hands at his sides, when he spoke to Tubal-Cain, his appearance seemed to change. When Enoch spoke, he would make direct eye contact and seemingly stand more erect. Not many would even notice. Tubal-Cain, on the other hand, stood with a slightly wider stance, hands on his hips. Enoch was older than Tubal-Cain, by maybe eleven or twelve years. But among early men, the age difference was hard to tell unless there was a great difference. It wasn't the age that brought about this chesty or proud mannerism because even more came over and they all acted haughty or lofty but, for some reason were curious of Enoch. Enoch thought maybe all people of the city were like this.

Jubal, Tubal-Cain's stepbrother, approached to talk to Enoch. Jubal was closer to Enoch's age. "I am Jubal. My father is Lamech. Adah, my mother and family wish to herd the cattle."

Jubal stepped in the group closer to Enoch and said, "Enoch, Here, you can have this." Jubal handed a pipe to Enoch. Enoch was puzzled. He slowly took the flute, examining it. It looked harmless enough.

Enoch said, "What is this?"

Jubal excitedly said, "Listen." Jubal pulled another flute and began to play a rapid, upbeat sound. Others around began to bounce, wiggle, and jiggle. Enoch saw that everyone's behavior was a little odd, but Enoch was very curious indeed. His immediate thought? He didn't like the sounds. People were acting very strange to the odd chirping sounds. His presence was no longer noticed by others. Enoch imagined the sounds could be made similar to that as some of the morning birds. Enoch loved hearing them. Even some of the sounds were close to that of the hawk or eagle. Enoch nodded, holding the flute so that Jubal could see he meant to keep the gift.

Jubal added, "Take care of that. There are only two. My father was shown the special metal and how to make these two flutes by one of the many gods. My father said they are special. See how the people move when I blow into the flute?" Then Jubal nodded back and kept playing the pipe. The others seemed to become oddly enchanted by the music. Some even began to sing:

Lamech has killed a man for wounding him
and has killed a youngster for bruising him
If vengeance was to fall upon anyone who kills
Cain sevenfold
Surely vengeance for Lamech would be seven-ty-seven times more

This was all too much for Enoch. It was making him feel awful that people could be this way. It seemed no one would notice, so Enoch had turned to walk away. He walked away, hiding the flute tucking it in his garment. For a moment, he thought the flute capable of different sounds. And that he could produce and create sounds which would carry through the trees. He could see this because he remembered the vibrations that sounds make in objects. Like the sounds and vibrations he made in the wood. The vibrations and sounds which accompanied the light and energy from Cherub and his sword. The vibrations seemed to carry sound like the waves in water. Except the waves could not be seen. Not just chirps and whistles but some beautiful sounds. He would try later when he was alone. The boy did not know that this would become an extremely special flute. It had to do with its creation sure. But in the wrong hands, it caused ungodly behaviors. He didn't know that one day, God's breath would flow through him and out the flute, changing the properties of the flute and the melodies produced to create divine events not ever dreamed possible to man. Was this flute truly meant for him or another? He had a feeling. He put his hand on where the flute lay hidden beneath his garment. Near his heart. He felt a type of tingling sensation all over his body. He was overcome with emotion to the point his eyes welled. It reminded him of the day He saw God. Why? Seth called to him. Seth could tell. He could always tell when the boy drifted to Yahweh. Not that it was a bad thing. It was just that in the middle of gathering, this group brought trouble. Seth knew there could be trouble for evil was nearby this night. Seth waved him over.

Enoch went and sat by the Elders. They were in deep discussion. He could not ask questions; they barely noticed he was there. He looked over in the shadows of some shrubbery nearby. He saw two very small felines lying tightly with a larger feline. The adult feline and he made eye contact. She started to back out. Enoch grabbed some fruit from the table and held it down by his leg. Acting like he wasn't doing anything, he turned his head toward the elders. He wasn't looking at the elders. He started to pay them no mind. Enoch was merely attempting to allow the feline to be at ease. She lay back down and nudged her kittens. The two kittens crept to Enoch's side as he looked ahead feeding them. He would reach for more small pieces of fruit with his right hand, switch the fruit to his left, and put it back by his leg. The kittens would gently paw the fruit from his fingers, bite and chew. So many questions. It was curious indeed that the city and he had the same name. Why? Enoch was very curious and had many questions. After senseless death and such odd behavior, this small act of sharing and camaraderie seemed to help Enoch find some peace.

He knew Tubal-Cain was not the one to ask the many questions he had. Tubal-Cain was too different than him. Tubal-Cain did reach out, seemingly warm and open. While Tubal-Cain spoke, Enoch had noticed the differences between Tubal-Cain and Himself. It seemed as though when Tubal-Cain spoke, he portrayed himself differently than what seemed to Enoch to be Tubal-Cain's true heart. It was as if Tubal-Cain relied on a weapon. Enoch liked Jubal and Tubal-Cain. Enoch had heard of temptation during training sessions but was too young to really understand how complicated being tempted can be. Why did Enoch take the knife? He put his hand on it a moment and wondered, well, it was a gift, and now it was his. So he had picked up and slipped the jeweled dagger into his garment while everyone was focused on preventing what seemed imminent between Enoch and Lamech. Enoch never wanted to hurt anyone one. The knife was not plain, though. The knife was adorned with ornaments. He took the knife because it was given to him, and he knew it could prove useful. Of course, Enoch did not really recognize that this was Enoch's first temptation. Too young. But it was very clear to Enoch, he did not like the inner swirl of excitement and emotions mixed with a great deal of curiosity. He sure had a lot of questions he wanted to ask someone.

On the way to their dwellings, all the elders were in very deep discussions, and others were troubled about the killing. When they got back, he tried to ask his mother about the city. She wanted to answer Enoch, but the discussion would be long and deep. She thought for a moment. "Enoch, it is late. You must try to go to sleep." When he got into the sleeping room with all his brothers and sisters, he tried to ask his eldest brother about the city. Many were already talking about the killing, and the blood of man spilled purposely on the ground.

Enoch whispered to his older brother, "Are all the people in the city bad?"

His brother said, "Not all the people in the city are bad. But to live in the city, they must follow man's laws. To survive, many submit to wickedness. Enoch, we must be quiet. Try to sleep."

Then his brother whispered louder, in control, "Everyone, go to sleep. Before Father comes." Enoch had a very hard time falling asleep. He was so curious and had so many questions. He thought, why would people choose to live under so many different laws, even unto death? Trading being able to make their own decisions for being told what to do and how to live. He rested for a long time with eyes wide open, unable to sleep.

The next day, he awoke to being shaken really hard. Startled, he opened his eyes to see Criggy shaking him. She was saying, "Wake up, Enoch. You are going to be in trouble if you don't get up and get to work." Then Keller put both front feet on his hanging bedding, causing it to tip and spill Enoch to the floor. Keller's size forced a laughing Criggy back out of the way so Keller could get into Enoch's face, giving some licks with his big, wet purple tongue.

At first, Enoch tried to block the licks with both arms raised and by moving his head from side to side. Finally, Enoch raised a hand palm out and commanded, "Stop, Keller." Immediately, Keller retreated backing up, worried he raised Enoch's ire. Enoch rose on his elbows; still prone on his backside, he began to giggle at Keller's rambunctiousness and stood to reach upward, hugging Keller around the neck. Of course all his brothers had gotten up and left already. If not for his friend Criggy, Enoch would've slept until missed and would've gotten into trouble.

He trusted Criggy. They were the best of friends. She liked to do the many things Enoch did and would marvel at Enoch's way with animals. She learned from Enoch, mainly by just spending time with him while he was with the animals. She rarely commanded the animals as Enoch could, although she frequently called them. Enoch would introduce her to some she did not know. He confided with Criggy. He wanted to see the city. There are times when youngsters respect each other so much they trust each other's decisions more than adults. After all, sometimes youngsters are astutely aware when adults make mistakes. We all witness the little back seat driver telling an adult they're speeding. Now even though these two were extremely young, Criggy witnessed some amazing interactions between Enoch and the animals. Even some adults were amazed at his relationships with the animals. Criggy was just an adorable, completely innocent little girl. She was amazed seeing God's Spirit in Adam, Seth, Kenan, and other descendants of Adam and believed strongly in righteousness. But still, she was young and enjoyed the fun, adventure, and Enoch's constant discoveries when she was with him. Enoch and Criggy knew the love they had for their family. It was real. They knew love was not tangible, but they could feel it in their heart. They both knew they loved each other. They were just too young to define what that would mean. They just knew they were more than brother than sister. Their parents could see it too. It was adorable. Criggy embraced a lot of respect for Enoch. Still, she was worried and very adamant that he should not go to the city.

Criggy said, "Please don't go to the city, Enoch. I'm afraid you could be hurt or tempted by wickedness. My father told me there is much wickedness in the city."

Enoch had questions. Enoch was very curious. Enoch reached for her hand. She placed hers in his. "Don't worry, Criggy. I must see. I must know of this city with my name. I will come home. Then I will have much to tell you. You will see."

ENOCH IS ATTACKED

He was about ten years old now, and the journey would be difficult enough. But he was alone, which meant he could actually carry
less—his flute, dagger, some glow rocks, and of course, his new staff
Da had made for him. The height of the staff still suited him fine.

Some animals seemed of no use to other people. They were not
pesky unless they ate of the fruit and vegetables that man toiled. For
then, of course, they might become an annoyance, and ways were
used to keep them away, mainly by training other animals to herd
them away from man's fruit and to other kinds available. There were
plenty of other kinds of foliage and fruit to eat that man did not prefer. He understood them better than others though. At his training
sessions the old man told him God said that all the animals were
to be dominated and subdued by man. Enoch believed. So the boy
would spend time with animals that seemed to have a more independent personality. When confronted about wasting his time, the boy
would say, "God has given these purpose too. We just don't know
what it is yet."

The little boy loved to play with the animals. He had many
favorite animals. His favorite though was his *Gidgag*. He like to call
him Gadder. Gadder would come leaping in giant bounds when the
boy called out for Gadder. Gadder had a family she would tend to
and sometimes the whole family would come when he called Gadder.
He noticed they were all uniquely different with different character traits accompanied with different facial expressions. So he would
name many of them too. Keller was hilarious. Ba'headge seemed to
always want to be in charge of the other Gidgags. They all didn't

seem to mind. At times, many would follow his lead. Although some would act like they knew he was in charge; when Ba'headge's attention was elsewhere, the others would frolic and play.

The young lad headed toward Mt Hermon. He would turn at the grove where he had met with Seth for a journey some years earlier. This time he would follow the smells of the styrax and galbanum then follow the Gihon. He had told his ma he wanted to go on a short journey by himself. At first his ma was worried, but all the animals seemed to really love her son. And when he became insistent, she relented. He wore his feathered garment to help stay dry and for warmth.

It was strange enough that a group sat by a fire instead of glow rocks, but it helped keep clothing dry and provided warmth away from the city. By the fire, there was discussion confirming rumors that there was one who stood face-to-face with the cherubim that guarded the entrance to the Garden of Righteousness. Then there seemed to be discussion of how valuable one might be with knowledge of another entrance to heaven. After all, no one else had survived after hundreds of the best had tried.

Enoch noticed a group of men approaching from the thicker cluster of trees coming into view, who were very different than he'd ever seen before. They were slowly making their way over fallen trees and stepping over boulders Enoch would have to climb to get over. They were coming up the side of the hill Enoch was on. One of them noticed one of the curious Gidgags. It was Keller. Then it became clearer to Enoch, Keller was intentionally gaining their attention, maybe wanting to play. That would be odd. Keller usually didn't go near strangers. Then Enoch noticed other Gidgags were stalking, hidden from plain view, positioning near the men. They remained hidden to the men, but Enoch saw them. Were the Gidgag intending to attack these men? Never had he witnessed them act like this against people. He had seen them herd large beast to protect the village, but they were extremely different now. They were readying to attack the men. Enoch did not understand why the Gidgag would prepare to attack these men. Maybe it was because these men were so different than any they'd ever seen.

The men were different than those from nearby villages. These men were of very large stature and were all beast of smooth dark blue skin with black hair and yellow eyes. These men were as big as some of the largest beasts Enoch had ever seen. Although they were extremely big, they were very agile. They were extremely muscular and looked very strong. They were moving quickly but carefully. Enoch was naively unafraid. They climbed over fallen trees and moving more limber than any he had ever seen. He remembered during training sessions that there many different kinds of people. Even Cain had spoken of children of gods. Were these Men of Renown: men who seek their name to be known on the earth forever? Enoch had never seen no one like this before. Enoch, of course, did what he would normally do. Enoch spoke out to the men, "Hello over there. Hey, you men." Some of them looked at Enoch. Other's didn't. They said nothing, but they kept coming. "Hey!" He was going to warn them of the Gidgag's behavior, to be careful. But before Enoch could get another word out, Gadder brushed Enoch's leg firmly, surprising Enoch, forcing him to pause, freezing in place. He couldn't help but look at Gadder. Gadder looked at the men. Not Enoch. What was she doing? She seemed to be preventing him from moving toward the men. Maybe protecting him? Enoch looked over at Ba'headge. Ba'headge was crouched like a lion before it leaps for attack. He was readied toward the direction of the men but was looking directly at Enoch. They made eye contact. Then Ba'headge was surprised at Enoch. Ba'headge stared at Enoch as if waiting. Gadder made eye contact with Ba'headge then looked back toward the men baring her teeth. Ba'headge bared his teeth too now. Now Enoch noticed Keller change. Enoch had never seen Keller so intense.

Suddenly about eight very large men drew weapons. Some had metal spears. These spears seemed very light and flexed. The spears had a manufactured long, sharpened tip, which glimmered a yellowish glow. The other end had a greenish feather shape like the feathers of a bird. But the greenish glow at the end was not feathers. The eight began charging toward Enoch. It was obvious now they were after him. Why?

Gadder stepped a little further out in front of Enoch. She was surveying what she knew would be a killing zone. Her long sharp spikes around her neck and shoulders straightened, moving into varying positions. She snarled softly but chirped loudly, showing her six- to seven-inch teeth toward the men. She set her front muscular legs on a log, sinking her four- to five-inch retractable claws deep into the wood. Ba'headge snarled, recoiled, then sprung leaping into action. He began by bounding, curving around trees while airborne. The Gidgag had a thin skin from foreleg to rear only visible when gliding. Similar to that of a flying squirrel. The Gidgag were landing then bounding and leaping across giant boulders. All the other Gidgag that followed were following Be'hedge's lead. All of them. The men's spears were extremely deadly accurate and whistled or zinged through the air. The spears thrown landed with extreme deadly accuracy. These men were not like other men at all. The men bounded over rocks to retrieve them quickly. Great long and high leaps. The Gidgags were extremely fast and agile too.

There was one huge problem. Keller. Keller was the closest when the fighting started and was in the midst of these men who were determined to kill. The men snarled and showed their teeth too. Keller had no choice; he had to attack the man closest to him. The man had no choice either. To get to Enoch, he had to kill Gidgags. Now to survive, this man had to kill Keller. Enoch could clearly see what that man and Keller both knew. Enoch could not just stand and watch. To throw a stone with great accuracy the distance must take into account knowing how much strength to put into the throw. Is it a clear throw? Through brush or over? The size and weight is a consideration. An odd shape of the rock may cause a curvature in flight. There would be no time. Enoch would take all the variables into account as he stepped and reached to grab the closest rock. But, he also knew he would have to trust in God. Picking up the rock and throwing it all in one motion. The rock arched high to reach its target and curved, slightly adjusted for the man's movement. The rock landed with great accuracy, striking the giant man above the left eye just before the man was to land a lethal blow to Keller with a very long, heavy cutting knife. The man missed, striking the ground instead. That knife would've cleaved Keller in two. Keller clamped his jaws on the man's arm. Keller began to pull the man to the ground. The man was dazed and confused from being hit in the head by a rock. But the pain brought realization to the man that he was going down. The man's eyes cleared to bring a fatal blow to Keller with the spear with his left arm. Just as he was beginning the thrusting motion, another rock struck him in the forehead. He still landed a full thrust into Keller. The force necessary to remove the spear quickly required the man to step on Keller's upper body. Repositioning for full body strength, the man slammed his foot down hard on Keller's upper body where he lay. Keller was not dead. Keller flexed "spikes" from around his neck outward as the man stepped down with full body weight. The man screamed in pain. This seemed out of the norm during the battle. The men seemed to be communicating but not verbally. The men did snarl and grunt during battle, but they never spoke out loud.

Previously, Enoch had thought these spikes were just like hair. Like the mane of a lion. He had caressed and petted them. Enoch never noticed these quills before. The hair must somehow stiffen. What seemed normally like hair as part of a mane, such as the male lion, were actually barbed quills. The force of the man's stomp had forced the quills all the way through his foot and were shining blue from his blood completely exposed out of the top of his combat sandal. It took all the man's strength to pull his foot from Keller. The quills came with his foot. Now the man was on the ground.

The second rock which hit the man dead center in the man's forehead may have helped. Keller was still alive. At least for now. Then for that one, the pain was over. Two Gidgags landed. One clamped its jaws on the arm which held the spear, easily pulling the man down sideways while the other leaped, clamping the man's throat. The man was not able to finish his sounds of anguish.

There was no man left standing in front of Enoch. Something seemed wrong. Enoch became a little focused on counting the men or scenes of carnage, a little confused now because he had overwhelming feelings or a rush of emotion for Keller. Suddenly he felt dirt and stone hit his side. It was from Gadder as she leaped, leaving

Enoch, heading straight left. Then Enoch knew what was wrong. Some men had circled (flanked their position) and were closing in on him and Gadder from their left side. Gadder was not going to let that happen. She would meet them on her terms, as far from Enoch as possible. The only thing Enoch caught a glimpse of was Gadder's hind quarters and tail as she disappeared over the edge down the hill top they both were on. He caught a glimpse of her spreading her front and rear legs to catch the wind as she leapt. Enoch still thought this amazing. Why was there so much he did not know about the Gidgags? There was no time to ponder.

On a dead run, Enoch tossed the staff from left hand to right. Into the air he went. He was airborne an extremely long time. He knew when he landed, he would have to flex his knees and roll to absorb such a long-distance jump. While in the air, he tried his best to do as the Gidgags did; he spread his arms and legs, letting his garments catch some wind so he could land near some bushes he saw on the right side of the two charging men. He did not realize until in flight, the feathers would actually allow him to glide where he needed to reach. What seemed as unfathomable as he left the ground somehow seemed possible now; he knew he would make it. He saw Gadder bounding left then right, back and forth as she charged the two men. The two men did not know which one of them was her target. They didn't seem to care except that she was an obstacle for their objective. Her back-and-forth movements were so erratic neither attacker could get a good throw off with their spears. They held off on their throw, waiting for her to choose which she would target, then the other would make the throw. While in the air, Enoch was gathering this all in, and while in the air, he had chosen his destiny. The shrubbery helped soften his landing. Enoch would've been well hidden in the shrubbery.

The day the two giant birds of the Red Trees (*sequoia*) fought, the bird had given him a feather. Enoch reasoned that the Giant Red and Green Bird meant to gather all the feathers strewn upon the ground for future use. The outer garment Enoch wore on this day was one his mother made from feathers gathered by Enoch. The feathers of Enoch's garment were affixed in such a way, unbeknownst to him or his mother, that when gliding they would uniformly unfurl just enough to allow almost the same responses as the winged bird in flight.

He knew Gadder would take the one on the left. He had already chosen right. While in the air, he had seen the fallen tree. After landing, he had never even had time to catch his breath before he continued. After his roll, up and on a crouched run again, he steadied readjusted a firm grip on his staff. He glanced at the man. *Good*, he thought. The man was focused in the other direction, trying to line a throw with his spear on Gadder if she were to choose his partner instead of him. Enoch was able to transition from the crouched run to a full upright sprint. A speed required to leap from the sloping tree, leaping from a point higher than the man's head and to cover the distance to reach the man on his right. Gadder's right. Completely surprising both men. At the last second, Gadder broke left and leaped, throwing her full body weight into the man on the left, still catching the men off guard. Not going for an arm or leg, she actually cocked her head to the side to land her cheek against the man's cheek, intending to bury her quills into his upper chest also the throat. The man did get the long cutting knife (sword) between himself and Gadder but not a thrust. Killing Gadder was not an option for the man. He couldn't; the knife was pinned between her and him. The spear was not an option; Gadder was too close. She was actually part of him now. He dropped the spear and let go of the knife. He was using every ounce of strength he had to pry her away from his chest. Extremely painful, unfortunately his only option. The man on the right was now distracted, confused, and now forced to choose. Throwing the spear at an animal stuck to your partner's chest doesn't seem like a good option. The man now took his attention to the bushes where he had last seen Enoch land, to finish what he had come to do. Enoch was nowhere near his landing spot.

Enoch was airborne, only several feet away, now coming downward with both hands on his sharp staff positioned above his head. Enoch was focusing on that area on the man's neck where all the blood flows. Enoch knew this because when that young server's throat was cut, he saw the tube (carotid artery) where all the blood spurted from. Enoch had been allowed to watch his father prepare woolly animals (sheep) as offerings to Yahweh and feast. Enoch had seen where to cut the throat. This was to be the exact spot Enoch would land his staff. The fact that the man turned his head at the last second made the strike easier. A direct hit.

Just prior to the point of impact, Enoch felt an arm gently wrap around his waist, slowing him and lifting him up and away. There was no jerk or jolt to a stop. It was done with perfect timing just as one of the beast with yellow claws and large sharp yellow teeth was readying the spear for a throw. Enoch's eyes widened in disbelief as the black unicorn had amazingly joined in unnoticed and charged at the odd man-like beast, piercing the man through the very center of his chest from behind with its horn. The black unicorn's eyes were blazoned red as smoke billowed from its nostrils. This couldn't have been the same unicorn, or could it? There were many unicorns, and Seth and Enoch did dismount the one they rode near its heard and saw it return with welcomed excitement to the herd. But on this day, Enoch had seen things from other animals that he did not realize they were capable of also. The unicorn simply with a muscled flick of its neck and head released the giant man through the air and he land in some foliage. The unicorn looked up at Enoch and who or whatever was carrying him and Enoch noticed its eyes change back to normal. Then the unicorn proceeded over to Gadder, maneuvering its log horn and prying Gadder away from a lifeless giant. Then Enoch remembered his previous digest, *Who or what was carrying him?* There was no worry now, only peace. During the traumatic and disturbing previous experiences, his heart was racing. He had been in some serious harm's way. Now his entire being knew peace and tranquility as he was being set down in a *green meadow area near still waters.*

He couldn't help the excitement from what his eyes were now filled with. He was with one of the two *winged angels* that were at God's right side from years ago. This one was in the same attire as years before and was standing with him only this time as a genuine living Creature. Like a man but not appearing as electrum (energy). Enoch also noticed his breastplate at this time was a dull metal with a natural physical fit, and it was not fiery as before. But he still had the length of golden rope at his side. Enoch stood very humbled, standing with an erect shoulder only because he stood with his staff his father had given him. Enoch burst forth, asking, "What is your name? What do I call you? What are you? Oh, please forgive me. That's not nice to ask. Do you know God? Did you? Where is God?"

Before the angel spoke, his wings folded inward and were absorbed as being part of the angel's physical makeup. The angel was thoroughly amused with the boy and replied, "Such a curious boy. So many questions for such young lad. One on Most High is giving me another appointment as we speak. But since I have been given yet a little of your time to be with you, I will answer. My name is Phanuel."

Enoch asked, "Was it you with One on Most High years before when I saw you? Do you change appearance?"

"Yes. If it be God's will, we can manifest in many ways, usually an appearance that suits the generation or one that suits God's pleasure and befitting betwixt the messenger and the chosen in time beyond the heavens."

Enoch felt trust and shared, "I was to go to the city, for I have heard many things good and bad. I have family there, and I was to learn of them." It was a tender conversation.

Phanuel said, "It is good to love all your family, but there are places you should not be for many reasons that you should not know yet. You have much to live through and much to learn. There are none better to teach you than Enos, Kenan, Mahalalel, and your father. The city is not your way."

Enoch was contrite and accepting. He asked, "Is God there?"

The angel said, "No, he sends us to be his eyes and ears. The city's ways are beginning to sadden God He desires a different way for you. Honor your mother and father. Stay and be with your family as long as you can. You need them. They love you. They need you, and before long, they will need you even more. Here. Look and listen." The angel gently put his hand on the boy's shoulder. Gradually, Enoch fell into a slight trance and could see his ma near their house, calling his da over and beginning to talk with his da. It became obvious what they were talking about. They held hands and walked to their family prayer area and went to their knees. Enoch could hear his ma's worry in her voice as she cried unto God for her son's well-being.

Enoch intentionally recovered to situational awareness on his own. Looked up at Phanuel he asked, "How can this all be?"

Phanuel replied, "It is God's spirit that connects us all, if it be his will. Enoch, you should go to them, for they love and worry for you now."

Suddenly Enoch felt a very strong desire to go with purpose to be with his family. Enoch replied, "Yes, I do very much want to go home. But will I see you again?"

Phanuel paused, looked to the sky, and said, "If it be God's will, but I do hope so."

Enoch knew it was time for the angel to leave, but he could not help expressing that he was upset and confused. Enoch asked, "Why did all this happen? Did Yahweh know this and let this all be?"

The angel replied, "Enoch, this is difficult for anyone to understand, especially one so young, so I will tell you in this way, You were going where you were not meant to go. There are times God's allows what is not his will. Those sons of those fallen are trying to live outside God's will. They are against what is *natural* (nature), and when they choose such ways, there will be ramifications, consequences, and repercussions, even unto death."

Enoch asked quickly, "What are ram-eek-teans or rea-pro-cusing?"

The angel said, "Like maybe bad things can happen, you see?"

Enoch said, "Like today."

Phanuel replied, "Yes, like today. Enoch, you seek God's ways, but you are young and have a lot to learn. He desires much for you. Now I must go, Enoch, for God's calls. You need to go too. But tend to your Gidgags first. Keller and Ba'headge need you."

Phanuel removed his hand from the boy's shoulder and stepped clear, unfurling his wings and soaring upward into *the cloud*.

That was a lot to take in, but Enoch began to turn his attention to searching the area for Gidgags that needed his help. He hoped he could be of some help. This was a serious and terrible battle. The noises and sounds had been horrible. The Gidgags had used fierce hunting strategies with teamwork that Enoch had not known they were capable of. They were singling out a prey, working in pairs and sometimes threesomes. Even though the size of Gidgags on all fours was the shoulder height of normal men, the Gidgags would stand on their hind legs to clamp their jaws on the arm of the weapons men held. In the meantime, others would tear off muscles at the ankles and at the backs of knees until the man would fall. In most cases, once the man was on the ground, it was over. Sometimes once in close range, the man would use all his strength for a steady and deadly thrust with his long cutting knife. When this would happen, it would seem to only hasten the Gidgag's attack. But it was over. It was just that Enoch had to force himself through the thoughts of the battle, which had since happened to be able to help because there Keller lay with a long metal spear, the likes of which Enoch had only seen on this day. Never before had he heard of such things. It was now he remembered that Cain had said, "Things were changing." Now he realized these were sons of gods which Cain had spoken about. It was then he saw Keller.

Enoch ran with leaps and bounds over to Keller's side. Ba'headge and Gadder slowly approached then lay close. Enoch had to put his foot on a nearby rock to pull the spear out. He removed his feathered cloak and his upper undergarment. He used it to push down hard to try and stop the bleeding. Keller turned his head up toward Enoch then gently laid it back down on the grass. There seemed an odd stillness, a great silence. Enoch had to push down firmly and slide the garment underneath the large body of Keller. The spear had gone through, and it was starting to set in. To all gathered around, this was a mortal wound. Enoch didn't completely understand yet that there were some living creatures made for only God's purpose. He never thought much about why he never saw any other Gidgags until now. It was all over. He remembered before the engagement, there was silence too, not even the sound of small creepy things like crickets or frogs or even birds, but now it was different. He couldn't stop the bleeding. Then he remembered the giant bird. Enoch removed the garment, put his hand directly into the blood and on the large gaping wound. As a tear rolled down his cheek, he began to cry unto God: Oh One On Most High, what you have done to let there be light and bring forth lots of fruit and water for all we need is amazing. God, you are awesome, and we are truly grateful. Thank you. God, I really don't know why you brought me a family of Gidgags, but you did. And I thank you. But God, if it be your will, I ask that you let Keller stay with his family and me. Please let Keller live."

As Enoch finished, it seemed as though Keller rested peacefully and stopped breathing. Instead of blood pressure, there was only an ooze, so Enoch gradually moved his hand and stood. Ba'headge looked at Enoch getting up. Enoch looked around, and there were some other Gidgags laying by the dead Gidgag. Enoch's heart sank as he thought, *All because he wanted to go to the city.* Then he heard Ba'headge yakking and chirping excitedly. He turned to look just in time to see Keller bounding toward him, gently knocking him to the ground and licking his face. Enoch looked at the wound. It was surely a fresh wound but seemed a week old. Of course, Ba'headge joined in, then all the Gidgags were bouncing around each other and rolling on top of Enoch. He could barely be seen. It was truly hard to stop enjoying the love being shared all the way around, but Enoch quickly got to his knees, and looking far away, he said aloud, "Thank you, One Who Gives Life." Enoch picked up the heavy spear then picked up his walking stick. Examining the two, he just pushed the spear away and let it fall. It was not to be his way. He started to walk toward home with his staff. The Gidgags stopped and saw the choice that was just made, and all stared at Enoch. Enoch looked back at them and then turned and bolted toward home with leaps and bounds. Ba'headge and Keller looked at each other and quickly shot to catch up. Enoch had to hurry home; his mother and father were worried.

THE MAN SEEMED CONTENT

The man definitely seemed out of place as he was seated at the table with a large locked wooden book. He had to refocus on where he was. It was this time and place. How could he tell them? He thought for a moment, *Thou preparest a table before in the presence of mine enemies.* But these were not his enemies. He was a witness, learning long ago we were all family. All the people were his family. He loved people. He loved all the people. Throughout his life, he had in many different ways served and helped people across the land. At least that's what he was always told. It was only recently he learned that by helping people he had been doing God's works almost his entire life.

How could he tell the people there was a way to unify the nation? He had written letters to senators, congressmen, radio talk show hosts, college student body leaders, college presidents, and so many more. He even called in by phone and got through to a television host and thought, *Surely, they'd be interested.* But as soon as he mentioned live on the air "a way to unify the nation" and started to make sense, he was taken off-air. The host and the producer talked to him off the air and into pursing a different avenue for the message. Which of course led to a dead end. He'd even written the past three presidents, beginning with President Barrack H. Obama. That letter earned him a spot on the "watcher's" list. The man has been under surveillance and experimental surveillance programs for nine years since that letter on August 12, 2012. It had been tough, and some of the experimental "watching" had been brutal, even unto high-tech collusion either wittingly or beyond their control to supernatural attacks. Granted, his first letter to President Obama was about veteran suicides. He even felt that after reading the letter, the president tried to do something about suicide prevention in the military. But the man was soon to learn from his friend, a local coroner who investigated both military and civilian deaths, that the civilian suicide death rate was by far exceeding the military suicide rate per day. At the time, veteran suicide rates were about twenty-two per day. Self-inflicted deaths had by far exceeded twenty-six to twenty-seven per day within a few years, which, in civilian comparison, would have about 1 million suicides per year and growing prior to the onset of COVID-19 in March 2020. The man was soon to learn that the government's decision was to keep the suicide rate across the nation from the public. The numbers were too disturbing.

Still seeking a cosponsor for the bill, he met with a congressman's staff member, and after a convincing discussion of the message of balance and unification, the staff member said, "The message would be moved forward." Interestingly enough, President Trump did not back the congressman during his reelection campaign, and the congressman even ended up losing the election to a candidate opposite the president's party. So he contacted President Donald J. Trump in writing, hoping for help with a cosponsor. He did get written responses confirming receipt but received nothing except more deeply involved and intimidating watching and surveillance. Then he saw on the news the new president, Joseph Robinette Biden Jr., was seeking unification, so he wrote seeking a cosponsor and also mentioning the breakdown of "love thy neighbor in communities" changing to "spy on the neighbor." No written reply from the White House came, but he heard news reports that President Biden was laughing and mocking that the people should watch their neighbors and report anything they see that was out of the "norm." By the way, what is normal and not normal for this generation? Friends, neighbors, and people on the street he had shared the message with said that "the message and amendment to the Constitution was sound and so good that his life would be in danger." This did turn out seemingly to be true. It seemed that those in power were actually afraid the message would take hold and give back self-governance, which over the years has slowly eroded, corroded, and been taken away from the people. It seemed those in political and monetary power and with much to gain were afraid that if the people were to actually participate during legislative sessions, there would be a *restoration of balance* to an unbalanced government and that the rich and politically powerful might lose power. It would only be through faith, belief, fasting, and prayer unto God by him and the people that the man did *sit at the table* with Congress.

Now that he was at the table, what would he say to Congress? It had been years since this message began evolving. Then he remembered, *"When they bring you in front of magistrates and powers, give no thought on what to say because God's breath will tell you what to say."* Before the man had even spoken a word to all in the room, a sense of serenity began to relax his entire being. He looked over at a clock on the wall. To him the second hand seemed to slow down. Making its way very slowly one second to the next. His throat seemed dry. Being thirsty would make sense, after all, this day did start with an unusually long walk. He casually turned his attention to a bottle of water. Not the bottle of water located on the table where he sat but one directly across from him. Ambient lighting from somewhere in the room was causing the water bottle to emit a soft glow. He began admiring the small occurrence of which he was certain no one else in the room would notice. *The water was clear*, he thought. Then the man reflected, *Water; as far as the eye can see with beautiful sunrises and sunsets. The Twilight colors of mornings and evenings of each day would be masterfully perfected by the most imaginative and creative One of all.*

Then the Man Heard, *"Finish."*

In the beginning, the Republic of the United States was established as a self-governing nation. Clearly established in the U.S. Consitution were three separate but coequal branches of government. It was also clear from the beginning that the people were written into the Consitution as the most critical component of the Constitution's "checks and balances" formula for success.

The People were to Begin the Process
of Self-governance by Voting

The people would vote for representatives so that their voice would be heard during governance. Chosen representatives would make decisions that reflected the will of the people. It was in this way the people would have a say in all government hearings, committees, matters of legislation, and development of law. Chosen representatives would create law, execute and administrate law according to the people's will.

For the law to be fair and just, required representatives to be somewhat immune from the influence of other branches. It was foreseen that determining equitable law did require that Legislators would have the ability to exempt or exclude themselves from certain enacted laws. To maintain balance required chosen respresentives to be somewhat immune from the law balanced by the people directly impacted by the law's effect. Chosen representatives creating the law would be balanced *with people* randomly selected as a duty to serve their community and country.

Jury Duty

As Jurist, not only were the people to determine guilt or innocence; degree of guilt, length of sentence, accountability and monetary damages but, also to determine if the law was fair and just. As a duty to serve, the people were to be the most critical *final check* of the "check and balances" formula. The people would have *the final say* determining if the law was Constitutional.

But then came **Jury Nullification**. The Judicial Branches across the country began to admonish the jury even before the case in court was heard. Jurys were being instructed to determine guilt or innocence based solely upon the law as explained by the court (judge). The Jury's Constitutional right to determine whether the law was fair and just was taken. *Thus, the final check by the people for the people in the check and balances formula was revoked.*

Of the People

The people were to be the *first concrete step* in the process of self-governance.

> For this generation there is a lack of trust in fair elections. The first step has been chipped away.

By the People

The will of the people was to be reflected by chosen representatives during all matters of governance.

> For this generation government is influenced by wealth, the powerful, influential groups, and corporations. This generation thinks they choose "leaders" to make decisions for them. This was never the intent.

For the People

The Jury was not only to determine guilt or innocence but whether the law was Constitutional, fair and just.

> For this generation their right to determine if a law is fair and just for their neighbors has been revoked.

The People were The Fourth Branch

A Government Without its People

The United States was no longer a self-governing nation. Inequities in law, in the courts and justice systems grew. Unfairness and injustice spread throughout the land. Lawlessness became rampant. The United States Government would try different remedies. Minimum Sentencing removed situational considerations heard by courts ultimately tampering with the justice system. Congress passed Federal Hate Crime Laws which amplified and intensified the existence of two different justice systems; the Federal Executive Branch and the Judicial Branch. The people's voice has been silenced and the people have no say. The people have been cut off from government. The exclusion of people from self-governance has caused a catastrophic imbalance. There was a clear sense that something was wrong but solutions eluded the people. The day had come that a nation of the people, by the people, for the people, was *without its people.*

Restoration

But there was a way to *restore balance* in the nation's government *with its people.* There was a way to *insert the will of the people directly into and during all legislative processes while remaining the final check of law.* The people would not only continue to serve as jurist but would also serve their duty as members of The Fourth Branch. The people would be a part of all legislative processes and vote on all legislation prior to the law's enactment.

The Twenty-Eight Amendment to the U.S. Constitution: A Government "With" The People:

> *The People are the Fourth Branch,*
> *To better define passage of laws and legislative bills which apply to the people in which they understand clearly the intent and application of the laws as they pertain to a free people and within their God given inalienable rights; The people have decided to directly insert their will during the legislative process by demanding the law's amplification, clarification, and justification prior to the enactment of law. The Fourth Branch will vote in all Congressional processes to include matters of*

Censorship and Impeachment. Each state will randomly select nominees meeting minimum requirements of current federal jury screening. Exceeding these requirements with political preferences, or any bias and prejudices with additional restrictive constraints will disallow nominees. The intent of Selected Nominees is to directly reflect the effectiveness of randomness and represent the widest range of citizens that live within each state. The Fourth Branch will consist of Two Bodies of the people whose right it is to serve their country for a period equal to a Congressional session; subject to extension matching Senatorial and House proceedings. An additional week of State Constitutional education, State Legislature orientation and procedural conduct; to include two weeks of U.S. Consitution and Senatorial and Congressional Legislature orientation and procedural conduct is to be served. And finally serve one additional week of service for formal discharge of services, debriefing and transfer of knowledge, experience, and wisdom for the incoming Fourth Branch.

The Qury: Consisting of 150 randomly selected U.S. citizens (three from each state). Selected as a duty to serve, by attending and participating in all House procedures, debates, hearings, committees and voting for or against passage of legislation.

The Query: Consisting of 100 randomly selected U.S. citizens (two from each state) selected as a duty to serve, by attending and participating in all Senatorial procedures, debates, hearings, committees and voting for or against passage of legislation.

All aspects of legislative procedure would no longer *close the door* on the people. The *door would remain open* and the people would participate in all hearings and vote for Supreme Court nominees. This Amendment would force Congressional debates and floor discussions to once again matter because the people would perform their duty by asking for amplification and clarification of legislation that would affect them and their children before it passes. And, vote on any matter before congress; as it pertains to government or the people. Security clearances would be granted on a need-to-know basis. It should be easy to understand the people would have a greater need to know the true basis and reasons for laws which govern them than anyone else. Sequestration, nonprofit, and confidentiality would of course be mandatory for those who would serve as members in the Fourth Branch. Just as Jury Duty the people will be compensated. The people who serve in the Fourth Branch will be appropriately and fairly compensated to include normal livelihood cost, periderm and cost of living expenses. The intent is not for profit but monetary hardships should not affect decisions but, sacrifice of time and absenteeism will be endured as a duty and service for country and neighbor. There would no need for profit from books, or interviews, etc., after serving.

This proposal intended that the United States could be from this generation forward: a *rededicated nation, under God, with a new birth of freedom, ensuring that a government of the people, by the people, for the people, "with" the people shall not perish from the earth.*

Was the man's journey over? Was it finished? Or, was the man's journey to a new beginning to continue?

Suddenly, the man knew that it wasn't going to work. What would have been the right intention was not going to work. The American people were always the fourth branch of the American government, but no one knew or understood. Even if the Twenty-eight Amendment was enacted in an attempt to restore balance, it could never fix that which was broken. There could be only one remedy because man simply could not govern. Man was not capable of governing. There could be only one solution:

The people are the fourth branch of Israel
and shall come upon you under the cloud.
Michael and Gabriel shall govern under the cloud.
Watchmen shall cry when they hear the voice of their Lord God
and the Lord shall reign over them.
The Law shall come out of Zion
and the Word of God will come out of Jerusalem.
He will teach us His ways
and we will walk in His paths.
The people will come from the North, South, East, and West
to hear His voice and be with Him.
But the Saints of the most High shall take the kingdom
and possess the kingdom for ever, even forever and ever.
God is sending His Son
to rule for a thousand years.
We have faith, hope, and believe Jesus is coming.
We know Jesus Christ is coming.
    So the end shall come
    So the beginning will come

ABOUT THE AUTHOR

As a young boy he saw God. He never really grasped the moment and failed miserably at being a witness with truthful testimony. As he grew his failures piled into his teenage years. He grew to break man's laws and on many occasions God's laws. He became known as an 'Unforgiven' according to man's laws. There were punishments with harsh realities known to many as life's lessons. Still longing to live life to its fullest he tried to thrive in the world with what he thought were integrity and character.

As a young adult he came to learn of second chances with limitations. He had no clue of what God's blessings, hidden treasures, mercy and Grace were. Gifts kept coming, he just didn't know the source. Much later in life after repeated failures and second chances then came what he thought was the final failure. This time there were certain unusual occurrences which caused deep reflection. It was then he began to realize that there were mind boggling events in which there was absolutely no way he could've lived or accomplished what he did. Not without divine intervention. What happened next can only be explained as being *Called by God and saved through Jesus Christ, Our Lord and Our Savior.* Then he felt moved by the Holy Spirit to write. Specifically, that it must be this book? No. Only that he must write. Can the author's writings prove God's existence?

No book proves the existence of God. Not even the Bible. The Bible which contains the Divine Word of God, helps others find God. Then through faith and belief, proof of God will only exist between God and whom the Creator has chosen or elected to receive proof of His existence. Proof or not doesn't matter, because it's through faith and belief we come to **_know_** God. By the way the author still fails almost every day but at least now he knows to thank God for everything daily.

Chief Mac Da'ibhidh

CPSIA information can be obtained
at www.ICGtesting.com
Printed in the USA
BVHW041251230323
661009BV00001B/83

9 781637 106235